Counseling in Marital and Sexual Problems

A PHYSICIAN'S HANDBOOK

Counseling in Marital and Sexual Problems

A PHYSICIAN'S HANDBOOK

Edited by Richard H. Klemer, Ph.D.

Department of Psychiatry, University of Washington School of
Medicine, Seattle, Washington

THE WILLIAMS & WILKINS COMPANY

BALTIMORE · 1965

Made in the United States of America

Library of Congress Catalog Card Number 65–12652

Reprinted December, 1965
Reprinted, 1967

Composed and Printed at
The Waverly Press, Inc.
Mt. Royal & Guilford Avenues
Baltimore, Md. 21202 U.S.A.

Preface

This book is intended as a useful source of practical ideas for the busy physician. It is not intended as an academic discussion of philosophies and rationales for various schools of thought in counseling and psychotherapy. Nor is it designed to analyze the latest research in the counseling field, although many of the chapters herein are based on just such research findings. Rather, this book has been written by its many contributors to provide sound, clinically-tested suggestions for helping the physician to help patients who have very real and very urgent marital and sexual problems.

Conciseness and clarity of expression, for quick idea absorption and immediate use, have been stressed throughout the book. In the early stages of the preparation of the manuscript, this emphasis on brevity concerned some of the contributors, all of whom are very able to be infinitely complex and meticulously thorough in their respective fields. Many of them wished to include in their original papers a paragraph expressing regret over the necessary condensations they had included.

But the editor prevailed upon them to eliminate these paragraphs by first promising that he would make note of their good intentions in this preface, and secondly by arguing that useful ideas, however simplified, which lead to successful treatment, need no defense. It is now for the reader to validate this premise.

Acknowledgments, too, can be very brief. Obviously, this volume now exists because of the thoughtful, and sometimes sacrificial, efforts of the contributing authors. The editor wishes to acknowledge not only their hard work and valuable ideas, but also their understanding cooperation and flexibility in allowing the editorial changes which permitted a cohesive, nonrepetitive manuscript and made the editor's task a relatively simple one.

Special recognition is due to Robert Rutherford, M.D., John Hampson, M.D., Joan Hampson, M.D., and Raymond D. Fowler, Jr., Ph.D., who contributed both editorial suggestions and general encouragement in addition to their well-written chapters; to Herbert Ripley, M.D., head of the Department of Psychiatry, University of Washington School of Medicine, who originally suggested preparation of this manuscript for publication; and to Mrs. Trudy Voogd, who assisted importantly in that preparation. Very special recognition is due to Margaret G. Klemer, R.N., M.S., both for her thoughtful suggestions and editorial help and for the generous sharing of her husband's time, which made possible his contribution as editor.

RICHARD H. KLEMER, Ph.D.

v

Contents

PART III—OTHER MARRIAGE PROBLEMS

PART IV—PREMARITAL COUNSELING

PART V—MARRIAGE COUNSELING INSTRUCTION IN THE MEDICAL CURRICULUM

APPENDIX

part one

COUNSELING IN
MARITAL PROBLEMS

chapter one

Treating the Patient's Marriage Problems—An Overview*

RICHARD H. KLEMER, PH.D., *Department of Psychiatry, University of Washington School of Medicine, Seattle, Washington*

When you include the psychosomatic reactions resulting from hidden marriage tensions, it seems very probable that more marriage problems are brought to medical doctors than to any other kind of professional helper.

Those who seek the physician's counsel on marriage problems have a great variety of complaints. Some openly ask advice about specific problems ranging from budgeting to mothers-in-law and from sexual techniques to how to cure an alcoholic husband. Sometimes these questions are related to the professional specialty of the physician, sometimes they are not.

There is another large group of people who do not ask directly for marriage help at all. However, the physician soon sees a tantalizingly obvious association between their functional complaints and the marital problems which they have either openly or guardedly revealed.

All of these people have one thing in common—they need some marriage counseling. But many of the physicians to whom they have come feel unprepared to deal with the problems presented and are reluctant or unable to refer these patients to others. Of 514 North Carolina physicians included in the recent study of Herndon and Nash,[2] 283 reported that there was little in their medical school training which had helped them to deal with marital maladjustment, and 342 reported that no helpful experience had been gained during internship or residency. Moreover, 78 per cent of those interviewed indicated that they rarely or never made referrals for marriage counseling, and 7 per cent of those interviewed said they refused to discuss marital problems even in response to the patient's request.

---

* Much of this material was originally published as Part I of "Marriage Counseling in Medical Practice" by Richard H. Klemer, Ph.D.,[1] in The Western Journal of Surgery, Obstetrics and Gynecology, March–April, 1963. Used by permission.

Clearly, there is a need for a greater understanding by the physician of what he can do with marriage problems, both in treatment and in referral. It is toward this end that the chapters in this book are addressed.

WHAT IS GOOD MARRIAGE COUNSELING?

Much of the reason why marriage problems are not more readily handled in medical practice—either by treatment or by referral—stems from the great confusion over just what constitutes good marriage counseling and who does it. Some physicians, as well as many patients, have shied away from recommending or using marriage counseling because they have been led to believe either that marriage counseling is too much like depth psychiatry on the one hand or is much too superficial on the other.

It is true that there are almost as many precise definitions of marriage counseling as there are practitioners. But that does not, *or should not,* diminish its effectiveness provided that the method, skill and personality of the counselor are adaptable to the problems, tension level and personality of the help-seeker. Many different counselors with widely differing professional backgrounds can do good marriage counseling in many differing ways, if they are realistically meeting the patient's present needs.

Obstetricians, for example, often use "marriage counseling" to describe their conferences with patients concerning sexual and contraceptive techniques. As a matter of fact, most medical specialists writing on marriage counseling tend to emphasize the physical and sexual aspect of the relationship, including frigidity and impotence. This is quite logical. These are the marriage counseling needs which their patients most often bring to them. By the same logic, a home economist writing on marriage counseling will heavily weight her paper toward budgeting and home management.

The term marriage counseling also is used by some psychiatrists and psychologists to describe individual psychotherapy with a married person whose problem, in the psychotherapist's view, has to do with his marriage. There are sometimes sound reasons for the psychopathologist's use of his psychotherapeutic skills and techniques in endeavoring to cure a marriage partner, since some marriage difficulties result from an emotional inadequacy of one partner or the other or both.

As a matter of fact, as a psychologist, the writer recently counseled a man and wife who were having severe difficulties. Most of their problems had inception in the aggravated inferiority feelings of the wife. It was very clear that she systematically destroyed her relationship with her husband by her constant withdrawal from social situations and her almost masochistic self-abnegation. She would not go out with her husband; she would not have acquaintances into the home; she was extremely jealous of his relationship with other women, even his own sister. She permitted— in fact almost encouraged—him to do things which inconvenienced her just so she could point out to herself, to her children and to him how abused she was. Only long-term psychotherapy for this wife could provide much benefit, either temporary or lasting, for this marriage.

But, with the popularization of marriage counseling in the magazines and television, more normal people (that is, those who fall within the normal range on relatively objective psychologic tests) have been asking for marriage counseling. A large proportion of these people seem to be above average individuals. They are the intelligent, problem-solving people. While they may have considerable current anxiety, they don't feel the fire of long-term emotional disturbance, so many of these folk are not motivated to lie down on a couch for extended psychotherapy. They want to get something done about their problems right now and divorce is a quick and tempting alternative if something else is not forthcoming.

And it is very true that sometimes the problems of these people cannot wait. When a young wife comes in to tell you that her husband is leaving tonight, there is no time for nondirective therapy or free association. Often it is just this kind of situation which is presented to the medical doctor. And often he must undertake to solve the problem himself, either because the patient will not accept referral or because no adequate source of referral is available in the community in which the physician practices.

This kind of emergency nonreferrable situation calls for a physician-counselor with hurrying patience and permissive directiveness. He needs to help the marriage partners to talk through their hostilities quickly and consciously, to help them to start listening to each other and trying to understand each other again, to help them to plan a course of action—again at the conscious level—which is mutually acceptable and which will resolve their present difficulty. He needs to help them to do all of this right now. To be successful in this kind of counseling, calm reassuring confidence is essential. Moreover, a very flexible and eclectic orientation and procedure are demanded for some actual education, some actual suggestion and some actual persuasion probably will be necessary.

It is true that a number of psychopathologically oriented psychotherapists have looked askance at the kind of marriage counseling outlined here. They see such counseling as only symptomatic relief of more serious emotional problems. However, the fact that marriage difficulties have now become a statistically normal problem of emotionally normal people in our society and no longer a probable evidence of psychopathology, seems clearly to justify this practical approach to marriage counseling. The evidence on this point is quite clear. Bossard and Boll[3] make a telling point against including all marriage problems in the realm of psychopathology when they point out that while Canada's rate of admissions to mental hospitals (and so the presumed incidence of psychopathology among its population) is approximately the same as our own, Canada has only one-fifth the rate of divorce. Even after making allowances for Canada's stricter divorce laws, it is still difficult not to conclude that in many cases the divorcee or potential divorcee (*i.e.*, the marriage counsel seeker) should have his relationship, and not necessarily his head, examined.

Some marriage counseling may well provide only symptomatic relief as charged. But in some cases this is all that is needed. After all, when the spots are gone so are the measles.

Practical marriage counseling with people who have marriage difficulty is as old as marriage itself. Some of its techniques actually preceded similar ones now used in abnormal psychology, and some of its methods have a procedural parallelism to those used in modern psychotherapy. However, there are several major differences between marriage counseling and individual psychotherapy.

It is tremendously important that the physician understand these differences. Otherwise, fearful that he might be entering the psychodynamic never-never land if he were to do a bit of marriage counseling, he may turn the patients away when he could have helped them to solve their problems. Evelyn Duvall has made this point very well:

"Many physicians would do more adequate counseling in their practices were they not afraid of encroaching upon the specialty of psychiatry which they have been rightly warned is no place for amateurs. This fear of getting involved in anything that approaches the psychiatric process cuts short many a counseling contact at the very moment that it might become helpful. As soon as the patient begins to express feelings or to indicate confusion in his personal or family life, the busy doctor may feel that his responsibility is to step out of the picture as gingerly as possible. Not being clear about the distinctions between counseling and psychiatric treatment, he hesitates to do anything when just a little of what he could do at the moment might be very helpful."[4]

DIFFERENCES BETWEEN MARRIAGE COUNSELING AND PSYCHOTHERAPY

In the first place, marriage counseling assumes that marriage relationship is the first concern of the counselor. It also assumes that this relationship is something different than the personalities of either or both of the partners. It is often pointed out that there are some very neurotic people who are happy together in marriage, while there are some seemingly well adjusted individuals who cannot relate to each other.

It is true that a marriage counselor may look for background factors in the childhood experiences of either or both partners, which predispose the marriage problem, in an effort to provide some insight into the nature of the difficulty. But the replaying of the childhood family drama, so important in much psychotherapy, is not ordinarily a function of marriage counseling. Nor is the individual personality reorganization of a partner a necessary goal of marriage counseling. In a large number of cases, if this is desirable, it follows the solution of the immediate marriage difficulty rather than preceding it.

There is a second major difference between marriage counseling and individual psychotherapy. As has been pointed out, because marriage problems often are brought to the counselor as an acute emergency, the counselor sometimes is much more directive in his approach to a solution to the problem than most psychopathologists wish to be in the initial stages of therapy. Moreover, while the marriage counselor may make deliberate or indirect use of the phenomenon of insight and its hopefully resulting change in behavior, he often finds that motivating the marriage partner to change his behavior even *before* he has achieved an insight is functionally effective. Surprisingly, it often brings on the desired insight more quickly than long hours of verbalizations and interpretations. Again, this is where there is no major psychopathology involved.

In addition to these two differences between marriage counseling and individual psychotherapy, Duvall has pointed out a number of others:

1. In counseling the counselor and counselee face each other and both are free to watch expressions, gestures and psychomotor tensions of the other.

2. In counseling there is usually a lapse of a week or more between interviews rather than the sometimes almost daily contact of deep psychotherapy.

3. In counseling there is much less interpretation of the patient's feelings and little effort to deal with highly symbolic material or to interpret dreams and fantasies.

4. In counseling there is no insistence on free association, although it may happen as a natural event.

5. In counseling there is considerably more use of direct educational materials with books and articles being referred to and discussed.

6. Counseling is much more liable to be of short duration, as a few weeks or a few months are acceptable for some cases.

What Does the Counselor Do?

Basically, marriage counseling is a method of education, a method of emotional tension reduction, a method of helping the marriage partners to solve a problem and a way of establishing better problem-solving patterns. In some cases, it is necessary to provide some education before the partners' tensions can be reduced (insight is self-education in its finest sense). In other cases, it is necessary to reduce the tension in the marriage before any education can take place. But in either case, whether education or reduced tension is primary, both must take place before problem-solving, either present or permanent, can take place.

To accomplish these objectives, the marriage counselor normally does seven things:

1. He creates rapport with his patient (a physician often has tremendous initial advantage in that the patient already has accepted him and related to him).

2. He provides for a ventilation of the marriage partner's hostilities toward his mate.

3. He provides the reassurance of acceptance of the patient's attitudes, and perhaps some additional reassurance as well.

4. He diagnoses the problem with the patient.

5. He encourages patient education.

6. He helps the patient to examine his strengths and his possible alternatives and to decide on action.

7. He motivates the patient to follow through on whatever course of action has been decided upon.

While all this may seem to be a rather large undertaking for a busy physician who is faced with the prospect of do-it-yourself, it is certainly less fearsome than the alternative of completely rejecting the patient. Naturally, where a sound referral source is available, it is probably in the patient's interest, as well as the physician's, for a referral to a professional counselor to be made, if only because of the physician's lack of time.* Herbert Otto discusses the process of referral in Chapter 9.

There are occasions, of course, when the professional marriage counselor himself will refer the physician's patient to a psychotherapist for individual treatment. Not infrequently, after a marriage counselor has diagnosed the marriage difficulty, structuring a resistant partner who has a personality malfunction for treatment by a psychiatrist or psychologist becomes the goal and end result of the marriage counseling. Many psychotherapists are finding that marriage counselors are an important intermediary in getting into treatment patients who otherwise might have rejected needed therapy.

There will also be some times when the physician will feel it is imperative to refer patients directly to a psychopathologist, regardless of the distance, inconvenience or expense involved. In Chapter 4 John Hampson

---

* The writer is presently a part of an interesting new practice arrangement—a psychologist-marriage counselor as an associate in an obstetric-gynecologic practice. While the arrangement is too new for a detailed report, there are many evidences of promising results in this effort to more nearly treat the whole person in her physical complaints, her emotional difficulties and her marriage relationship malfunctions.

will discuss the patients who are maladaptive to their total living experience—the psychotic and severely neurotic—who must have hospitalization
or psychotherapy. In Chapter 5 Joan Hampson will discuss those people
with character disorders that make them maladaptive in any interpersonal
relationship—marriage or other—and so they are remotely improbable
candidates for help by marriage counseling.

But in Chapter 6 by John Cuber and in the writer's Chapter 3, there
will be a discussion of those relatively normal people who are maladaptive
in their *present* marriage relationship, and are very much in need of marriage counseling. It is those patients to whom the physician can probably
be of the most help in straightening out the marital difficulty. In fact, in
some cases, he may be in a better position to help than anyone else. There
are at least six unique advantages which the physician has over other
helpers when he is serving as a marriage counselor. These have been
pointed out by Duvall:

1. In the first place, just by virtue of being a physician, a medically
trained and experienced doctor ordinarily enjoys the respect of the
community. Moreover, he is state licensed (at the present writing only
one state, California, licenses its marriage counselors), and in most
communities his very status endows him with an ability to make some
difficult interprofessional arrangements which can help solve marriage
problems.

2. For a second asset, Duvall points to the tremendous readiness for
help with which the patient comes to his doctor. He is used to the notion
that he needs help from the physician and he professes this readiness for
professional attention by his coming to the physician. Moreover, he offers
himself as a whole person, not just one organ or set of feelings, but as
himself with all of the complexities within him—physiologic, psychologic,
emotional, social, and cultural. He comes in humility with the expectation of getting help, and thereby gives the physician an advantage rarely
enjoyed by members of many other helping professions.

3. The physician also can get most patients to cooperate in a full exploration of the trouble before any serious attempt is made to diagnose or
prescribe. Many people are impressed with the various tests employed to
investigate them physiologically and some point with pride to the extent
to which a doctor has explored their complaints. As Duvall points out,
"this expectation that the physician will explore a problem over a period
of time is conducive to continuing cooperation and patient acceptance
of both a delayed diagnosis and a careful review of all relevant factors
highly significant in the good physician-counselor relationship."

4. The physician's association with the stereotyped concept of illness,
convalescence and recovery helps the patient to curb his impetuous demand for immediate and miraculous results from counseling.

5. The physician's familiarity with psychosomatic medicine, functional disease and the emotional basis for health help him to see problem causes and make associations which might be missed by the helper not trained to such depth in physiologic complaints. Moreover, his very association with physiology enables him to be far more direct, especially in the sexual area, than counselors from other backgrounds might feel comfortable in being.

6. Another advantage that the physician has over other professional workers is that he performs many other services that are closely related to a family's life. He helps the infertile couple to have children, he performs surgery on the grandparents, he enters into the preparations for marriage by making premarital examinations, he officiates at births and deaths and he deals with the problems of middle and later life. Very often the family doctor is felt to be almost a family member and obviously has much greater claim to being chief family counselor.[5]

Much of the rest of this book will be concerned with detailing some techniques which the physician can use in marriage counseling. But while these techniques will be catalogued, it should be pointed out at the outset that there is no one set of standardized techniques which will be successful in all marriage counseling cases. The best way of counseling is the effective way. And the effective way is that way which is congenial to the personality of the counselor. While the counselor's technical skill in handling difficult situations and specific marriage problems can be increased by education and experience, ultimately it is his personality which will provide the acceptance, reassurance, cooperation and motivation needed to help the patient solve his marriage problem.

As several writers, including Jerome Frank,[6] have pointed out about other helping relationships, an important part of the counselor's ability to help his patient by marriage counseling comes from the strength of the counselor's belief in his own ability to help and from his ability to transmit that hopeful belief to his patient. Stated more briefly, the more self-confident marriage counselors are often the more successful.

Yet it takes more than optimism and self-confidence. The marriage counselor—or the physician serving as marriage counselor—who can help the patient is the one who is also a warm, understanding person, who knows himself and his limitations, and who has made himself competent. It is with these goals in mind that the following chapters are presented.

REFERENCES

1. KLEMER, R. H.: Marriage counseling in medical practice, Part I. Treatment or referral? West. J. Surg., 71: 96–99, 1963.
2. HERNDON, C. N., AND NASH, E. M.: Premarriage and marriage counseling: a study of practices of North Carolina physicians. J. A. M. A., 180: 395–401, 1962.

3. Bossard, J. H. S., and Boll, E. S.: *Why Marriages Go Wrong*. The Ronald Press Company, New York, 1958.
4. Duvall, E. M.: Physician-counselor roles in modern settings. West. J. Surg., **61:** 430–436, 1953.
5. Duvall, E. M.: The physician as marriage and family counselor. West. J. Surg., **62:** 443–452, 1954.
6. Frank, J. D.: The dynamics of the psychotherapeutic relationship. Psychiatry, **22:** 17–39, 1959.

chapter two

What Has Happened to Marriages?*

RICHARD H. KLEMER, Ph.D., *Department of Psychiatry, University of Washington School of Medicine, Seattle, Washington*

Just as it is necessary for the physician to know something about the etiology and course of any disease if he is to effect its cure, so is it important for the marriage counselor—or the physician serving as marriage counselor—to understand what has happened to marriage in the United States in recent years. Only when there is an awareness of why modern marriages are becoming the breeding ground for so many problems can successful marriage therapy be undertaken.

Marriage difficulties between men and women have, of course, existed since Adam and Eve. In the years since the industrial revolution, accelerated social changes—and the consequent changes in status relationships between men and women—have enlarged the problems tremendously.

It seems to the writer that what has happened to marriage in America best can be understood in terms of three major social changes:

1. The decline in understanding between marriage partners.
2. The loss of determination to stay married.
3. The development of unrealistic marriage expectations.

We will examine each one of these three changes in turn, starting with the loss of understanding.

DECLINE IN UNDERSTANDING

In marriage counseling today we see a great many people who actually and literally do not understand why their partners behave as they do.

A classic example of this often occurs in sexual relationships. A young husband will come in for counseling help and complain that he is baffled by his wife's sexual behavior. Last night, he relates, he was making a sexual approach to his wife and she apparently rejected him. Seeking to

* Much of this material was originally published as Part II of "Marriage Counseling in Medical Practice" by Richard H. Klemer, Ph.D.,[1] in The Western Journal of Surgery, Obstetrics and Gynecology, May–June 1963. Used by permission.

be considerate and feeling that perhaps she was tired, he rolled over and tried to go to sleep. Whereupon his young wife sat up and cried the rest of the night.

Her side of the story is that she should have been so irresistibly fascinating that her husband would have persisted despite any obstacles she put in his path. She does not understand why he did not. Obviously he did not love her enough, she thinks.

What this young husband really does not understand is why such gestures of the depth of his affection are important to his wife's emotional security. In his childhood family he never really became aware that some little girls, including the one he later married, are conditioned to need aggressive reassurances of their desirability and worth. Meanwhile, he was conditioned by his mother to seek a woman's love by being supplicative and considerate and nondemanding. Now both the young man and his wife are confused and frustrated when their techniques for getting response do not produce the expected results.

Such misunderstandings certainly are not limited to sexual activity. A wife sometimes will complain about a husband who goes out and buys a car the family cannot afford. She does not understand her husband's highly competitive business world and his need for recognition and prestige. If she had been raised as a boy in his home, she would have understood. But she was not—so she does not.

One recent development has enormously increased the magnitude and importance of these basic man-woman understandings today. Now the understanding problem has been complicated by the marriages of many more young, relatively immature partners who come from widely different backgrounds—racial, religious, socioeconomic and ethnic. As our population has become more mobile and more cosmopolitan, people have become less critical in their choice of marriage partners. In the old days when marriage mates more often came from the same neighborhood and the same cultural background, with relatively the same values, they had a much better understanding before their marriages of what the other partner's genuine attitudes and undisguised behavior would be later.

Not so today. Let me give you a case in point: a young husband came in threatening divorce and complaining that he had the most spendthrift woman that was ever put on this earth. "She can't keep track of a single nickel; money goes through her hands like water," he said. "Imagine," he concluded, "she won't even sew up a hole in a torn sheet!"

The wife in her turn said something like this: "I am married to the worst miser and the most miserable tightwad that there ever was. He hoards everything. He even expects me, in this year of 1965, to sew up a hole in a torn sheet!"

When, in the course of counseling, the backgrounds of these two people became known, the reason for their misunderstanding became apparent. He was the son of a widow from a small community in New England where the greatest cultural value was "wear it out, make it do." His mother had to support herself and five sons. She constantly impressed upon the developing consciousness of her boys the importance of putting money by for the inevitable rainy day.

This mother could not have known that this one of her sons would marry the easygoing daughter of a suburban California family where the highest cultural values were "gracious living," "spend it now, it's later than you think" and "what is money for but to spend?" Besides, in California, if one spends money today for real estate, for example, he may get it back next year greatly appreciated in value.

Because these people came from such widely divergent backgrounds, they did not even begin to understand each other's internalized attitudes and so were on the verge of divorce.

It is not necessary, though, that two people come from distant parts of the country in order to have difficulty in understanding. I am presently counseling a married couple in which the partners came from the same state. He is the son of an old-time downstate farmer; she is the daughter of a "modern" metropolitan banker. Neither one understands the other's attitude about such things as his going on long hunting trips, her spending money, his desire to be the boss in the family, her insistence that she be consulted about decisions.

Over and over again, this story is repeated. When such a marriage partner can be brought to the intellectual realization that his partner is not trying deliberately to punish him by exercising his "silly notions," but instead is emotionally conditioned to behave this way, there can be at least some progress toward a more complete acceptance of his behavior.

It almost goes without saying that before understanding there must be communication. One of the big problems of marriage today results from the inability or unwillingness of people to talk to one another. Some of this silence is a result of deeply ingrained inhibitions—as, for example, in the sexual area. Much more of it, however, results from the failure of one partner to create the climate which is conducive and receptive to the other's ideas and feelings. Both dreams and confidences are fragile things. Once ridiculed or threatened, they will be shared again only when their owner is convinced that the other partner has learned to be accepting.

Still more uncommunicativeness results from the lack of common understanding brought on by the partners' working and living in two different worlds nowadays—he in the shop or office, she in the home or a different office. This is why the effort to develop common interests becomes essential in marriage counseling, in addition to the enlargement of communication about present interests.

It is sometimes startling to see how much can be accomplished merely by getting the partners genuinely to accept each other's feelings, ideas and experiences, and thus to understand each other. This is true because, in a sense, they are really counseling each other.

removal of outside force

LOSS OF DETERMINATION

A second new concept important in the marriage counselor's understanding is that of the loss of the determination to stay married current today. Fifty years ago one of the highest values in marriage was stability. Both partners married with the intention of staying married. Even if they were inclined to change their minds, they soon found that society had many obvious and/or subtle pressures for making sure that they did not.

Today, however, most of the bonds which once held marriage together from the outside—including strict divorce laws and the necessity of staying together for protection and in order to produce enough to avoid starvation—have faded away. Now the major bond—perhaps the only bond—that holds most marriages together is the emotional satisfactions which accrue to the partners.

Personal and individual happiness have replaced stability as our highest marriage values. The moment that either partner feels that he is not as happy as he could be if he were unmarried or with another mate, he begins to think about divorce. In fact, in many cases, he has considered the possibility of divorce before he even gets married.

Historically, it probably is not as surprising that we have young men who marry on the basis of "this-one-will-do-until-the-next-one-comes-along," as it is that we have young women who are willing to get a divorce at the drop of a hat. This is something new in the history of civilization. Until modern twentieth century America, every woman everywhere was dependent upon some man—be it father, husband or brother—for her literal existence. Today, however, any woman can pack up almost any time she wishes, move a thousand miles away, settle down and support herself in some culturally approved occupation—not as a prostitute or a slave—and often make more money than the man whom she left. This has had an enormous effect on the instability of marriage relationships. For it is always an implied threat which, even if never voiced or used, creates doubts and frustrations within the marriage relationship. It might well be argued that marriages are better today because of the freedom of the partners to secede; it also may be pointed out that the very permission to fail leads to many marriage failures.

change choice?

UNREALISTIC MARRIAGE EXPECTATIONS

Perhaps of all the problems created by the changing social conditions of marriage, none is more important for the marriage counselor to understand than the unrealistic expectations of marriage roles, of marriage satisfactions and of the marriage relationship itself which both partners often bring to marriage today.

True satisfaction comes from knowing what is expected of you and then doing it better than anyone expected you could. If too much is expected, so that one cannot possibly attain an excellent level of performance, can there be any satisfaction? Herein is a major source of marriage difficulty today.

It is literally true that in order to be a good husband 50 years ago a man didn't even have to smell good. Today, he is constantly being compared, because of our mass communications, to the best athlete's manliness and the finest gentleman's manners. It goes without saying that relatively few men in our society can stand such a comparison. This very evening all over the country, there will be little girls sitting down to watch the latest television hero and to dream about the men they are going to have in marriage. Their men not only will have all of the resoluteness, decisiveness, intelligence, perception—indeed the omniscience and omnipotence—of the television hero, they will also have all the good attributes of their fathers.

Perhaps the expectations are even more unrealistic in the opposite direction. All over the country tonight there will be little boys watching the glamorous television heroines and dreaming about the wives they will have who will be just such paragons of personality, charm, poise and elegance; in addition, they will have unquestioned skills as homemakers, wives, mothers, sex partners, walking encyclopedias, appliance mechanics, chauffeurs, child psychologists, psychiatrists to their husbands and experienced purchasing agents. Moreover, they will be warm, tender, submissive, agreeable and adaptable, and will want only to make their husbands' every wish a command.

The fact that too much is expected of each partner is only a part of the problem. Another factor is that there is a wide disparity between the marriage partners' expectations of how their mates should behave.

As Robert Blood[2] has pointed out, the fact that role expectations are acquired unconsciously in childhood gives them the appearance of absolutism, which they hardly deserve. But this appearance is convincing enough to give the marriage partners a sense of self-righteousness and moral indignation toward a spouse, which infuriates him, since he holds the same attitudes in return. By this process, anger, hostility and resentment are engendered, almost always enough to trigger emotional upset and quantities of adrenalin into the bloodstream, and often enough to lead to marriage disruption and dissolution. The fact that these differing expectations and the consequent seeds of marital discord are planted very early in life is evidenced by studies of high school boys and girls. It has been shown that by this age, differing expectations of marriage partners' roles between the sexes are well developed and tend to exist regardless of background or place of residence.[3]

It is small wonder that there is so much confusion between the partners over what is proper role behavior. There is a great deal of confusion on the part of our society as a whole over what are the proper expectations for marriage partners in modern society. Many young women are tortured by guilt feelings if they do work outside the home, many are troubled by guilt feelings if they do not. Our society has not made up its mind. Many marriages are currently in trouble because one partner or the other cannot make up his mind whether the husband is expected to be boss and to make resolute and courageous individual decisions, or whether the wife wants to be consulted at every point and be considered a democratic partner. Again, our cultural norms are in a state of flux. Time and time again, I have counseled women who chose a husband because he was "so considerate" when he was courting, only to reject him after marriage because he looked to her for her opinion and failed to tell her what to do and make her like it. You will find more about this in John Crist's Chapter 24 on the overdominant and the oversubmissive partner.

To add to the list of unrealistic marriage expectations such things as the American ideal of constantly increasing romantic love and "togetherness" would be to labor the point. We shall leave it here.

THE COURSE OF THE MARRIAGE DISEASE

But, if it is important to know that these unrealistic expectations are a major cause of marriage disease in our society, it is also important to understand the insidious course of the disease. What happens is this: two young people going together in school or college believe that they meet each other's expectations completely. After all, does he not know just when to bring the flowers, just what to say at the dance, just how to conform to the peer group rules of social etiquette? Does she not know just how to accept compliments demurely, to set the table carefully and to say the right thing at the right time? Starting from these basic signs of reciprocal expectation-meeting, the young man and the young woman generalize to the conclusion that they will meet each other's expectations after marriage.

By this time they are joyfully in love and the conviction grows that they were just made for each other. By a process of autosuggestion they build in their own minds an idealized picture of perfection for the mate which is far beyond anything that could be realistically expected. So they are married.

For the period of the honeymoon, their mate's behavior may actually exceed their expectations. Very soon, however, one partner may begin to recognize that his mate is not a super human being, but is actually mortal with all the imperfections and jealousies and weaknesses common to mortal men and women. The halo fades.

While it may not be intentional or even conscious, one partner or the other begins to have something less than complete acceptance—complete hero worship—for his mate. If it begins with the wife, the husband soon senses this change of attitude and begins to protect himself, again perhaps only half consciously. In turn, the wife protects herself against the husband's slightly changed attitude which she is now experiencing. Then he adjusts again, and so forth. This goes on until the partners have arrived at a state of complete hostility—or worse, apathy—in their efforts to protect their own egos against their mate's disillusionment.

In this process no single rejection may be important in itself, but ultimately there is one incident which represents the final denial of expectation, the ultimate disenchantment and perhaps the last straw.

This pattern of disillusionment sometimes sets in rather early in marriage In Blood and Wolfe's[4] cureful study of a sample of Detroit married women, it was found that 52 per cent were very satisfied during the first two years of marriage but only 6 per cent were still so completely satisfied 20 years later.

Often the men suffer disenchantment earlier than the women; perhaps their expectations have been even more unreal.[5] However, which is the first to be disillusioned is unimportant. Sooner or later it will affect the other partner and the relationship will begin to suffer. Then the modern marriage disease will have claimed another two victims.

Our examination of modern marriage sums up to this: the counselor who wants to help people with marriage troubles is faced with the basic problems of helping them to improve their understanding, helping them to stimulate the determination and helping them to adjust to a more realistic expectation which will be less subject to gross denial.

There is a reading list of books on the psychosocial background to marriage problems in Section IA of the Appendix.

REFERENCES

1. KLEMER, R. H.: Marriage counseling in medical practice. Part II. Marriage disease —its etiology and its course. West. J. Surg., **71**: 154–157, 1963.
2. BLOOD, R. O., JR.: *Marriage.* The Free Press of Glencoe, New York, 1962.
3. DUNN, M. S.: Marriage role expectations of adolescents. Marriage and Family Living, **22**: 99–111, 1960.
4. BLOOD, R. O., JR., AND WOLFE, D. M.: *Husbands and Wives, The Dynamics of Married Living.* The Free Press of Glencoe, New York, 1960.
5. PINEO, P. C.: Disenchantment in the later years of marriage. Marriage and Family Living, **23**: 3–11, 1961.

chapter three

Marriage Counseling Techniques*

RICHARD H. KLEMER, Ph.D., *Department of Psychiatry, University of Washington School of Medicine, Seattle, Washington*

There are three general objectives for marriage counseling implicit in the conclusion that most marriage problems result from the partners' lack of understanding of each other, lack of determination to stay married and lack of realistic expectations for marriage.

For, if these are the major areas of difficulty, increasing understanding through communication, stimulating determination by emphasis on positive attitudes toward the partner and developing more realistic expectations through re-evaluation of marriage satisfactions should—and do—lead to an improved marriage. These are realistic and attainable goals for practical marriage counseling.

But when you are facing the patient across your desk, fine sounding objectives are not enough. Equally as important, if not more so, are the actual techniques and procedures to be used in achieving those objectives. What should be done? How do you begin?

THE FIRST STEP

The first step, obviously, is to assess the problem. This is as true for the physician who intends to refer the patient for treatment by a marriage counselor as it is for the physician who, by choice or necessity, is to serve as counselor himself. For it is important to know both the depth of anxiety and the complexity of the situation in order to make an appropriate referral or to get started in counseling. Not only is this important for the referral and for the physician's records, but also for the morale of the patient. The patient wants to know that his physician is at least interested enough in his personal life to listen to the details of the problem which he finds so upsetting.

* Much of this material was originally published as Part III of "Marriage Counseling in Medical Practice" by Richard H. Klemer, Ph.D.,[1] in The Western Journal of Surgery, Obstetrics and Gynecology, July–August 1963. Used by permission.

Unfortunately, though, most patients are not good reporters even when they are not emotionally involved. Often they want an excessive amount of time to tell the most rudimentary facts. But, with practice, the physician can develop a skill in asking a few direct questions which will help the patient to give him a brief but adequate understanding of the marriage relationship. Interestingly, even though it is necessary sometimes to interrupt the patient gently with these questions, more often than not this is interpreted as a sign of intense interest on the part of the physician.

In addition to such obvious questions as "What bothers you?" and "Why do you feel that he behaves that way?", I have found great advantage in asking a patient such things as, "What would he say about you if he were sitting here?" and "If you could have any solution you desire, what would you like?" These questions not only get facts, they also reveal a great deal about the patient's emotional state and sometimes provide him with the material for self-examination and later insights. Sometimes these very questions lead to an alleviation of the problem before further counseling is necessary. Such questions also are useful in some cases in revealing gross irrationalities in the patient's thinking and behavior which point to the desirability of referral to a psychopathologist. There is much more about this in John Hampson's Chapter 4.

Because the aim in marriage counseling is to counsel the relationship and not just one individual partner, it is generally necessary to talk with both partners before any wholly valid diagnosis of the difficulty can be made. However, for the purpose of this early assessment, at least some basic estimate of the extent of a problem can be made even if only one partner is available.

Once the physician has an adequate understanding of the complexity of the problem, he is ready for the next step. Sometimes, as has been indicated, this will be referral, but sometimes this may also mean the beginning of marriage counseling by the physician.

Techniques that produce results in counseling are not always universal. Successful counselors differ widely in their methods and procedures. However, all of them do some sort of tension reducing and some sort of educating (if only through insight), and all of them try to provide the patient with a solution for his present problem as well as a better method of solving his problems in the future.

To do this, ordinarily, the seven functions pointed out in Chapter 1 are necessary: (1) creating the climate in which the patient can talk about his problems, (2) providing for ventilation and emotional catharsis, (3) providing the reassurance of acceptance of the patient's attitudes, and perhaps some additional reassurance as well, (4) diagnosing the real problem with the patient, (5) encouraging patient education and evaluation, (6) helping the patient to examine all of the possible alternatives and to decide on a specific action, and (7) motivating the patient toward completing the chosen action.

CREATING THE CLIMATE FOR COUNSELING RESULTS

Basic to any successful marriage counseling is the establishment of a secure permissive atmosphere in which the patient can talk freely about his problems, and basic to the creation of such a climate are three factors:

1. The security given to the patient by the confidential attitudes and the physical surroundings in which the counseling takes place.

2. The interest and the concern exhibited by the physician-counselor.

3. The nonjudgmental attitude of acceptance with which the patient's statements are received by the counselor.

It is tremendously important that the patient be able to express himself without having to weigh all of his thoughts and to measure his words lest they be offensive to someone else. For this reason, it is vital that the counseling take place where conversation will not be overheard and the sessions will not be interrupted. In the early stages of counseling I have generally found it preferable to see one marriage partner by himself and to talk to his spouse at another time. (But be sure to see Gerald Leslie's Chapter 7 on counseling the partners together.) Sometimes, in the beginning, having the spouse present in the counseling room leads to interruptions and contradictions which actually preclude any counseling progress. Later, of course, for some purposes—such as evaluating progress in communication—it may be wise to see both partners together. The decision as to whether to see the partners singly or jointly may well depend on the counselor's experience and skill.

Of equal importance with confidentiality in a counseling situation is the attitude and interest of the physician-counselor. Most troubled people are extremely sensitive to the slightest implication that their problem is not sufficiently important to warrant the doctor's attention. Consequently, an alert participation on the part of the physician—something more than listening—is imperative if there is to be any real success in marriage counseling. While the therapeutic aspect of just-letting-the-patient-talk is not to be underrated, neither should the importance of demonstrating interest and helpfulness by asking pertinent questions be overlooked. Sometimes these questions can have other functions as well. Dean Johnson[2] distinguishes between clarifying questions (How did that come about? Why was he so angry?), reflective questions (You feel he hates you?), counseling questions (You feel there is a connection between the coming of the baby and your marriage difficulties?), information-gathering questions (What do you do?) and confronting questions (Is that what you really want?).

The third factor important to the provision of the secure climate is a nonjudgmental and permissive attitude on the part of the physician-councelor. This is something more than a calculated calmness and lack of shock reaction. This is genuine acceptance of the patient's feelings as being understandable even if not entirely appropriate.

This kind of acceptance of the patient's attitudes and behavior must arise from the counselor's own self-understanding of his biases, and from his ability to tolerate ideas and behavior which conflict with those biases. For this reason, the physician-counselor needs to spend some time in self-evaluation so that he is aware of the points at which he is emotionally unable to keep his values and predilections from intruding into the counseling situation.

Even an experienced counselor is startled sometimes by a question that he asks and must constantly be saying to himself: "Why did I ask such a question? Was it really to help the patient get a new insight into his behavior, or was it because I was just curious?"

VENTILATION AND CATHARSIS

Having created the secure climate, the next step in functional marriage counseling is to listen carefully as the patient ventilates his hostility against his marriage partner. Often this hostility is veiled or disguised with such a beginning as "He is such a wonderful man." Or, "I am sure it must be all my fault." In marriage counseling and in psychotherapy, there is a great deal of catharsis in the process of the expression of real feelings and the airing of suppressed hostility. The patient sometimes immediately feels better after such a session. It is not surprising to find an occasional patient who will announce that this was all he wanted from counseling and who actually goes away with an improved marriage relationship.

PROVIDING ACCEPTANCE AND REASSURANCE

The next function of the physician-counselor is to provide supportive acceptance and reassurance for the patient. Some form of reassurance is implicit in every form of counseling, including deep psychotherapy, although plain old-fashioned Pollyanna type reassurance has justly fallen into disrepute because of its previous overuse and misapplication. But as Frederick Thorne, among many others, has pointed out, ". . . reassurance is a natural psychological antidote for the negative emotions of fear, worry, doubt and uncertainty." [3] Since these emotions often must be set aside before any constructive progress can take place in counseling, reassuring support for the patient, in a proper degree, is often indicated.

In practical marriage counseling, as in psychotherapy, at least some of the necessary reassurance comes from the quiet acceptance of the patient's attitudes and verbalizations by the counselor. That the counselor is willing to hear such hostile and guilt ridden thoughts and not pass judgment is often enough for the patient.

Sometimes, of course, patients will have come to see you wanting something more than passive acceptance. Indeed, some will be seeking a kind or a quantity of reassurance that is impossible to give them. It will be necessary to point out to them—for their own good—that to expect some guarantee of the unpredictable is not realistic, or that to expect the counselor to take sides in an argument just to make them feel better will not solve the problem.

Yet, in working with nonpsychopathologic patients there is almost always (I am tempted to say "always") something positive in every situation. The counselor, being further removed from the emotional trauma of a situation, can usually see and provide some new interpretation of the problem or give some new direction to the patient's thinking. This can lead the patient out of his inaccurate rut or away from his dead center vacillation and back toward those emotional attitudes which will allow him to take positive action to solve his problem.

Herbert Otto, who has written two chapters in this book (Chapters 9 and 27), has given much study to discovering and making use of the strengths and positive factors in the marriage relationship. In an unpublished paper he says, "By virtue of their training and orientation, most counselors develop a sensitive awareness of the problems, difficulties, dysfunction, and personality pathology of individuals who come to them for help. The more extensive their experience, the more refined are the counselors' clinical perceptions in diagnostic skills. However, the able counselor is aware not only of the dysfunction but also of the resources or assets of his patient. What abilities, skills or capacities are manifest? What are the strengths or assets in the patient's background? What are his positive personality attributes?

"As an integral part of the counseling process, the patient should be helped to assess and take stock of his assets and strengths. He should be encouraged to explore possible methods of employing these resources in relation to his problem or difficulty. There are strengths within his relationship with his partner as well as within himself. Relationships between people have discreet qualities. It may have qualities of trust, warmth, honesty and spontaneity to name a few. In any particular marriage situation, the counselor will want to assess the strengths in the relationship and to find out how these strengths can be brought to bear on the problems and difficulties." [4]

The matter of what else is reassuring to the patient will require some careful thought. The patient is not necessarily reassured by telling him that his difficulties are less than he believes they are. This only leads him to believe that the counselor does not understand the depth of his problem.

Moreover, some counselors have fallen into the trap of trying to be reassuring according to the statements of the patient, rather than according to the patient's real meaning. A case of which I know involved a young man who had been told by his physician that he had an incurable disease. One night his wife awakened to hear him sobbing. She inquired as to what was the matter. He replied that he was very concerned that she and the children would not be able to get along after he was gone. "Oh, don't worry about that, dear," said his wife brightly, "I am quite capable of taking care of the children." This statement, while calculated to be reassuring, was not.

While the use of reassurance must be both well considered and limited, it is still true that this is a major function of the counseling procedure. It is important in reducing tension so that progress can take place. It is also all but prerequisite in establishing better patterns of behavior, the ultimate objective of the counseling. Thorne has said it well: "The whole practical psychology of learning depends heavily upon rewards in the form of assurance and reassurance to reinforce the first timed efforts of learners . . . ."

Diagnosing the Problem

The next step in the marriage counseling procedure is the diagnosis. The first concern of the marriage counselor is a *clinical* diagnosis. This refers to the symptom complex; how does the marriage problem manifest itself? It is from this working understanding of what appears to be wrong with the marriage, that the counselor can, with the full cooperation of the patient, arrive at some conclusion as to what is wrong in the relationship and what alternatives are available for helping this patient.

This is the point at which it is necessary to focus on the extent of the patient's lack of understanding, his lack of determination and his lack of realistic expectations. How well does this patient understand the real reasons for his mate's behavior? How much is he willing to sacrifice to improve the relationship? How congruent are his expectations for his role in marriage with those of his mate? How realistic are both partners' expectations of what marriage can provide? These are important questions in arriving at a diagnosis.

But as John Cuber will later point out in Chapter 6, it is important to understand the total marriage configuration, as well as the specific problem, if the diagnosis is to be meaningful in treatment. It is the existing condition of the marriage, as well as the specific problems, which portends the prognosis. Just as with individuals, some marriages can stand terrific shock and not be sick; others dissolve with half the trauma an average marriage might stand.

Cuber proposes a five-category classification of marriage, including the *conflict habituated* (fighting is incessant and expected), the *devitalized* (resignation and acceptance of less-than-hoped-for satisfaction), the *passive-congenial* (not disillusioned, they never really did expect satisfaction in marriage), the *vital* (successful acceptance and understanding) and the *total* (total fulfillment in the relationship for both spouses; rare).

The counselor who diagnoses only the immediate problem without reference to the total condition of the marriage may have little result to show for his diagnostic accuracy. Cuber points out that whatever the specific diagnosis is for a conflict habituated couple, for example, telling them to "talk it over" is not apt to solve their problems in itself. Such a prescription, on the other hand, might have real merit for the same diagnosis in another marriage relationship. Failure to consider the overall configuration of the marriage can lead to disappointment and discouragement for both the physician and the patient when it comes to treatment.

Some counselors who are oriented toward psychopathology try to arrive at what might be called a dynamic diagnosis even in marriage counseling. This is used to describe one or the other partner's (or both partners') mechanism of adjustment, or, you might say, his habitual way of solving his frustrations. This often portends a diagnostic labeling with psychiatric terms. While this may be useful, if correct, in referrals to the psychopathologist, it is rarely useful in marriage counseling. For, unhappily, some marriage counselors, as well as some psychopathologists, have fallen into the habit of believing a day's work is well done when they have arrived at a diagnosis such as "compulsive person," "frigid wife" or "latent homosexual," or, perhaps, "psychopathic personality." As Cuber[5] has pointed out elsewhere, even if these labels were precisely valid, they are by no means an end objective, and they are not likely to prove effective by themselves in solving a relationship problem. In fact, they often create aggravated anxieties in the patient and a skepticism concerning the marriage counselor's ability to tend to the problem at hand.

Education and Insight

Once the diagnosis is made and tested for validity, the educational process begins. Sometimes straight information giving is needed on the part of the physician-counselor. This can be information about sexual techniques, methods of adjustment, or even knowledge of hereditary characteristics. Sometimes what is required is education about the dynamics of human behavior, so that the marriage partners can better understand why their mates behave as they do.

Sometimes the information giving process is furthered by giving the patient carefully selected books to read, or suggesting self-study and self-analysis. Books, while valuable, should be meticulously screened. Often a patient, in the process of acquiring new understanding of his present problem from one area of a book, will acquire a whole new set of imagined symptoms by reading another section of the same book.

It should be noted that what has been called "insight" is in fact a form of self-education. It is probably the most effective kind of learning. A physician-counselor, like all other person-helpers, depends in large measure for his effectiveness on the patient's ability to gain new perceptions in the process of exploring himself or his situation.

PLANNING ACTION

Once the patient has altered his perceptions of his situation, through education or through insight, planning a new course of action becomes the next step.

Actually, some patients already know all the possible alternatives for action when they come in to see the counselor. What they need is the re-assurance of a sympathetic listener before they can make a decision.

But there are other patients who may have overlooked important alternatives which the counselor can suggest. While it is undoubtedly desirable for the patient to arrive at all of the alternatives in his own thinking, this often requires a luxury of time that is not available. So, many physician-counselors will sometimes want to point the patient's thinking toward an alternative which seems to offer a good chance of improving the patient's relationships.

This is not to say that the counselor can provide a total ready-made solution for the patient. Often such attempts end in failure just because the overeager counselor attempts to solve the problem for the patient. As Otto points out, to answer the question "Doctor, what should I do?" is often to fall into a trap. For it is possible that the patient will be unable to follow through with whatever advice is offered. This may result in the accusation, "You should not have given me this advice—you should have known I would be unable to carry it out!" Pointing out alternatives is one thing; dictating a solution is quite another.

Some counselors "steer" the patient indirectly and rationalize that they really did not have anything to do with the decision at which the patient arrived. Actually, some direction is almost unavoidable, even in so-called nondirective counseling, because counselors are human beings with values and prejudices.

Needless to say, it is hoped that the physician-counselor can be as objective as possible and aware of his own, as well as his patient's, values when he is serving in a counseling capacity. But when problem-solving and the teaching of decisiveness are called for, being timid and evasive is probably not being wholly helpful.

MOTIVATING THE PATIENT

Finally, it is the responsibility of the counselor to motivate—you might even say inspire—his patients to follow through with whatever course of action has been decided upon. This is perhaps the hardest and yet the most important function of all, for usually any improvement in interpersonal relationships requires some self-sacrifice and the change of long-standing habit patterns.

This brings up one important aspect of relationship counseling which should not be overlooked. While not wholly axiomatic, it is probable that if one partner can be induced to change to any significant degree, the other partner will not long be able to maintain his same attitudes and ways of behaving.

Thus, it is often both possible and wise to have behavior change *precede* insight when you are counseling a relationship. That is to say, if a wife can be induced to start being nice to her husband, she may soon find that he is in return somewhat nicer to her. She *then* can gain the insight that her behavior was the cause of the unpleasantness in the first place.

This is the point at which the use of some actual direction and persuasion by the counselor not only seems justified but also is probably inevitable. Very often it is the counselor's willingness to reenforce the patient's decision which provides the impetus for the patient to carry his plans through to a successful conclusion.

It is true that one of the ultimate aims of marriage counseling is to help the marriage partners to establish better long run problem-solving patterns. So, therefore, it is not helpful for the physician-counselor to continue to motivate the patient time after time to do what he has decided to do. But in the initial phases—in the learning to walk which precedes the learning to run—the confirming reassurance of the physician-counselor will be what makes for successful counseling.

Naturally, this requires considerable self-confidence on the part of the counselor himself. As was indicated in Chapter 1, the more self-confident marriage counselors are often the more successful ones. An important part of the counselor's ability to help his patient comes from the strength of his conviction of his own ability to help, and from his willingness to transmit that hopeful belief to his patient. As Jerome Frank[6] has pointed out, this is a major success ingredient for all forms of the person-helping process.

In general summary, it might be said again that no one standardized set of techniques will be successful in all marriage counseling cases. The best way to counsel is the effective way. And the effective way is the way congenial to the personality of the counselor. In the end, it is the physician-counselor's personality, his warm self-confidence, which will provide the acceptance, the reassurance, the cooperation and the motivation to help marriage partners solve their problems.

It is probably not necessary, desirable or even possible for the physician-counselor to assist in the resolving of *all* the partners' difficulties. Once several of the major stumbling blocks to marriage harmony have been removed and patterns of communication and problem-solving have been successfully established, the partners themselves should be able to deal with other minor irritations and new situations as they arise. Consistent failure to do so should realert the physician-counselor to the probability of personality disorder in either or both of the partners (Chapter 5), and should prompt a reevaluation of the need for referral to the psychopathologist.

There is a reading list of books on marriage counseling in Section IB of the Appendix. There is also a reading list of books for the married partners in Section II of the Appendix.

REFERENCES

1. KLEMER, R. H.: Marriage counseling in medical practice, Part III. Marriage counseling technics. West. J. Surg., **71:** 198–202, 1963.
2. JOHNSON, D.: *Marriage Counseling: Theory and Practice*. Prentice-Hall, Inc., Englewoods Cliffs, New Jersey, 1961.
3. THORNE, F. C.: *Principles of Personality Counseling*. Journal Clinical Psychology, Brandon, Vermont, 1950.
4. OTTO, H.: Unpublished memorandum on counseling. 1964.
5. CUBER, J. F.: *Marriage Counseling Practice*. Appleton-Century-Crofts, Inc., New York, 1948.
6. FRANK, J. D.: The dynamics of the psychotherapeutic relationship. Psychiatry, **22:** 17–39, 1959.

chapter four

Deciding Who Must See the Psychiatrist— A Brief Diagnostic Guide to Psychopathologic States

JOHN L. HAMPSON, M.D., *Department of Psychiatry, University of Washington School of Medicine, Seattle, Washington*

The physician who is approached by his patients for marriage counseling will want to ask himself: "Is this truly a marriage problem that can be handled by the techniques of marriage counseling, or are the marital problems a concomitant of a more serious underlying psychologic disturbance for which the patient must be referred elsewhere?"

Just as some emotionally ill persons may present themselves to doctors with predominantly *somatic* complaints, so too others can only bring themselves to ask for emotional help in terms of *marital* complaints. Moreover, there are others who, unaware of their own emotional and psychologic handicaps, all too readily focus on only the marital aspect of interpersonal difficulties when in fact most, if not all, of their other interpersonal relationships have also been seriously affected. Although the physician may find it necessary or advisable to take on marital counseling as a part of his job as family doctor, he may be less willing to become involved in the management of serious psychiatric illness.

Although the task of deciding whether a given individual is psychiatrically ill is not always easy, there are certain time-tested guidelines which can prove useful. It is perhaps only restating a truism to say that nothing quite takes the place of a good history—one obtained as much by listening as by asking questions.

The following outline is offered, at the cost of oversimplification, as an additional guide to augment life history data and to provide a diagnostic framework against which one can put case material into proper perspective.

CLASSIFICATION OF PSYCHOPATHOLOGIC STATES*

I. *Disorders Caused by or Associated with Impairment of Brain Tissue Function*
  A. *Acute brain disorders*
    Disorders due to or associated with infection, intoxication, trauma, circulatory disturbance, convulsive disorder, disturbance of metabolism, growth or nutrition, new growth, or unknown or uncertain cause.
  B. *Chronic brain disorders*
    Disorders due to prenatal (constitutional) influence, due to or associated with infection, intoxication, trauma, circulatory disturbances, convulsive disorder, disturbance of metabolism, growth or nutrition, senility, new growth, or unknown or uncertain cause.
II. *Mental Deficiency*
    Intellectual inadequacy of unknown or uncertain cause with the functional reaction alone manifest, hereditary and familial diseases of this nature.
III. *Disorders of Psychogenic Origin or without Clearly Defined Physical Cause of Structural Change in the Brain*
  A. *Psychotic disorders*
    1. Involutional psychotic reaction
    2. Affective reactions
    3. Schizophrenic reactions
    4. Paranoid reactions
    5. Psychotic reactions without clearly defined structural change other than above
  B. *Psychophysiologic, autonomic and visceral disorders*
    Disorders due to disturbance of innervation or of psychic control (psychophysiologic skin, musculoskeletal, respiratory, cardiovascular, hemic and lymphatic, gastrointestinal, genitourinary, endocrine, nervous system and organs of special sense reactions).
  C. *Psychoneurotic disorders*
    Disorders of psychogenic origin or without clearly defined tangible cause or structural change (anxiety, dissociative, conversion, phobic, obsessive-compulsive, depressive and other psychoneurotic reactions).
  D. *Personality disorders*
    Disorders of psychogenic origin or without clearly defined tangible cause or structural change (personality pattern disturbance, personality trait disturbance, sociopathic personality disturbance and special symptom reactions).
  E. *Transient situational personality disorders*
    Temporary alterations in personality which arise in response to a life predicament; the personality changes constitute the individual's way of coping with an overwhelming situation.

TECHNIQUES FOR EVALUATING EMOTIONAL AND PSYCHOLOGIC DISTURBANCE

Although there is no adequate substitute for a thorough case history, there are certain methods of evaluating emotional and mental status which have stood the test of time. The greatest obstacle to using these

* Adapted from *Diagnostic and Statistical Manual of Mental Disorders*,[1] published by the American Psychiatric Association, Washington, D. C.

methods is likely to be the doctor's own reticence about asking such questions of patients he has perhaps known for a long time.

Sometimes one can discover a great deal about a patient's mental status in the course of an ordinary conversation without the patient being aware that he is being so examined. Thus, it is possible to inquire about dates, phone number and knowledge of recent news events, from which one can make certain inferences about the patient's memory, grasp of events and even his prevailing mood. Other times, though, a more straightforward approach is required and the family doctor is likely to be the least threatening person available to assess certain aspects of his patient's mental functioning.

It is a mistake to avoid discussing mood disturbance, suicidal preoccupation and thinking difficulty if one has the slightest concern about such matters in his patient. An honest but tactful approach at the beginning will preclude alienating one's patient.

The following examination techniques are good to have on hand as ready guides to:

1. The patient's intelligence level—this should be estimated primarily from the patient's school and job record, his awareness of current events, the vocabulary he uses and so on. Test results should be evaluated in the light of this clinical estimate. For subjects of marginal or defective intelligence, language tests should be interpreted cautiously.

2. Whether the patient's grasp of events is more defective than his level of intelligence would warrant—a sign of organic or toxic brain disease. Patients with organic brain damage tend to minimize or conceal their defects; therefore, they often do much worse on testing than the examiner anticipates. Clues regarding organic or toxic factors are given by the test of recent memory (No. 2, below), retention of digits (No. 3, below), the serial subtractions test (No. 4, below) and the absurdities test (No. 5, below).

3. Whether the patient's grasp of events is distorted or odd—a sign of schizophrenia. Clues to this are given by the absurdities test and by the proverbs test (No. 6, below). Distorted intellectual functioning is shown particularly by difficulty in forming concepts or making abstractions. Whatever way the ability to form abstractions is judged, one must be fairly certain that the task is within the patient's intellectual grasp before much significance may be attached to the distortions themselves. However, even in the case of low intelligence, highly personalized interpretations may be useful in detecting deviations in thinking.

4. Whether a patient is suffering from a sweeping mood disturbance, as in depression. In this condition, the patient complains of a more serious disturbance in mental functioning than is apparent on testing; *e.g.*, he

may insist that he cannot concentrate or remember, yet he may do serial subtractions adequately and do well on the digit span test.

It is seldom necessary to use all the tests on any one patient. Rather, those tests which are most useful for a given problem should be selected. In testing for schizophrenia the proverbs test is used, preferably when the estimated intelligence level is average or better. The examiner should first formulate his own clinical impressions and questions based on them, and then select some tests accordingly.

The following kinds of test questions have been found helpful by psychiatrists and psychologists for making such evaluations. It should be remembered that they are useful only for making rough estimates, and to check clinical impressions. More detailed and finer measures are provided by standardized psychologic examinations.

1. The orientation test. The patient is questioned regarding his orientation to time, place and person. He is asked his name, what day it is, where he is and similar questions. Patients with organic or toxic factors may be confused or give grossly inaccurate answers, especially for time relationship questions. Schizophrenics may say that they are someone else, that they are in a prison, or otherwise reveal their twisted orientation to the world around them.

2. The remember 3 things test. This is a test of recent memory. The subject is told that the names of an object, a color and an address will be given to him and that he will be asked to repeat them in a few minutes. The patient is told something like, "table, green, 609 Broadway." He is asked to repeat these to make sure he has heard and understood the 3 things mentioned. The interview is then resumed and after 3 to 5 minutes the patient is asked to name the 3 things. Patients with intact recent memory should remember all 3. Impairment of recent memory is frequently found in cases of senility, cerebral arteriosclerosis and in other organic brain conditions.

3. The digit-span test. Another test which measures concentration and attention span, as well as the ability to retain material just learned, is the digit-span test. A series of randomly selected digits is recited to the patient, beginning with 3 digits. They should be given at the rate of about one a second without grouping. The patient is required to repeat the digits in proper sequence. If the patient repeats 3 digits correctly, a new series of 4 digits is given, then 5, 6 and so forth. If the patient fails one series of a given length, another series of the same length should be given. If 2 series of the same length are failed, the patient is assumed to have reached his capacity and the test is discontinued. The same procedure is then repeated, except that now the patient is asked to say the numbers backwards. Be sure that the patient knows what is meant by backwards, as some fail to reverse the sequence until the task is explained or an illustration is given. Start with 3 digits. If the patient fails, go back to 2.

The adult of normal intelligence repeats about 6 to 7 digits forward and 5 to 6 backwards. Individual differences in ability and concentration make for some variation in these figures. If a patient cannot retain 5 digits forward and 3 backward, then it is probable that the patient will be found to be feebleminded or emotionally disturbed. High anxiety may interfere with concentration. People with organic brain conditions frequently do much more poorly on digits backward than digits forward. If the difference between digits forward and digits backward is more than two, then brain pathology should be considered.

4. The serial sevens test. The patient is asked to take 7 from 100, 7 from the remainder and so forth. *To perform this test adequately, a degree of intelligence approaching normal and a grade school education are required.* If the subject has difficulty in subtracting 7 from 100, or is unable to do so, then ask him to start with 20 and subtract 3's in the serial manner as above. If the subject cannot subtract 3 from 20, he is probably in the mentally defective range. Length of time required to complete the task, and frequency and kind of errors made are noted. Essentially, the test involves the ability to concentrate and to stay with a task. If a patient makes a few errors, only slight in degree, and corrects them himself, then we can infer that concentration is only slightly impaired. If errors are gross and the patient seems unaware that he is making mistakes, then the thinking processes may be more severely disturbed. If the serial subtractions are very slow, the answers correct and the subject excessively concerned about his precision, then the question of depression should be raised.

5. The absurdities test. This test detects the extent to which a patient will recognize logical absurdities. The patient is told: "I am going to say something foolish, and I want to see if you can tell me what is foolish about it." After giving the absurd statement, ask: "What is foolish about that?"

This test is useful primarily for detecting schizophrenics. These patients fail to see why the statements are absurd, or they offer farfetched explanations of them. One of the common characteristics of the thinking of schizophrenics is that they are able to maintain two opposite or logically contradictory notions at the same time, and in such cases the irreconcilable elements of the above situations would not be recognized as such. The following are some examples of absurdities: (a) They found a young man locked in his room with his hands tied behind him and his feet bound together. They think he locked himself in. (b) A wheel came off of Bob's automobile. As he could not get the wheel back on by himself, he drove his automobile to the shop for repairs. (c) Bill Jones' feet are so big that he has to pull his trousers on over his head. (d) The fireman hurried to the burning house, got his fire hose ready, and, after smoking a cigar, put out the fire. (e) In an old graveyard in Spain they have discovered a small skull which they believe to be that of Christopher Columbus when he was about 10 years old.

6. *The proverbs test.* This test may be useful for detecting schizophrenics whose estimated intelligence level is *average or better.* The patient is told that the proverb, "Large oaks from little acorns grow," means that great things may have small beginnings. He is then asked to tell what the following proverbs mean: (a) A burnt child dreads the fire. (b) He who would eat the kernel must crack the nut. (c) A drowning rat will catch at a straw.

Schizophrenics frequently are unable to formulate the principle involved because the ability to think at abstract levels may be impaired. Frequently, they see the point only insofar as it applies to something concrete or specific in their own lives. At times their answer will be given in such a way as to demonstrate their personal application, or they will read into the statements meanings in terms of their own preoccupations. Sometimes they will tend to see the same meaning in more than one proverb, reflecting such preoccupation. Sometimes the answer will be entirely irrelevant, but they will seem to be perfectly confident of its correctness or indifferent to its incorrectness. At worst, the answers are confused, incoherent or very peculiar.

Recognizing the Patient with an Organic Brain Disorder

The number of conditions falling into this category is almost infinite in variety. The diagnosis and treatment of such conditions may be extremely easy or may defy even the expert. The basic syndrome for all organic brain disorders, whether acute or chronic, consists of the following:

1. A lowered level of awareness which is constant or progressive in the chronic brain disorders and fluctuating in the more acute disorders. This may range all the way from difficulty in concentration to partial or complete loss of orientation.

2. Impairment of memory—particularly recent memory.

3. Impairment of such intellectual functions as ability to learn, comprehend and calculate.

4. Impairment of judgment which affects not only day to day living but extends to matters of social judgment as well.

5. Changes in affect (mood)—emotional shallowness and lability are the most constant affect changes seen.

The symptoms of an organic brain disorder are related more to the individual's preexisting personality than to the degree of brain damage *per se.* In all patients over the age of 50 whose complaints involve inter-personal difficulties, it is well to give some thought to the possibility of an organic brain disorder as a contributing factor in the total picture.

PSYCHOTIC DISORDERS

The most severe of the functional emotional disorders, classified as psychoses, are characterized, in general, by regressive attitudes and be-havior, an unusual capacity to distort reality, diminished control over impulses and desires and, frequently, such gross disorganization of the personality that delusions and/or hallucinations become conspicuous features. The major "functional" psychoses include the *affective reactions* (including depressions), the *schizophrenias* and *paranoid states.*

RECOGNIZING THE DEPRESSED PATIENT

About 15 per cent of psychotic patients admitted to public mental hospitals are classified as depressions of one type or another; the ratio of females to males is nearly 2 to 1. The term *depression*, though, is simply a description of the dominant mood and as such may be symptomatic of a great many psychologic problems and accompany many clinical conditions. To complicate things still further, many patients—particularly men, since they lack cultural sanction to express sadness and other extremes of mood—cover up depressive feelings with a facade of gaiety and joviality. Still others focus on bodily complaints, fretful indecisiveness and even paranoid delusions as an alternative to depression, so that one must be on the constant alert for the patient with a "depressive equivalent."

Most typically, depression is characterized by: (1) a prevailing mood of sadness and despair, and (2) a general slowing down of intellectual and overall behavior. At times, however, the depressed patient can be so anxious and agitated that the retardation and depressed mood is obscured. A depression often starts with such symptoms as fatigue, insomnia and loss of appetite and later other somatic complaints. His ability to concentrate on current activities becomes impaired, but his past misdemeanors seem to loom over him like a dark cloud. The patient may begin to drink excessively in an effort to ward off depressive symptoms. He sees his future as gloomy and himself as a continuing burden to his family. His self-preoccupation becomes painful not only to his wife and family but to the patient as well. In such a setting the suicidal danger becomes acute.

A CHECKLIST FOR EVALUATING SUICIDAL RISK

1. Does the patient have a history of suicidal attempts in the past?
2. Does the patient talk openly of suicide? Contrary to popular belief, suicidal patients do communicate their intentions in most instances.

3. Does the patient see his life situation as overwhelming or hopeless; does he blame himself for what he is doing to his family?

4. Does the patient have a history of "acting out" impulses and feelings—such as by excessive drinking, reckless driving or dramatic behavior?

5. Has the patient shown an unexpected shift in mood, behavior or contentment from one interview to the next—either for the better or the worse? (Patients often appear better once they have worked out a suicidal plan; sudden weight loss and insomnia during the course of a depression may presage a suicidal attempt.)

6. Is the patient in the recovery stage from a profound depression? Having lost his indecisiveness and retardation, a patient may be better organized to carry out latent suicidal intentions.

7. Is there a family history of suicide or a recent suicide by a friend or acquaintance? Such occurrences seem to enhance suicidal motivation by tacit sanctioning of the act.

8. Does the patient have meaningful personal and occupational involvements in his life?

In some depressed persons, though by no means all, there is a tendency for depression to alternate with manic or hypomanic moods. The manic state with its overly affable, elated overtalkativeness is easy enough to diagnose. The hypomanic state is more of a problem and a patient may hover for months in a hypomanic state that so closely approximates normalcy that family, friends and doctors alike fail, for a time, to recognize the element of pathologic irresponsibility in the patient's behavior. Such patients appear happy and optimistic about everything. They show a great push to accomplish, and in conversation they jump from topic to topic. The great danger in this period lies in alcoholic and sexual excesses, extravagant use of money, reckless driving and an irritable, quarrelsome demeanor which can destroy a reputation, disrupt a marriage and even bring the patient into conflict with the law. The hypomanic person's delusions and behavioral abnormalities are often not gross enough to seem very psychotic to the layman. The patient himself has no insight into his mental condition and commitment for proper psychiatric care is often difficult to obtain.

Recognizing the Patient with Schizophrenia

Schizophrenia is a common mental disorder. About five persons out of a thousand are alleged to have the condition. Many times it is mild and may go unrecognized, while at other times hospitalization is mandatory. Schizophrenia is not so much a single disease as a *group* of mental illnesses, each differing in some way from the others yet sharing certain common features. Schizophrenic symptoms involve three basic kinds of disturb-

ance: (*1*) *thought*, (*2*) *emotions*, and (*3*) *volition*. The diagnosis of schizophrenia is based on the presence of one or more of these basic disturbances.
Some schizophrenic persons, however, display additional secondary (or
accessory) symptoms: (1) delusions (false, unshakable beliefs and peculiar
interpretations of events), (2) hallucinations (false perceptions), and (3)
catatonia (disturbances of posture and motor behavior).

The disturbance of *thinking* may be shown by thought blocking or an
unusually marked "pressure" of thoughts. The schizophrenic's thought
associations may be so difficult for a normal person to follow that they
have often been termed "meaningless" or "bizarre." In less pronounced
cases, the patient's interpretation of a proverb may bring out an extra-
ordinarily inappropriate answer. Still others, operating within an elabo-
rate system of denials, dissociations and barriers against associations,
evolve a language of their own, which is in part verbal, in that he attaches
peculiar meanings to words or phrases, and in part a magical sign language
of posture and gesture.

The disturbance of *emotionality* is usually perceived by others as an
inappropriate affect in which the emotions appear either out of keeping
with the situation or blunted. Such emotional blunting may result in
loss of sympathetic feelings toward family and friends, or even in a lack
of fearful, angry or erotic feelings.

The disturbances of *volition* refer particularly to an apathetic indifference and a loss of initiatory verve.

Traditionally, schizophrenia has been divided into four clinical types:
simple, hebephrenic, catatonic and paranoid.

In the *simple* type emotions are shallow and bland. The person has
little drive to accomplish, so he appears shiftless and lazy. He complains
of fatigue and boredom, but seldom does such a patient display delusions
or hallucinations.

The *hebephrenic type of schizophrenia* characteristically begins in adolescence
and the diagnosis is aided by the unpredictable giggling, silly behavior
of the individual.

Catatonic schizophrenia can be recognized by the characteristic waxy
flexibility of the limbs and periods of mutism which alternate with periods
of excitement.

Paranoid schizophrenia is typified by delusions of persecution and sometimes of grandeur. Ideas of reference and hallucinations are common.
The individual may become excessively religious and may display an
expansive delusional system of omnipotence, genius or special ability.

In recent years other variations have been described. Hoch and Polatin[2] drew attention to the fact that neurotic symptoms sometimes serve as
defenses against an underlying schizophrenia. From this the term *pseudo-*

neurotic schizophrenia has come into popular usage in psychiatry. Similarly, the term *pseudopsychopathic schizophrenia* calls attention to the observation that many latent schizophrenic thought disorders find expression in antisocial behavior. In other instances, where a mood disturbance such as depression predominates, the term *schizo-affective disorder* has been applied.

RECOGNIZING THE PATIENT WITH A NEUROSIS

In actual practice it is a moot point as to where the line should be drawn between "normal" and "neurotic." Both terms are abstractions which we have inherited from the past and which at times have little usefulness.

A neurosis is, for all practical purposes, only an exaggeration of characteristics which everyone has had to a lesser degree at one time or another. The spectrum of symptoms which patients experience encompasses a diversely disagreeable range from anxiety, depression and alterations of consciousness to disturbed body functions, repetitive thoughts and difficulties in interpersonal relationships.

The contemporary view of neurosis is that the primary underlying factor is anxiety. Anxiety may be directly felt or may be dissipated unconsciously and automatically via one of many psychologic "defense mechanisms" (*e.g.*, dissociation, repression, depression, avoidance, ritualistic behavior and so forth). Other times anxiety acts directly to disturb physiologic body systems and bring about functional changes in one or another part of the organism.

The names of the common neuroses derive from the predominant symptom. Thus, unmodified anxiety is called an *anxiety state;* excessive repression may "convert" anxiety into functional symptoms involving sensory or motor functions—*conversion reaction or "conversion hysteria."* Other common neuroses include *dissociative reactions, phobic reactions, obsessive-compulsive reactions, neurotic depressive reactions* and *somatization reactions.* (This latter term is used to refer to disordered autonomic functioning, *i.e.*, psychophysiologic disorders.)

In addition to these common symptom-neuroses, another term has come into recent usage in psychiatry—*character neurosis.* In the character neurosis the most striking thing about the individual is his repetitious overuse of some characteristic behavior to the extent that not only does it lead to excessive suffering for himself or his family, but his "public image" is colored by it as well. Such persons have major problems in getting along with other people because of their unhealthy patterns of behavior and their temperamental and often pathologic emotional responses to life situations. The dividing line between a "character neurosis" and a more malignant, deeply ingrained "character disorder" is often difficult to distinguish.

The following descriptions of the major neurotic reactions may serve to sharpen the clinical picture of these conditions somewhat and to help in diagnosis.

Anxiety Reactions

Palpitation, dizziness and fear of fainting are typical complaints which bring the anxious patient to the doctor's attention. Typically, the anxious person is in a state of apprehension, tension, uneasiness and uncertainty. He feels helpless and fearful but can never designate the object of his fears.

Dissociative Reactions

At times, anxiety states may become so intense as to result in a temporary gross disorganization of the personality of near-psychotic proportions. Thus, the anxious person may feel "outside" of himself (depersonalization), and may develop amnesic symptoms, the habit of sleep walking and dream states. Troublesome though such symptoms are at the time, the ultimate prognosis is good.

Conversion Reactions

In some individuals anxiety is not experienced consciously but is converted by massive repression into functional symptoms which lessen the anxiety which the individual feels. Often the symptoms symbolize the nature of the underlying emotional conflict and result in a more or less obvious solution to the conflict (secondary gain). The three main types of symptomatic manifestations are: (1) involuntary movements (tremors, tics, catalepsy and epileptoid seizures), (2) loss of motor functions (paralysis, monoplegias, hemiplegia and aphonia), and (3) alterations in sensation (pain syndromes, paresthesia, anesthesia, anosmia and hysterical blindness or deafness). The somatic conversion reactions simulate known medical conditions more or less expertly according to the patient's medical knowledge and sophistication. With the popularization of medical information in magazines and newspapers, the conversion symptoms as displayed by patients are becoming increasingly difficult to diagnose and distinguish from structural diseases.

Phobic Reactions

Phobias arise through a process of displacement of internally engendered anxiety to situations or things such as heights, dirt, animals and enclosed spaces. Ashamed of the irrational character of their fears, the phobic person often hides his illness from himself and others by avoiding situations where symptoms might be expected to occur. The unin-formed or intolerant spouse of such a person sees this kind of behavior as willfully uncooperative and negligent. Oftentimes phobias acquire an obsessive-compulsive quality and thus combine with the reaction type described below.

Obsessive-Compulsive Reactions

An obsessional idea is one which is persistent and unwanted and which recurs, like an annoying tune, to the distress of the individual. Often, obsessional thoughts are linked to a need to perform repetitive acts or rituals, such as touching, counting and hand washing (compulsion). Like phobias, obsessive-compulsive symptoms, despite their nuisance value to the individual, seem to resolve and dissipate the anxiety stemming from internal conflicts.

Neurotic Depressive Reactions

In some depression-prone individuals the anxiety originating from in-ternal conflicts appears to be partially relieved by depression and self-depreciation. The depressive reaction is triggered by some stress in the environment and is often associated with marked feelings of guilt over past failures or misdeeds. Gross psychotic symptoms are absent. Not in-frequently the neurotically depressed individual vacillates between pe-riods of free-floating anxiety associated with obsessive-compulsive and phobic symptoms.

THE PERSONALITY DISORDERS

The personality disorders doubtless represent the single most important group for the doctor who engages in marriage counseling. These disorders are manifested by lifelong patterns of behavior, rather than by mental or emotional symptoms. It is true that sometimes organic brain disease will simulate the clinical picture of a personality disorder, but the history and diagnostic examinations readily distinguish the person with organic brain disease from the person with pathologic personality structure. Because of the special importance of personality disorders in the terms of reference of this book, they will be discussed separately in the next chapter.

PSYCHIATRIC TREATMENT

Just as not every physical condition warrants treatment, so too not every emotional disorder requires treatment. There are many minor neuroses and other emotional maladjustments which are quite compatible with a happy and productive life and, unless there are clear-cut indications for psychotherapy, it may oftentimes be better not to interfere. There are two useful criteria that one can use in arriving at a judgment in such matters which can be put to oneself in the form of a question:

1. Has the patient's emotional disorder led to—or is it likely to lead to—an unhealthy social adjustment for the patient, his family or society?

2. Has the patient's emotional disorder led to—or is it likely to lead to—physical pain or discomfort so marked as to affect his enjoyment of life?

With increasing understanding of their patients' emotional problems, many psychiatric disorders are now being handled quite satisfactorily by family doctors in the course of general medical treatment. Referral to a psychiatrist should not, however, be done as a measure of desperation; conversely, one should avoid conveying to the patient that the psychiatrist can cure any and all emotional ills. The emphasis in a psychiatric referral is usually best placed on obtaining a psychiatric opinion, leaving open the possibility of psychiatric treatment.

There is a reading list of books on psychopathology in Section IC of the Appendix.

REFERENCES

1. *Diagnostic and Statistical Manual of Mental Disorders.* American Psychiatric Association, Washington, D. C., 1952.
2. HOCH, P. H., AND POLATIN, P.: Pseudoneurotic forms of schizophrenia, Psychiat. Quart. 23: 248–276, 1949.

chapter five

The Effect of Character and Personality Disorders on Marriage Relationships

JOAN G. HAMPSON, M.D., *Department of Psychiatry, University of Washington School of Medicine, Seattle, Washington*

Implicit in the very nature of man's existence as a social creature are certain adaptive necessities. Inevitably there will be some people who consistently fail to adjust—they repeat maladaptive failures.

Some of these people exhibit major maladjustments sufficiently severe and serious enough to have been long since awarded a "disease label." Neuroses, psychotic reactions—and some psychosomatic disorders—all have been recognized as somehow fitting into the spectrum of emotional illness or disease. Such conditions have been dealt with in the preceding chapter. The physician will almost always find it advisable to refer these patients for psychiatric help.

There are, however, a multitude of people chronically repeating minor maladaptive failures in interpersonal relationships who only in recent years have come to be regarded as serious enough to require specialized help. Such minor but firmly entrenched maladaptive patterns originate in basic patterns of behavior which the individual has learned in the course of growing up; and, since they are repetitive, they color his whole personality and character. For this reason, such individuals are referred to as having a character or personality disorder.

It is one of the ironic features of these people that, while they are not customarily seen as being disturbed or ill in any traditional psychiatric sense, they are nonetheless almost invariably destined to have some degree of difficulty—ranging from trivial to profound—in their relationships with other people. Since marriage is surely the most intimate and demanding of interpersonal relationships, it is not surprising that they often ask for help with marriage problems. But with these people, it is a mistake to assume that, because a problem is presented primarily as a marriage difficulty, they can make effective use of the kind of marriage counseling advice and guidance effective with better adjusted, more adaptable people.

This is not to say that the physician serving as a counselor cannot have some psychotherapeutic role with patients who have character and personality disorders. Ameliorative help for any emotional or personality disturbance can often be given by the physician who has lots of time, is very interested and is sympathetically supportive.

But, in order to avoid disappointment and wasted effort, it is important for the physician to recognize the existence of these chronic maladaptive repeaters. If brief, practical marriage counseling is the physician's objective; he should learn to differentiate as soon as possible after starting counseling, those with character and personality disorders from those adequate problem-solving individuals about whom Dr. Klemer was writing in the first three chapters and about whom Dr. Cuber will be writing in the next chapter.

It is beyond the scope of this chapter to describe all the possible variants of personality and character which may contribute to marriage difficulties, but some of the more important patterns can be discussed briefly. First, though, something should be said of the symbiotic nature of marriage.

THE SYMBIOTIC NATURE OF MARRIAGE

As the dictionary defines it, symbiosis is "the living together of two dissimilar organisms in close association or union, especially where this is advantageous to both, as distinguished from parasitism." The successful marriage established by two psychologically mature partners is almost, by definition, a felicitous symbiosis. Psychologic maturity implies that a person is capable of caring for and respecting the needs of a marriage partner as much as he is concerned with fulfilling his own needs and interests. The choice of marriage partner is, however, often determined by the character patterns of the individuals. A psychologically immature person may, possibly unconsciously, seek a mate who seems to offer the promise of fulfilling his neurotic needs, a marriage partner who will fit into his particular mode of distorted personality functioning. A case in point is the domineering, aggressive woman who is likely to seek a subservient, passive husband, or the hostile, punitive man who manages to find a wife with excessive need to be long-suffering and martyred.

It is possible, though by no means inevitable, that two people, each with a particular kind of character disorder, may fortuitously arrive at a marriage with a degree of mutual symbiotic advantage if the unhealthy personality traits of each partner happen to be congruent. But the equilibrium of this partnership would be unstable and the balance of such a marriage precarious at best. A relatively slight challenge or provocation may shake the whole structure of such a marriage, showing its true basis of neurotic needs and demands. Or, in a greater number of instances where a character disorder exists, even a shaky symbiosis will not be established. Rather, there will be clearly exposed the pathologic relationship shown by the individual who seeks only his own personal gratification, being either unwilling or incapable of concerning himself with the needs of his partner—a condition which is essentially a psychologic parasitism. Problems related to the basic personality or character of one or both of the marriage partners may be presented as marital problems but, clearly, are not to be resolved by environmental changes or social manipulation. Advice and guidance alone are seldom sufficient.

PATTERNS OF PSYCHOSOCIAL IMMATURITY

Whether any human being ever attains complete maturity of personality is perhaps a problem for philosophers to debate. The physician not infrequently, however, encounters individuals whose behavior could appropriately be described as adolescent, childish or infantile. But, because psychologic maturity is so often an ideal rather than an actuality, we are often hard put to define a patient's level of personality maturation with the scientific preciseness that one might desire, because the process of emotional maturation is not necessarily in step with the chronologic age of an individual, nor is it necessarily dependent on intellectual maturity. Whitehorn[1] has described a useful four-stage scheme for characterizing immature levels of personality functioning, which he has designated the infantile level, the childish level, the early adolescent and the late adolescent level.

Infantile Level

At the infantile level one expects from others a limitless amount of service and consideration without feeling any reciprocal obligation. Case example:

A 58-year-old wife of a prominent and successful lawyer had spent her childhood coddled and pampered by her socially prominent parents. Her marriage, though conforming to all requisites for social success in the eyes of her prestige-oriented Southern family, was, despite external appearances, a long-term fiasco. She found childbearing and motherhood a "miserable experience" about which she complained to all who would listen. She produced three children but remained a petty despot by virtue of her incessant whining demands and imaginary physical complaints. When her children finally married and her retinue of faithful domestic servants diminished, she gave up all pretense of meaningful social functioning and lapsed into a pattern of total dependency. In desperation her husband hired a full-time "companion" for his wife who, in fact, funtioned essentially as a nursemaid, catering to her whims both day and night.

Childish Level

At the childish level there has developed some sense of responsibility, but of delegated responsibility, the kind that is completely erased by a good excuse. The alibi habit is a characteristic manifestation of this stage. Great circumstantiality of speech is a useful clinical clue. Persons at the childish level expect complete reliability in others but only make excuses or token efforts themselves. They may expend more effort in framing acceptable excuses than might be required to get a job done. Obsessiveness as a substitute way of establishing merit is rather characteristic of this level. Praise or blame is the focus of attention. Case example:

An attractive 35-year-old woman complained that her life was made miserable by her husband's inconsiderateness. She felt sexually unresponsive because her husband was "not romantic . . . peremptory and oversexed." Though a conscientious mother to her two youngsters, she felt trapped by domestic responsibility but, childishly, held out the expectation that most of her problems would be solved if only her mother would babysit for her more often and "just give me a little sympathy." Once, while her parents were out of town and her husband at work, she naively invited the local supermarket manager to go with her to her parents' home to help her feed the cats for whom she was acting as temporary custodian. She was only mildly surprised when her invited guest seduced her. Later she rationalized to the psychiatrist, "After all if my husband won't be romantic no one can blame me if I fall for a guy who will be." The marriage was an on-again, off-again affair with both husband and wife alternately stalking out of the house and declaring themselves through.

Clearly, neither of the partners was either psychotic or classically neurotic. Equally clearly, though both talked about needing help with the marriage, the underlying problem was one of a persistence of immature patterns of social behavior—a problem unlikely to be resolved either quickly or easily by literal-minded attention to the presenting complaint.

Early Adolescent Level

At the early adolescent level exhibitionism and prestige seeking are the outstanding manifestations. There is a strong push to assert one's personal significance, and to sustain it by repetitive demonstrations. Badges and trophies have high value as demonstrable symbols of prestige. The striving for self-importance requires extrafamilial supports and these are characteristically found in idealistic hero worship and in gangs and clubs. Case example:

A professionally well established surgeon in his early 40's became mildly depressed and sought advice after his wife filed for divorce. He claimed to be surprised and was certainly indignant that his wife would want to break up their marriage of eight years and move away with their three children. Dr. K. boasted a long string of professional associations as well as membership in a half dozen civic organizations. A country club man, too, he made sure that all of his colleagues and most of his patients knew of his enviable golf handicap and he grumbled conspicuously of the tribulations of maintaining his expensive foreign sports car. His enthusiasms were often transient but sometimes newsworthy, as when he organized and led a skin diving expedition to locate sunken treasure vessels off the Aegean Islands. His wife had been dazzled and charmed by his boyish enthusiasms during their courtship but had gradually become disenchanted and told her lawyer that she was "tired of waiting for her husband to grow up."

Late Adolescent Level

The late adolescent level is the stage of "-isms,"—romanticism, idealism or cynicism, for example. The sense of social responsibility has become more diffused, usually in the form of loyalty to a cause. His earlier dependence on heroes, gangs and clubs is becoming more sophisticated and consumes a smaller proportion of his total energies. The tendency to excess is still present, as in early adolescence, but it is doctrinaire excess rather than strenuous physical excess. The pseudosophisticated line of talk, the wisecrack and the sophomoric savant are easily recognizable manifestations. Sexual interests are expressed in pairing off and in courtship behavior, but success in this field, or the anticipation of success, may have the emotional quality of a conquest rather than of mutual devotion. Case example:

A 32-year-old brokerage firm assistant sought psychiatric advice, feeling that he needed professional help in examining his growing conviction that his marriage was unworkable and that divorce was, for him, an appropriate and reasonable step. Though he presented many complaints pointing up his wife's "immaturity," it soon became clear that the responsibility for the failing marriage was far from one-sided. His wife, when interviewed, described the man as self-centered and unreasonable. His interest in his home and children had never been great, but had dwindled to the point of extinction during the past several years as he had immersed himself in an ever enlarging statewide campaign to interest sportsmen in a wild life conservation program. Hard working and respected for his business ability, he was much in demand as a luncheon and dinner club speaker. He was never able to resist an opportunity to display his debonair and witty style in pleading the conservationist cause.

It was only after many interviews that the patient was able to recognize that his overzealous dedication to his outside activities was working to the detriment of his family relationships.

Since our American culture sets a high value on nonconformity and independence, the characteristics of the late adolescent's style tend to extend into the adult years. Even so, most individuals, as they get into their late 20's and 30's, lose some of the urgency and competitiveness of their earlier years and become more or less reconciled to the realities of the world about them and to their own limitations, without feeling depressed or discouraged by it. The social needs for affection, security and personal significance, characterizing immature stages, are not outgrown in the mature individual. Rather, the means to their satisfaction have been found in a fairly wide range of personal relationships and in a greater flexibility in acting out social roles which satisfy these needs.

The real usefulness of the above schema is not simply as an aid to diagnosis or labeling, but as a guide to appreciating and understanding the basis of a person's distress in personal difficulties. The problems of many patients become understandable when one relates them to the degree of maturation of their psychologic development and to the degree to which their sense of well-being depends on preserving a social environment better suited to a child or an adolescent.

Thus, against the background of a crude scale such as this, one can understand better how a chronologically adult person whose personality development has been arrested at an early adolescent level, for example, heavily dependent on the need to assert one's personal significance, might alienate those about him who were more mature. How the infantile person comes to a marriage relationship with little real capacity for closeness, stability and comradeship may also be understood. The high premium which our American culture places on preserving characteristic adolescent values, such as excesses of competitiveness, assertiveness and love of prestige has caused countless problems in American marriages. The adolescent preoccupation with more and more sexual conquests and romanticism has proven troublesome time and again when it persists into chronological adulthood. Many of the sexual maladjustments encountered in today's marriages are expressions of arrested emotional development. No marriage manual and no amount of advice giving will solve the marital problems of such individuals unless basic progress in maturation of personality and social attitudes can somehow be brought about.

The Histrionic (Hysterical) Personality

The histrionic personality style is a rather colorful, dramatic variant of the emotionally immature personality and, as such, deserves separate mention. The physician will encounter the histrionic personality in a variety of symptom-settings, ranging from serious marital conflicts to problems of sexual adjustment, as well as in somatic conversion syndromes. The histrionic personality is not the exclusive prerogative of the female sex but is very nearly so. Sexual and social anxieties early in life appear to play a role and the psychiatric literature is replete with speculations regarding the psychosocial dynamisms involved. The unique problems implicit in becoming a girl and woman in our society doubtless provide the focal points where social learning during the growing up years can go awry, leading to a lasting personality style of the sort to be described. In general, the hysterical personality in adulthood is an immature, shallow person, self-absorbed to the point of egocentricity. Such individuals can often be singled out by their flair for the dramatic in manner, dress and speech. One writer has aptly described the shifting feeling states of the hysteric as "emotionally capricious." The female hysteric is often a caricature of "sexiness," dressing and acting in a sexually provocative manner but, paradoxically, becoming frightened and perplexed when her provocative behavior evokes an appropriate masculine response. Such individuals are often unexpectedly emotionally labile. Their immaturity is additionally exemplified by their strong suggestibility and an astounding tendency to represent fantasy as fact.

Of importance to the physician are the psychopathologic potentials in such individuals. The enormous capacity of the hysterical individual to repress and deny anxiety-provoking insights leaves them vulnerable to dissociative and amnesic phenomena as well as to the conversion of anxiety into physical dysfunctions such as pain syndromes, hysterical paralyses, aphonia and so on. Their immaturity is evidenced in other ways, too, such as their poor ability to assume responsibility. Though not always readily apparent, the hysteric is not infrequently a socially fearful individual who, in self protection, establishes superficial relationships and finds the greatest difficulty in the more mature, warm relationships demanded in a marriage. Despite their sexually provocative behavior, sexual expression, even in marriage, can be a problem for these individuals, finding expression in such difficulties as frigidity and dyspareunia in women and impotence in the hysterical male. Case example:

A serious-minded graduate student in English came to discuss his relationship with a young woman with whom he had been living for some time at her suggestion in a "trial marriage" to "test their compatibility." As the end of the trial period approached, he found himself increasingly disquieted by his fiancee's behavior and dubious about the wisdom of embarking on a more formal marriage. At her suggestion the couple had established their menage on a houseboat despite the inconveniences of sharing these cramped quarters with her two Afghan hounds. Initially fascinated by her unconventionality, he had at times been embarrassed by her flamboyant manner of dress, as when she reproached him as a stuffed shirt for questioning her going to a rather formal Christmas party in black leotards and kid boots. He was troubled, too, by her unabashed flirtatiousness with his student colleagues and her temper tantrums when he had voiced his objections. Twice she had dramatically taken about 25 aspirin tablets after a quarrel and, during a party on the houseboat, she had taken undue insult at a facetious comment by a guest and, in a fit of pique, had jumped overboard, necessitating a potentially dangerous rescue operation by bewildered guests. He was by now aware that her feelings for him did not run very deep and he questioned her capacity for the mature relationship he envisioned in marriage.

The physician who approaches the management of symptoms in the hysterical personality, as he would in any other patient, through the traditional methods of advice giving and education, is apt to be disappointed. The remarkable ability of these individuals to dissociate and repress, and the profound difficulties they have in establishing a healthy doctor-patient relationship sometimes requires the greatest skill in handling. All too often the doctor is trapped into a situation where the patient becomes too dependent and perpetuates inappropriately immature patterns, to the patient's own disadvantage.

THE SOCIOPATHIC PERSONALITY

Although in times past the terms psychopath or psychopathic personality were used to designate individuals with this kind of personality disorder, contemporary nosology employs the term sociopathic personality disturbance to refer to essentially the same behavioral phenomena. Awareness of sociopathic character traits is not new. As long ago as the eighteenth century, doctors recognized this group of individuals as somehow different from other people, and in 1835 Prichard described what he called "moral insanity" so well that we can hardly improve the definition even today: ". . . the moral and active principles of the mind are strongly perverted or depraved; the power of self-government is lost or greatly impaired and the individual is found to be incapable not of talking or reasoning upon any subject proposed to him, but of conducting himself with decency and propriety in the business of life." [2]

Today we view the sociopath as an asocial—and sometimes actively antisocial—highly impulsive individual who behaves irresponsibly, lacks guilt or anxiety about things he has done or plans to do and who somehow fails to learn from experience that certain kinds of behavior are socially unacceptable or irresponsible and must, therefore, be suppressed. In some such individuals the deviation from reasonable social behavior is so marked that Cleckley[3] was provoked to title his book on the subject *The Mask of Sanity*. The sociopath, however, is "insane" only in the sense of being a severely unhealthy personality. He is not psychotic (although it is possible for him to become so) in the sense of having lost contact with reality like the schizophrenic or in the sense of having profound emotional transformations like the manic depressive. The sociopath retains, at some level, an awareness that many of his actions are not acceptable to society. This intellectual insight, however, remains superficial and without emotional involvement, so that he fails to act upon his awareness. Being free of normal anxiety, he has no reason to refrain from immediate gratification of his urges.

It should, at this point, be made clear that not all individuals who manifest rebellious, antisocial behavior are true sociopaths in whom there is a basic character disorder. There are individuals whose asocial and antisocial behavior is symptomatic of underlying neurosis or psychosis.

Typically, the true sociopath is a person of average and sometimes unusually high intelligence. He often has great personal charm and an easy social manner. His freedom from the socially inhibiting effect of anxiety allows him to succeed brilliantly for awhile in all his human relations, including even his work and studies. Inevitably and repeatedly, however, he manages to sabotage his life, to lose his job, to alienate his friends, often to appear in the office of the doctor or marriage counselor on the verge of losing his wife and children as well. Thus, these individuals display a tragic paradox in that for limited periods of time they may succeed, only to prove themselves inadequate as time goes by.

In addition to passive, inadequate sociopaths such as this, there is another variant, easier sometimes to recognize, in which the individual repeatedly commits aggressive antisocial acts. Some are petty thieves, check forgers and swindlers who easily become involved in serial common-law marriages, bigamy and sexual escapades. Others attract public attention through more shocking crimes, usually with little or no provocation or motivation.

Less flamboyant, though more frequent than these rather spectacularly acting-out sociopaths, are those basically sociopathic persons whose character disorder takes the form of a less public variety of maliciousness—the sadistic child beater, the pinball wastrel, the alimony evader, the irresponsible nonprovider and the uncooperative passive aggressive.

Perhaps the hardest thing for the average person to comprehend is the coexistence in the same individual of familiarity with correct ethical rules of behavior and an ability to formulate in words rules of conduct and plans for the future, but with an utter incapacity to follow through in his own life.

The results of attempts to help the true sociopath have not been good, so that at present the doctor must be satisfied if he can recognize such individuals among his patients and, when possible, relieve the pressures on the sociopath's children and spouse.

THE OBSESSIONAL PERSONALITY

There are individuals whose most characteristic personality functioning might be described as obsessional or obsessive-compulsive. We speak here not of those individuals so severely handicapped by obsessive-compulsive symptoms as to be clearly neurotic (*i.e.*, so controlled by their symptoms that their day to day functioning is severely impaired). Rather, the term obsessive-compulsive personality is used here to describe a distinctive mode of negotiating life and relating to others.

Psychiatrists have described over 40 traits as being characteristic of the obsessive-compulsive individual though, of course, they are not necessarily all present in any one person. The major personality traits of the obsessive character include meticulousness, overorderliness, persistence, stubbornness, inflexibility and procrastination. Such people live by routine and are upset if the routine is disturbed; they are fond of discipline, adhering dutifully to rules and regulations themselves; they are sticklers for the same precise kind of performance in others. Since they seem to be unable to leave well enough alone, they are always busy and never finished. Fearful of error, they are often indecisive, insecure and hesitant, extremely dependent on the approval of others though they try to hide their uncertainty and, paradoxically, may give the impression of being self-possessed and confident to the point of appearing smug. Although, in general, the obsessive personality is not given to quixotic mood changes, he can at times be malcontented, irritable and morose. On the other hand, it should be stated that they are often highly intelligent, sensitive and capable of unusual tenderness.

A person in whom a constellation of these traits is pronounced may attempt to justify his behavior by pointing to his efficiency and accomplishments. Up to a point, his careful attention to detail and conscientiousness may indeed be useful, but it is important to understand that serious discomfort and personal limitations can result both for the individual and his spouse if these personality traits operate beyond the level of social usefulness. Precisely what this level may be cannot be delineated unequivocally for all individuals and every situation, as people vary in their tolerance for personal idiosyncracies. It must, however, be recognized that marriages not infrequently founder when the relationship is strained by such personality traits in one of the marital partners. Control or modification of these traits is seldom possible simply by conscious effort, no matter how earnest these efforts may be. With expert help some modification can be brought about to the benefit of all concerned.

This chapter, then, presents four of the more important types of personality traits and character disorders encountered in clinical practice. The shy, schizoid, isolated individual, the morbidly jealous person, the offensively domineering woman and other personality variations which may be crucial in marriage problems have not been dealt with because of space limitations. What has been said, however, will hopefully suffice to guide the physician to an awareness that a frontal attack upon what may be presented as a marriage problem may be thwarted by ingrained disorders of personality and character. In instances where character disorders are evidenced, the chances of a rewarding outcome are slim unless attention is focused beyond the presenting problem towards an understanding of the unique personal character of the two people involved. Psychotherapy with these people is not impossible; it is, however, a more time-consuming and more intensive process than the physician-counselor ordinarily wishes to undertake.

But there are increasing numbers of people, as Dr. Klemer has pointed out earlier and about whom Dr. Cuber will report subsequently, who have normal adaptive ability, and who could not justifiably be diagnosed as having character or personality disorders, and yet who still have marriage problems. These are the likely candidates for marriage counseling. The remaining chapters emphasize methods and procedures for helping them.

REFERENCES

1. WHITEHORN, J. C.: A working concept of maturity of personality. Am. J. Psychiat., **119:** 197–1202, 1962.
2. PRICHARD, J. C.: *Treatise on Insanity.* Sherwood, Gilbert and Piper, London, 1835.
3. CLECKLEY, H.: *The Mask of Sanity.* C. V. Mosby Company, St. Louis, 1955.

chapter six

Three Prerequisite Considerations to Diagnosis and Treatment in Marriage Counseling

JOHN F. CUBER, Ph.D., *Department of Sociology and Anthropology, The Ohio State University, Columbus, Ohio*

The physician who is accustomed to diagnosing and treating medical problems of individuals is faced with unfamiliar difficulties when he attempts to assess the marital problems of his patients. Typically, husbands and wives manifest contrary subjective symptoms, and the stated symptoms, even when agreed upon by the pair, present unusual problems of interpretation.[1]

Despite a helpful legacy from psychology and psychiatry, and more recently from psychosomatic medicine, there remains a continuing need for creative research to facilitate diagnosis and treatment in marriage counseling. The writer's recent study of middle-aged men and women tends to confirm three pertinent observations which the physician-counselor may find helpful:

1. The marriage partners' behavior is strongly conditioned by their *relationship*, as well as by their personalities.

2. Those who seek marriage counseling are not likely to have radically different sexual and marital histories than so-called "normal" people.

3. The *total* marriage configuration provides the context for understanding the patient's behavior and attitudes.

These three conceptions grow out of the findings of our study of 437 eminently successful business and professional people who were between 35 and 55 years of age, and married, single, widowed and divorced, in the approximate proportions found in the total American population.[2]

RELATIONSHIP, NOT PERSONALITY

There is a common supposition that all behavior somehow resides in something we call "personality"—that people are intrinsically stable, energetic, conventional, cold, highly or lowly sexual, and so on, and that because they "are" this way they behave as they do. A *prima facie* plausibility supports this: almost everyone has observed that a person more or less predictably acts in certain ways. Hence the strong, familiar case for the concept of "personality" which has usefulness in some therapeutic situations.

But the focus on the marriage *relationship* sees people differently—and more realistically for marriage counseling purposes. The actual interpersonal behavior which occurs, according to this view, is substantially accounted for by the reciprocating *interaction* with the *other* person involved. A case may sharpen the point.

Early in our study we worked with a woman interviewee who had been married for 13 years and also had been involved in an affair for about half of that time. In the marriage she had been throughout the years essentially frigid. Not only did she almost never experience orgasm, she was more totally asexual; she tried to keep sex out of her mind in all ways. She was nevertheless an exceedingly efficient housekeeper and mother of several children. In the other relationship, carried on simultaneously, she almost unerringly experienced multiple orgasm and a high frequency of sexual intercourse. Now, is this woman "naturally" frigid or is she sexually active? She is both—but she is each within a given relationship only.

To put the point both generally and simply, we have abundant evidence that man-woman behavior is often unique to the particular pair. The easy supposition which sees behavior as the outgrowth merely of a "personality" can thus be misleading. At least it is misleading for relatively normal people; neurotic people may be so rigid and inflexible that as they move from relationship to relationship, they impose the same imprint upon each in succession. (See Chapter 5.) We have found in our nonclinical sample abundant evidence that the *interplay of two people,* and not simply the personalities of either, resulted in the kinds of relationships which exist. Much more often than not, *the same person showed radically different behavior with different persons of the opposite sex, whether they followed in sequence or occurred intermittently with one another.*

Why is it, for example, that two persons who meet in middle life, each having experienced a variety of partners and situations with which they were only minimally content, can discover a whole new world of total living, with dimensions and intensities of sorts which, a month or a year earlier, they would have denied were possible? No analysis of either's personality would have formed an objective basis for anticipating such an outcome.

Personality, however much we know about it, is simply not enough to understand whole people in the man-woman dimension. Whether we are considering fulfillments or frustrations, sex or decision making, the same subtle interpersonal dimensions intrude and tip the balance definitively.

What Is "Normal" in Sexual and Marital Behavior?

A second prerequisite to adequate diagnosis in marriage counseling is an understanding of what is "normal" and "functional" in sexual or in more diffuse male-female behavior. Table 6.1 contains seemingly an odd miscellany of items. Some are sex practices, some represent outcomes of sexual behavior, some represent circumstances rather than practices which are inappropriate and some, like divorce, involve more than sexual aspects. What all of them have in common, however, is that each is almost universally regarded as undesirable, many downright immoral, and there is a widely held opinion that people in whose lives these things have occurred are not only different from "normal" people but are different in ways which are likely to bring them serious trouble.

The table compares a random sample of 45 nonclinical cases ("normal" people who sought no counseling help) from our study and 45 cases also selected at random from clinical records of people who sought help at a marriage clinic.

From the table, even without formal statistical measures of significance,

TABLE 6.1

Miscellaneous background factors in clinical and nonclinical cases*

Factors	Clinical	Nonclinical
Divorced and remarried............................	13	16
Extramarital coitus (in a "love" relationship).........	18	21
Extramarital coitus (for thrill or situational)..........	22	16
Frigidity (present and considered "a problem").......	8	6
Impotency (present and considered "a problem").....	5	8
Incest (with consent, with parent)...................	2	1
Incest (with consent, with sibling)...................	5	8
Induced abortion (pre- or postmarital)..............	5	5
Masturbation.......................................	36	32
Mouth-genital sexuality.............................	21	19
Premarital coitus (in a "love" relationship)..........	39	41
Premarital coitus (for thrill or convenience)..........	34	37
Premarital pregnancy...............................	7	9
Voyeurism (compulsive).............................	10	7
Voyeurism (noncompulsive but deliberate).	15	18
Median age	42.3	41
Married at some time	100%	100%
Married at interview time...........................	39	43

* Of the 45 cases in each sample group, 22 were male and 23 were female.

it is obvious that the differences between the clinical cases and the "normal" cases are virtually nil. The clinical and nonclinical samples which appear in the above table, though random, are small. Conclusions based on them are not, therefore, reported as definitive. Even, however, should larger samples reveal some differences, there remains the hard fact that these and other items of history have occurred generously in the lives of the 437 "normal" people we studied and, aside from some practical inconveniences here and there, have caused them no serious trouble. A further reinforcement is suggested by the fact that these findings were what the research man calls serendipitous—they were discovered accidentally while we were looking for something else. This tends not to happen when the matters involved are trivial.

The implication from this aspect of our study seems clear: much deviant behavior is, in fact, neither really deviant in a statistical sense, nor is it *necessarily* pathologic. To insist that it is both deviant and pathologic by so diagnosing the patient often means perpetuating marriage problems rather than curing them.

In counseling, a serious clinical error still tends to be repeated and may result in serious and unnecessary trouble for the patient. When a woman presents an ill-defined complaint which is clearly psychologic or vaguely psychosomatic, some clinicians jump too soon to the inference that *because* she had a divorce or *because* she had an abortion 10 years ago or *because* he knows she is having an affair, these items of history are necessarily what is giving her trouble. It then becomes easy to commit what has been called the "self-fulfilling prophecy"—giving the patient the feeling that she *ought* to feel guilty and be disturbed, thus forging a false link in her mind between two things which may have been unrelated. Shortly, she will in fact be troubled because she is made to feel she should be by the counselor's diagnosis of the problem. This may leave much more real and serious causes of her marriage relationship problem undiscovered. Clinicians should observe a far greater burden of proof when connecting unconventional behavior and current difficulty than is, regrettably, sometimes the case.

The Total Configuration of the Marriage Relationship

Effective diagnosing in marriage counseling must consider the pluralistic structure of modern marriage. A diagnosis can be considered "good" only as it facilitates correction of the felt malfunction. An analogy to physical medicine is striking. If a pathogenic systemic condition in one patient can be corrected by injection of thyroid, to use an oversimplified illustration, it does not follow that the injection of thyroid for someone else would necessarily be corrective—it might, in fact, be severely malfunctional. The physician needs to know both the total configuration and the specific problem before he can know what to prescribe, for whom, and in what dosage.

Just so, the marriage counselor needs to know the total configuration of the marriage before he can adequately diagnose the specific marriage problem, or, more probably, problems. An incident that could be designated by the partners as a cause for divorce in one marriage could be barely noticed in another because of the differences in the accepted patterns of the relationships. What *might* cause difficulty in a marriage has little importance; what *does* cause difficulty is crucial.

The most generic finding of our study is that relationships between men and women in marriage are highly variable, despite the monolithic character of legal requirements, ecclesiastic teachings and conventional expectations. Our 437 case records were based on long and intimate conversations with the subjects and contained about 100 for whom we have a 25 year running record. We selected from the group those marriages which had endured 10 years or more and which the spouses considered to be satisfactory and likely to endure. Relationship within these "satisfactory" and enduring marriages, we found upon closer examination, fell into five distinct "conditions" or "types," with only a few which did not permit such classification:

1. The conflict habituated. This is a configuration in which verbal conflict is a continuing, almost incessant condition between the pair. Efforts are made to keep the conflict concealed from friends and relatives and children, but this is seldom successful over long periods. The subject matter of the conflict seems to matter little. In their other interpersonal relations most of these people are not hostile or argumentative or chronically in conflict. It is chiefly *in the marriage* that this form of conflict has become habituated.

2. The devitalized. Devitalized marriages are marriages which, rather soon after establishment, lost the close sharing, identification and deep feeling which the partners had for one another at the outset. For reasons which we did not determine to our satisfaction, but also confirmed by other investigations, the devitalization tends to begin to be felt with the advent of parenthood.[3] For whatever reasons, the present interaction is characterized by resignation and apathy and a rather dogged determination to accept the modest gratifications which present circumstances bring and to turn attention outward to other aspects of life for basic fulfillments.

3. The passive-congenial. The passive-congenial relationship is much like the devitalized with the exception that the relations between the couple never were really vital, not even during courtship, and therefore they have no feelings of disillusionment or regret or other negative sentiments. They never had it otherwise. Typically, they assert that they don't want it otherwise and doubt that other "mature" people do. They are content to meet as mates on the peripheries of their lives. Their children, their homes and their joint property, however, are important to them— for the women, especially, they tend to be central.

4. The vital. These are marriages in which the man and woman deeply invest their total personalities in one another; they empathize in the deeper feeling states of their spouses. They typically spend a great deal of time together, but this is not what makes them vital; it is more the desire and the need and the successful expression of accepting, understanding association which forms the vital bond. Their sex lives tend to be important to them, and when they have problems here they usually work them out well because of the strongly empathic nature of their association.

5. The total. All that needs to be said here is that they are much like the vitals with the addition that the association and the psychologic investment in the mate more nearly encompasses the total needs and fulfillments of each of the spouses. This kind of mating is rare, but it does exist, despite its utter incomprehensibility to people in the passive-congenial or devitalized roles.

One important perception regarding the above is that the people in all of these five types are at least minimally satisfied with them, and once the relationship is so established it tends to endure in that form over long periods. While, of course, there are exceptions, the overriding fact is that couples get adjusted rather early to some one of these patterns of gratification, defend it and do not take readily to changes in it. There are, of course, exceptions; sometimes they are "unequally yoked" and such people are the ones who may want a second chance or who are suffering one way or another. This minority suffers, however, not because the mode itself doesn't work, but only because it doesn't work *for them.* It manifestly works for many, many others.

It can readily be seen from the foregoing that counsel or practical assistance given to people with specific problems in marriage cannot be good counsel or poor counsel *per se,* but is good or bad only *as it fits the larger life expectations and habituations* of the specific person or pair with whom one is dealing. To suggest to the conflict habituated, for example, that they "talk it over" is simply to continue an already pointless procedure. (It is doubtful whether any real harm is thereby done because these people have already learned how to live with conflict.) The common suggestion that the couple should spend more time together or involve themselves more deeply with each other can actually worsen the situation for the passive-congenial and the devitalized, who in their own intuitive way have already made the important discovery that the way *for them* to live with a minimum of inconvenience and frustration is to avoid the spouse as much as they possibly can while still carrying out their other life needs. Nor is it necessary to tell the devitalized to "act their age" or "be mature"—they have already been pulling this off with remarkable adroitness. Sexual advice which might be appropriate to a vital couple— who almost never need it anyway—would be almost impossible for the passive-congenial to understand, much less carry out; the attempt to do so would likely be seriously disruptive. And so on.

Having examined the condition or the total configuration of the marriage, it is then possible to proceed to the specific marriage problem with some hope of arriving at a reasonable prognosis. To ignore the total configuration and treat only the presenting symptoms could (and, unhappily, often does) lead to disappointment both for the patients and for the physician-counselor.

Summary

Our studies of these normal and successful people have caused us to question certain traditional clinical assumptions and strongly to suggest new concepts which are useful in diagnosing marriage problems.

1. The evidence suggests strongly that actual behavior (good or bad as judged by some external criteria) derives importantly from the way in which two persons "come through" to one another and not simply from the kinds of "personalities" which each has. Unless this is understood with precision and objectivity, adequate diagnosis or helpful therapy is impossible.

2. Clinicians probably should rely less on the assumption that kinds of behavior that are conventionally designated as objectionable are necessarily indicators of psychopathology. Obviously aberrant sexual practices are hard for some to be casual about, but the principle is still there. It is supported not only by our own research, but is also clearly implicit in the Kinsey data as well as elsewhere.

3. Our close, intimate and detailed examination of the ways in which men and women with continuing marriages actually associate with one another revealed a typology of actual interactions which are radically and dramatically different. Yet they are not idiosyncratic; there are clear types or syndromes, recurring and repetitive modes which last over long periods, if not for entire lifetimes. Awareness of these types can serve an important purpose in differential diagnosis.

REFERENCES

1. Cuber, J. F., and Harroff, P. B.: The more total view: relationships among men and women of the upper middle class. Marriage and Family Living, **25**: 140–145, 1963.
2. Cuber, J. F.: *Marriage Counseling Practice*. Appleton-Century-Crofts, Inc., New York, 1948.
3. Blood, R. O., and Wolfe, D.: *Husbands and Wives, the Dynamics of Family Living*. The Free Press of Glencoe, Illinois, 1960.

chapter seven

Should the Partners Be Seen Together or Separately?*

GERALD R. LESLIE, Ph.D., *Department of Sociology, Oklahoma State University, Stillwater, Oklahoma*

Physicians working with marital and sexual problems constantly face the problem of whether to see the husband and wife separately, or whether to bring them into the office together. Obviously, it would save time if they could be seen together. On the other hand, the exclusiveness of the patient-physician relationship would be altered and the whole counseling process might be affected. Since much of this book analyzes the fundamentals of counseling and emphasizes the one to one relationship, this chapter will deal specifically with the advantages and limitations inherent in the use of joint marriage counseling.

THE DEVELOPMENT OF JOINT INTERVIEWING IN MARRIAGE COUNSELING

During its early years, marriage counseling was unique in its emphasis upon relationships. After all, it had come into being to treat relationship problems rather than personal problems. Obviously, counseling planning involved working with two persons, but it also involved working with the relationship as such. To provide a framework for analyzing the marital relationship, marriage counselors turned to the concept of the social system.[2]

When marital interaction is viewed as a social system, the individual no longer is the basic unit of analysis and less emphasis is placed upon personality factors alone. Both personality and relationships are conceived as distinct entities, each being composed of simpler elements or systems and each having dynamics of its own, such that neither is completely

---

* The basic ideas in this chapter apply equally to medical and nonmedical counseling and were originally published as "Conjoint Therapy in Marriage Counseling" by Gerald R. Leslie, Ph.D.,[1] in the Journal of Marriage and the Family, February, 1964. Used by permission.

reducible to the other. These systems are overlapping, of course. Social systems are made up of roles, and roles, as patterns of behavior, are elements of personality.

Viewed as a social system, the marital relationship has properties of its own, resulting from the interaction of two personalities in a particular social context. The relationship possesses dynamic force in its own right and influences the way in which personality is manifested. A man, for example, who has neurotic difficulties may or may not give malignant expression to those difficulties, depending upon the particular woman he marries and the developing relationship between them. Moreover, to "cure" his neurosis may disturb the relationship between them to the point where either or both display symptoms more serious than the original ones. Adequate evaluation involves making integrated appraisals of both partners and the relationship so that counseling of the partners may be coordinated and gains in one area of personal or marital functioning may be used to consolidate gains in other areas of living.

From the beginning, marriage counselors typically worked concurrently with both partners in a relationship. Until recently, however, their use of joint interviews has been tentative and hesitating. In conventional marriage counseling practice, the couple often was seen together for an initial interview to define the problem and to assess each partner's attitude toward it and toward the marriage. Then, ordinarily, the counselor proceeded by seeing each partner separately, with only occasional joint interviews. Toward the end of counseling, more joint interviews might be used to consolidate the gains achieved and to redirect the dependence upon the counselor to dependence upon the partner.[3]

Gradually, many marriage counselors are exploring the more systematic use of joint counseling. It is the thesis of this chapter that the potential of joint counseling is considerable and that most of the limitations on its use are not yet known.

Conjoint Marriage Counseling

The term conjoint counseling is not precise. Its essence is the systematic use of joint interviews in which the counselor simultaneously interviews two or more persons, usually the marital partners. In purest form, conjoint counseling involves *all* interviews being conducted as joint interviews, with neither partner being seen in individual sessions. Such pure conjoint counseling is feasible in a small proportion of cases. Occasional couples whose problems are acute rather than chronic, who focus consistently on a particular problem area and who are both motivated to strengthen their relationship by working out their problems, appear to be good risks for pure conjoint counseling.

Most counselors, most of the time, prefer to do some individual inter- viewing of the partners early in counseling. In these individual sessions, excessive hostility to the other partner is drained off through catharsis, "privileged" communication permits the revelation of attitudes and be- havior that would not be revealed to the partner, and thorough evaluation of each of the two partners is done. Then, when the counselor believes that the couple can work efficiently in joint sessions, joint interviews be- come the sole or major technique for most of the counseling. Joint inter- views become the major vehicle for insight development, and further individual interviews are used only when anxiety in one of the partners mounts to the point of interfering with progress in the joint interviews.

It has not yet been determined whether the alleged advantages in this combination of joint and individual interviews are really advantages to the patients. Few would question the legitimacy of the cathartic and personality assessment functions of the individual interviews, but there is some doubt about the need of counselors to "know the whole story" through the revelation of material that is not to be shared with the partner. That some counselors feel more comfortable when they know more about their patients may partly reflect the counselors' discomfort in working with the unfamiliar, new technique of conjoint counseling. A less charitable interpretation would stress the elements of psychologic voyeurism in- herent in marriage counseling[4] and indicate that the counselor's need to know is not necessarily consistent with his patients' welfare. More ex- perience with conjoint counseling should illuminate this question but, in the meantime, experience indicates that some individual interviews mixed with more frequent joint interviews are the most widely applicable form of conjoint counseling.

Finally, conjoint counseling shades off into the conventional marriage counseling technique when joint interviews become occasionally inter- spersed among individual interviews. For the remainder of this chapter, the term conjoint counseling will be used to refer to the first two patterns only.

ADVANTAGES OF CONJOINT COUNSELING

It is probable that there never will be a universal answer for the question "Should the partners be seen together or separately?" But it is clear that in some circumstances and with some patients conjoint counseling offers important advantages.

In my own experience I have found four areas in which conjoint counseling often has superior promise. These areas are:

1. The identification of distortions.
2. The handling of transference reactions.

3. The understanding of conflict.
4. Focusing on current relationships.

The Identification of Distortions in Conjoint Counseling

Marriage counseling patients present themselves to the counselor in ways that involve considerable distortion. The identification of and working through these distortions is an involved problem even when the patients are emotionally healthy, and may be prolonged where there is much pathology.

Many patients distort consciously and perhaps intentionally. Virtually all patients—indeed, all people—have done many things of which they are not proud and which they do not wish known to others. Desiring and needing acceptance from the counselor, they conceal damaging information. Even when patients are able to avoid the temptation to conscious concealment, they are apt to present themselves in one-sided, biased fashion. No matter how hard they try to be objective, they are too entangled in their conflicts to see themselves adequately. It is common in marriage counseling to hear the same relationship described by husband and wife in such different terms that the counselor must force himself to realize that the partners are really talking about one another. And finally, of course, there are distortions that derive from repression. These may be mere fragments or they may be systematic and comprehensive. Obviously, these present the greatest problem.

Individual marriage counseling may proceed indefinitely without the counselor being able to break through the barriers presented by these distortions. It is my experience that in conjoint counseling such distortions tend to be fewer and less extreme, and that partners cling to them less tenaciously. When the same counselor is seeing both partners and when, at least part of the time, they are being seen in joint sessions, there is less possibility of and less need for concealment. Each partner is forced to hear descriptions and interpretations of his behavior that differ from his own. Too, the rapport that develops between each patient and the counselor is not based upon such a partial, favorable revelation of self. The patients confirm directly that the counselor can accept them in spite of the things that they wish to conceal.

Just as surely, the unintentional distortions of each partner are quickly revealed. Whether these are merely problems of perspective or whether they result from repression, neither partner can escape the fact that distortion is occurring. To the likely criticism that such rapid confrontation is apt to result in even more serious symptoms, we can only reply that we have not usually found it so. Ackerman's[5] observation that so-called family secrets, allegedly very dangerous, are neither very secret nor especially dangerous is pertinent here.

The situation in traditional counseling practice, where the counselor must lengthily unravel and work through distortions with each partner before bringing them together, is largely cut short. What might otherwise drag on and on frequently is accomplished in a very few sessions. Moreover, the counselor in conjoint counseling is not placed in the position of constantly having to restructure his relationship with each of the partners.

Transference Reactions in Conjoint Counseling

Even in conventional marriage counseling, incipient transference reactions tend to be checked by the participation of the other spouse. Joint participation discourages the development of a "private world" between the counselor and the patient. In conjoint interviews the physical presence of the other partner is an even more effective deterrent. Each spouse's efforts to maneuver the counselor into private roles run head on into the counselor's relationship with the other partner. Thus, too much regression is discouraged and the partners are encouraged to work on their problems at more current relationship levels. Where the counselor still becomes a parent surrogate, he is more likely to become a joint parent and to reinforce the relationship between the partners.

With some marriage counseling patients, transference becomes pronounced even in conjoint counseling. And the interplay between the counselor and two patients occasionally gets exceedingly complicated. Traditionally oriented counselors to the contrary notwithstanding, however, most counselors handle these multiple transference situations about as well as they handle other transference problems. The additional burden of having to work through distortions with both partners is at least partly counteracted by the lesser likelihood of the counselor becoming unwittingly caught up in either partner's distortions. Not only do many common forms of transference become very obvious to the counselor during conjoint counseling, but many common forms of countertransference are quickly identified also.

Conflict in Conjoint Counseling

A third effect of the systematic use of conjoint counseling is to bring the marital conflict into the open and into the counseling interviews. Herein lies both a major advantage of conjoint counseling and a major source of resistance to its use by some counselors.

Marriage counselors long have known that when angry partners are seen together they are apt to begin to fight. Traditional practice is based upon the assumptions that if the partners fight their relationship will deteriorate, the counselor will lose control of the counseling sessions and that, as he loses control, he loses his ability to aid the patients. Two of these assumptions may be challenged and the third may be shown to have little to do with conjoint counseling *per se*.

It is true that many couples in joint session will fight. It does not follow, however, that the fighting need produce deterioration of the marital relationship. The question is not simply whether the couple will fight, but only whether they will fight in the presence of the counselor. They have been fighting at home and will continue to do so. Moreover, while the deteriorating effects of the conflict upon their relationship is what brings them into counseling, we should not overlook the ability of most couples to tolerate prolonged, severe conflict. They are both afraid of their fighting and they are used to living with it. When a counselor excludes that conflict from the counseling sessions, he may unintentionally heighten the patients' fears. On the other hand, when the counselor can accept the fighting without alarm, its effects upon the partners tend to become less malignant.

There is no good reason why arguing in the counseling sessions should cause the counselor to lose control. He permits the expression of other feelings without losing control because he does not become entangled in those feelings. But when patients begin to fight they often trigger both anxiety and hostility in the counselor. Counselors often are rather controlled people to whom outbursts of direct hostility are threatening, and whose own tendencies to respond in kind, or perhaps to withdraw, are uncomfortably close to the surface. When this happens, or when the resulting anxiety is communicated to the patients, the counselor may indeed lose control of the sessions and the confidence of the patients. But this is a counselor problem and not a characteristic of conjoint counseling as such. Not only do many counselors quickly become comfortable with conflict in the counseling sessions, but they learn to use it to good advantage.

Whereas in conventional marriage counseling there may be prolonged inconsistency between the behavior of patients in the counseling sessions and their behavior outside the sessions, conjoint counseling admits the counselor directly to current squabbles. When the partners find that the counselor can understand each of them without taking sides, they can become more objective both about the partner and about themselves. Each can be helped to make tentative gestures toward a less hurtful pattern of behavior and find that the other partner reciprocates. This process, in time, becomes cumulative and circular. Gradually, the couple can be led out of conflict according to dynamics analogous to those which led them into it originally.[6]

The partners' interaction during the sessions provides a model for interaction between sessions. Each partner becomes, with the counselor, a kind of co-counselor working throughout the day and week. And because both partners are involved, alliances involving the counselor are avoided. More of the responsibility for solving their problems is shifted to the patients, where it belongs. Less dependence upon the counselor is encouraged, and eventually less weaning away from the counselor is necessary.

Focusing on Current Relationships in Conjoint Counseling

A final important feature of conjoint marriage counseling, and one that has been implied above, is the emphasis it places on current relationships. The term "current" here does not imply momentary, ephemeral or trivial. Roughly, it marks off the period from the time of marriage forward. Spouses seen together do not receive great encouragement to relive their early family experiences. The emphasis is upon what hurts them as a pair. They will, naturally, seek out the bases for their conflicts both in what has happened between them and in the experience which each partner has brought into the marriage. They will develop understanding of the effects of childhood experience, but the emphasis is upon the contribution of childhood experience to the marital problems and not upon early frustration or personality problems as such.

It should be clear that personality reconstruction is not a primary goal in marriage counseling. Most couples learn to become more comfortable with their own dynamics, with those of the partner, and with the common product. That change is inherent in this process is obvious. There is no sharp line between marriage counseling and reconstructive counseling. But there are differences of degree and emphasis. The point is simply that with a marriage counseling emphasis, conjoint counseling has many advantages that are just beginning to be appreciated.

Limitations in the Use of Conjoint Counseling

We should not let our limited successes with conjoint counseling blind us to its limitations. The temptation is there, but to portray conjoint counseling as a panacea will only bring discredit upon it and delay its taking its proper place in the counselor's tool kit. Unfortunately, the full limitations upon the use of conjoint counseling are not yet known. There follow some suggestions to these limitations based upon my own experience.

Greater Difficulty of Conjoint Counseling

Because of traditional emphasis on one-to-one counseling and interviewing, few counselors—or physicians serving as counselors—have much skill in the conduct of joint interviews. Consequently, their first efforts along these lines frequently result in disappointment. The resulting threat to professional self-image encourages the rejection of the technique rather than acknowledgment of the need to develop new skills.

It should be admitted at the outset that conjoint counseling is inherently more demanding upon the counselor. He must respond continuously and rapidly to an exceedingly broad range of stimuli. He must almost simultaneously hear, accept, and reflect the communications of both spouses; he must protect each partner; and he must continuously support the relationship. It is demanding work for which some counselors may not be suited.

LACK OF PATIENT PREPAREDNESS

Patients, as well as counselors, have problems in accepting conjoint counseling. Some patient problems undoubtedly make the systematic use of joint interviews unprofitable.

Among marriage counseling patients, the motivation of the partners is important. If it is true that marriage counseling patients hurt less, on the average, than many psychiatric patients, and sometimes have to be "coaxed" to work determinedly on their problems, the more rapid confrontation inherent in conjoint counseling may tend to drive some of them out of counseling. Since the prognosis for such patients is not usually good, the question may be asked whether this is really a disadvantage.

There is a more subtle problem related to the nature of the patients' motivations. It may be assumed that many people who come to a marriage counselor need to work out their problems within the marriage. But some marriage counseling patients come specifically seeking support for the termination of an intolerable marriage. And, at various levels of awareness, these motives may be mixed and confused. Patients who are committed to separation or divorce may be only handicapped by joint sessions. And those whose motivations need to be worked through and clarified, may do so far more efficiently in individual sessions.

There are also forms of patient maladjustment that contraindicate the use of conjoint therapy. How many such patterns there are and how severe the maladjustment must be are not yet known. There follow just two recurring examples from my own practice. Patients in whom there are integrated paranoid features, not surprisingly, tend to interpret the conjoint situation as conspiratorial. Whether these delusions could eventually be worked through in conjoint counseling is less relevant than the fact that whatever advantages ordinarily accrue to conjoint counseling are lost in this instance. Other than thoroughly trained, highly skilled counselors would do well to refer such clients for psychiatric evaluation.

Similarly, patients who have suffered such severe early deprivation that they are seriously crippled emotionally, cannot participate actively in conjoint counseling any more than they can in individual counseling. When such persons are brought into conjoint counseling with antagonistic partners, the overwhelming need for protection of the disabled spouse blocks the development of the desired cumulative circular interaction.

REFERENCES

1. Leslie, G. R.: Conjoint therapy in marriage counseling. J. Marriage and the Family, 26: 65–71, 1964.
2. Parsons, T.: *The Social System*. The Free Press of Glencoe, Illinois, 1951.
3. Skidmore, R. A., and Garrett, H. V.: The joint interview in marriage counseling. Marriage and Family Living, 17: 349–354, 1955.
4. Grotjahn, M.: *Psychoanalysis and the Family Neurosis*. W. W. Norton and Company, Inc., New York, 1960.
5. Ackerman, N.: *The Psychodynamics of Family Life*. Basic Books Inc., New York, 1958.
6. Kirkpatrick, C.: *The Family: As Process and Institution*, p. 210 and *passim*. The Ronald Press Company, New York, 1963.

chapter eight

The Marriage Problems Physical Examination

WALLACE A. COBURN, M.D., *Seattle, Washington*

Some patients are well aware of the nature of the marriage or sexual problem which brings them to the physician. Some may even be aware of the cause of their problem, be it physical or psychosomatic.

But there are others who come with functional complaints and vague aches and pains, not realizing that the tension which produced this psychosomatic distress had its inception in the hidden resentments of their marriage or sexual relationships.

In all of these cases, a thorough physical examination is the first prerequisite. For even in cases where the relationship difficulties are an obvious source of the patient's problem and marriage counseling is clearly indicated, sometimes unsuspected physical problems (only indirectly contributory to the major relationship complaint) are uncovered in such a physical examination. A wife whose major problem is lack of sexual interest may be found to have a borderline anemia, for example. Treatment of her physical condition may add enormously to the success of later counseling treatment for her frigidity problem.

In other cases, the need for the physician to assure himself that there is no anatomic or physical basis for the complaint may be an equally important reason for the priority of the physical examination. Only when this has been done can the physician have the self-confidence and assurance on which successful counseling in marriage problems may hinge.

There are a number of other reasons, physiologic and psychologic, for careful attention to the initial physical examination. For example, reassurance to the patient that he or she is physically normal is of great psychologic value in itself. Moreover, in the course of the examination, the physician may come to an awareness of other underlying psychologic causes of much of the patient's difficulty. The woman patient who defends herself dramatically against a routine pelvic examination may be giving an important clue to her childhood conditioning and her resultant sexual problems.

The remainder of this chapter will discuss some of the physiologic and psychosomatic symptoms of marriage problems, both in cases where the presenting complaint is obviously marriage-related and in those cases where the patient's functional distress can only be indirectly traced back to its source in the personal difficulties between husband and wife.

It almost goes without saying that a thorough medical and marital history taking should be the start of the marriage problems physical examination. Because this topic is so well covered in several other chapters (notably Dr. Kavinoky's Chapter 17), it will not be discussed here. However, it should be noted that the history form outlined on pages 168 and 169 is a good example of a comprehensive checklist for such an examination.

Physiologic Causes for Marital Problems

Almost any physical complaint, from herpes to hangnail, can have a deleterious effect on a relationship as intimate and as sensitive as marriage. Irritability, fatigue, hypo- or hyperthyroidism, anemia and any other partially disabling condition are among them. To treat the patient with a marriage problem, it is necessary to be aware of any condition which detracts from his buoyant good health. Any subnormal physical function should be treated by appropriate therapy so as to help rule out all possible sources of marriage irritant.

However, in the sexual area, there are some special difficulties. These are worthy of particular mention because of their evident shock to the marital relationship. These problems should be of unusual concern to the physician who suspects or knows a marriage problem exists.

The first of these important problem areas is the anatomic anomalies of the male and female sexual parts. Ordinarily, any anatomic irregularity causes concern among the partners, and often surgical intervention is indicated. Some good corrections can be made. Masters and Johnson,[1] among others, have reported on the functional effectiveness of artificially created vaginas. Because of the complexity of the erectal function, a complete correction of male sexual anomalies is often more difficult if not impossible. But whether or not correction can be made, it is imperative that the physician give attention to supportive counseling with the partners. In few other areas of human experience are emotions so close to the surface as in irregularities of sexual function.

However, it should be noted that the mere presence of any congenital defect should not always be considered as presumptive evidence of a marital problem. The writer has seen patients with complete absence of a vagina who have reported that both they themselves and their husbands were satisfied by some substitute sexual release and they were consulting the doctor only because of having been unable to conceive.

This in itself is presumptive evidence that the physician can, sometimes at least, help those other partners who are having difficulty because of uncorrectable anomalies to reevaluate their relationship. Perhaps they never should have married, true. But also, perhaps their relationship is more important to them than their form of sexual release.

An indirect cause of some anatomic anomalies of the sexual parts is gonadal defects. In recent years an interesting series of discoveries pointing to the apparent chromosomal etiology of gonadal defects has led to better understanding of these problems. Techniques for identifying and counting chromosomes are rapidly expanding the physician's ability to diagnose and classify numerous congenital abnormalities, including gonadal digenesis or Turner's syndrome, for example, which has long puzzled geneticists. This classic syndrome consists of short stature and sexual infantilism, manifested by absent or greatly diminished breast tissue, infantile genitalia and at least one other congenital abnormality, the most common of which is webbing of the neck. Vaginal smears reveal a marked estrogen deficiency, and the urinary excretion of gonadotrophins is high in older individuals exhibiting Turner's syndrome.

The major problem for these patients, however, is the short stature and the failure of sexual development. Little can be done for the short stature, as there is usually early closure of the epiphyses. However, the administration of estrogens in a cyclical fashion results in a withdrawal type bleeding and an appreciable growth in the development of the vagina and breasts. This, together with some helpful guidance from the physician, often enables these individuals to marry and have normal relations, and, except for their absolute sterility, lead normal lives. There are, of course, male abnormalities of the gonads as well, and even the slightest suspicion of anatomic irregularity should be investigated.

But anatomic anomalies account for only a minor part of the physical problems causing marital distress. Of far greater relative importance are the more commonly seen genitourinary and gynecologic pathologies which in the female result in physical dyspareunia and consequent loss of sexual desire. Included in this list would be conditions causing pain during intercourse such as vaginal cysts, ovarian cysts, endometriosis and the wide variety of microorganism caused pathologies included under the general heading of vaginitis. Parallel pathologies in the male would include prostatitis, orchitis and various venereal diseases. Fortunately, modern surgical techniques and antibiotics, including the oral trichomonicides, have greatly improved the physician's ability to treat pathologies affecting the sexual function.

However, even with such effective pharmaceuticals, a counseling need often remains. For one thing, it may be necessary to talk extensively with the husband in order to enable him to see the need for *his* taking the trichomonicides, or to avoid sexual relations until the vaginitis is cured.

Also inhibiting complete sexual satisfaction for both partners, if only esthetically, is abnormal uterine bleeding. Aberrations of menstruation are usually divided into classifications according to whether or not ovulation occurs. Functional uterine bleeding in which ovulation occurs may be of an excessively heavy or prolonged type—hypermenorrhea; a markedly diminished flow—hypomenorrhea; increased frequency of the periods— polymenorrhea; and, of course, menstrual cycles occurring at intervals of 35 days or more—oligomenorrhea.

There is no doubt that hypermenorrhea may be associated with psychogenic causes; however, the large majority of cases usually has an organic basis and this should be ruled out before accepting a functional basis. A trial of progestogen therapy may result in a more normal period.

Hypomenorrhea is usually not of clinical significance except for those individuals who just don't seem to feel well without a heavy monthly bloodletting episode. A decrease in the amount of menstrual flow without a change in the cycle is often seen in women in their mid-30's and can continue this way for many years. Assurance concerning the normality of this is usually all that is needed. In most cases, it would be ill-advised to attempt hormonal therapy.

Polymenorrhea, the least common of the functional uterine problems, is significant mainly in problems of infertility. It is usually due to a shortening of the follicular phase of ovulation, and responds well to cyclical hormone therapy.

Oligomenorrhea is bleeding commonly occurring three or four times per year at irregular intervals. When such menstruation does occur, it is usually of a normal type and has been preceded by ovulation; these patients do not seem to have much difficulty in achieving pregnancy if enough sexual activity occurs. Commonly, these patients are quite surprised when told that they are five or six months pregnant. Oligomenorrhea may be associated with pituitary tumors, hypothyroidism, psychiatric disorders and liver disease. Polycystic ovary syndrome frequently includes this type of menstruation.

The most common menstrual irregularity is dysmenorrhea. While there can be extrinsic or secondary dysmenorrhea associated with a pathologic state within the pelvis, usually it is the primary or intrinsic type of dysmenorrhea which plays havoc with a marital relationship. Because this is psychogenic in origin, it is the point at which a discussion of the relationship between physical and emotional problems in marital distress and the resultant need for counseling can clearly be demonstrated.

Psychosomatic Factors in Marital Distress

The great majority of women with painful periods have no demonstrable pelvic disease. Most observers agree that psychologic factors play a significant role in primary dysmenorrhea, yet no clear-cut psychiatric pattern is evident. However, some characteristic emotional conflicts do appear frequently in patients with painful menstrual periods. Sometimes these women give a history of psychologic maladjustment as children. Often it is evident that if nothing else happened to these women during their childhood years, they certainly got a terrible indoctrination about the evils of the sexual function or genital play.

Other dysmenorrhea patients seem to have acquired resentments about their feminine roles, so that menstruation is taken by them to indicate that "woman's fate in life is one of suffering." Occasionally, psychologic conflicts involving guilt, sexual phantasies, incestuous desires, sibling rivalry and past traumatic experiences appear to be related to dysmenorrhea.

Management of primary dysmenorrhea is largely psychologic, but most women can be helped without formal psychiatric treatment. Many patients acquire insight into their own emotional problems regarding menstruation if given the opportunity by a sympathetic, interested physician, and will often freely discuss them.

The damage which dysmenorrhea does to the marriage relationship is often not immediately evident. It is obvious that sometimes the husband's patience is stretched to the breaking point by the wife who takes to her bed for the best part of a week out of every month, or by the woman who is constantly complaining about the fate which inflicted "the curse" upon her. But sometimes the subtle damage to the male sexual drive, caused by the unconscious rejection he feels as a result of his wife's overdramatized suffering from what he may interpret as a sexually related function, can be even more devastating. This should be pointed out to the young wife in helping her to see the importance of establishing a pleasure—not pain— association with the genital parts and their function, both for herself and for her husband. Instruction in the importance of keeping the sexual relationship esthetically desirable fits in well here, too, and in many cases some advice regarding feminine hygiene can be an important aspect of the counseling with the young wife.

As far as medical treatment of primary dysmenorrhea is concerned, simple analgesics should be tried, but the use of narcotics should be scrupulously avoided because of the danger of addiction. If simple measures fail, it is logical to suppress ovulation as anovulatory menstruation is painless. In the past, estrogen suppression was helpful in a certain number of patients, but recently the progestogens in doses of from 2 to 10 mg. daily, from day 5 to day 25, are being used extensively to inhibit ovulation.

There are, of course, other sexually related psychosomatic problems which cause much, or perhaps even more, difficulty in marriage than dysmenorrhea does. Vaginismus, and dyspareunia due to vaginismus, can be of major consequence.

Vaginismus, an involuntary spasm of the vaginal muscles causing more or less complete closure of the vagina, is always of psychogenic origin. As Kroger and Freed point out, "Although vaginismus is a symptom of hysteria, many of the patients are not neurotic. As a matter of fact, once the spasm disappears, the sexual adjustment of these individuals is often satisfactory, since over one-half are able to obtain orgastic gratification." [2]

In the marital-sexual relationship, vaginismus may be used to describe the condition in which the spasm is so intense as to absolutely prohibit entry of the penis, or else where either the muscular tension or the fear associated with that muscular tension causes dyspareunia even though intromission is accomplished.

Vaginismus is often noted during the physical examination when merely touching—or even threatening to touch—the labia produces a spasm and pain, and the introitus becomes so constricted that the admission of even the smallest speculum would be impossible.

Most women who exhibit vaginismus believe that they are "too small inside" and for the time the spasm exists, they are. While vaginismus may serve the unconscious purpose of keeping out the penis, it should be noted that true vaginal spasm cannot be produced voluntarily, and so cannot *consciously* be used by a woman to avoid intercourse.

Since vaginismus (although not dyspareunia) is always psychogenic in origin, counseling with the patient, and often with her husband, is the most important treatment. Rarely, if ever, will such hoary old prescriptions as "Get yourself a little drunk before attempting intercourse" do anything more than make the problem worse and lose the patient's confidence as well. Many young women with vaginismus had overly rigid moral training to begin with and the suggestion of drinking is liable to be as abhorrent to them emotionally as is the intercourse which is the cause of their problem.

The first step in successful counseling with the patient afflicted by vaginismus is a careful explanation of the genital parts and of the effect of anxiety upon them. Diagrams are often useful. Next is a thoroughgoing questioning of both partners as to their knowledge of marital techniques and some explanation of those procedures which will induce erotic arousal in the female and reduce her tension at the same time. Very often the physician, in the very process of talking to the wife and the husband, can help to reduce their anxiety about what is appropriate and proper to the point where the probability of vaginismus at the next intercourse is much reduced. The physician's own gentle, sympathetic approach in discussing the problem can also serve as a model for sexual communication between the patients. (See Chapter 12.)

Naturally, such practical suggestions as the use of a lubricating jelly will be a part of the educational process in counseling. Sometimes it is helpful for the patient to convince herself of her own capacity by privately inserting dilating tubes of increasing diameter at prescribed intervals.

There are, of course, some cases in which the vaginismus has such a deep-seated and guilt- or anxiety-ridden origin that only long-range, depth psychotherapy will be beneficial. But, in most cases the physician-counselor will be able, with kindly understanding, to accomplish a very great deal toward helping these patients.

Lack of sexual desire on the part of the female is often associated with vaginismus. While Masters and Johnson will thoroughly discuss the treatment of various levels of frigidity in Chapter 13, some additional comments might be noted here.

Until relatively recently, no great amount of enthusiasm for sex was expected of the good wife. It was enough that she "submit" herself to her husband's marital embrace and if she happened to like it, so much the better. Fifty years ago the husband who considered himself an absolute failure because he did not bring his wife to a climax would have been more of a rarity. Now, however, in this age of orgasms for women, a young man more often believes that he is something less than adequate unless he can turn his wife into a raging tigress during sexual relations, and very often the woman herself expects him to provide this kind of stimulation, too.

But while the expectation for male and female sexual behavior has changed, often the conditioning which is given young boys and girls has not. It is, therefore, not too surprising that both partners are ashamed— she because she has not been able to respond in the manner he thinks is appropriate, and he because he has failed to make her that responsive.

In itself, the fact that they are ashamed would be no great tragedy. But that shame leads to worry, the worry to tension, and the tension to even more inadequate sexual performance. Maximum ability in the sex act, as well as maximum enjoyment of it, results from a complete self-confidence and a belief that the partner is pleased by his mate's performance. Today, the minute either the man or the woman has any doubt about his sexual ability, or his ability to please the other with his sexual performance, that performance may become a source of worry. In cases where there is deep concern, either conscious or unconscious, this can lead to frigidity or impotence.

Manifestly, then, at least part of the counseling which the physician may wish to do with the partners who are having sexual difficulty will consist of building—or rebuilding—their confidence in their own ability to perform adequately. By the very nature of his status as a physician, sometimes the physician's assurance that they *can* be successful, and with proper communication, education and experience they *will* be successful, is the most important medicine the patients could receive. The physician can only give this assurance, of course, after the marriage problems physical examination. If there were no other reason for the examination, this would be reason enough in itself.

It would be difficult to overstress the importance of giving this assurance of adequacy, for once either partner begins to feel inadequate, he may withdraw, thus not only perpetuating his own sense of failure, but also evoking the same feeling within his partner. Unless the physician's good counseling intervenes, this can lead to a long spiral downhill, ending in a broken or unhappy marriage and psychologic depression. But many people, physicians as well as patients, find it difficult to believe that such disastrous consequences can come from so simple a cause as seemingly trivial worry.

If there be a luxury of time in any counseling case, it may be profitable to explore the psychologic conditioning of the individual that led him to the lack of self-confidence which permitted his original concern over sexual adequacy. But most cases can and must be handled less elaborately. The simple belief in success, engendered by the physician's assurance, plus a few successful experiences, may go a long way toward the improvement of sexual ability and sexual desire in both marriage partners.

Diagnosis of low sexual desire ordinarily offers no problem, since one partner or the other usually is acutely eager to suggest this possibility. However, there are physical indicators as well. One of the definitive physical indicators of low sexual desire in the female is a persistent lack of sufficient lubrication for easy penetration of the vagina and comfortable intercourse. Masters[3] has shown that in the normally responsive female, individual droplets of lubricating material appear on the walls of the vagina within 10 to 30 seconds after the initiation of physical or psychic sexual stimulation. In the past, some authors have regarded the cervix as the main source of vaginal lubrication and at other times Bartholin's glands have also been allotted a major role. But now it appears that neither of these sources is of real consequence in vaginal lubrication. As sexual stimulation continues, the droplets on the walls of the vagina coalesce to form a smooth glistening coating for the entire area. While the true source of this vaginal lubrication is still in doubt, its production is an obvious indication of sexual responsiveness and its lack of production is a clear indication of lack of adequate sexual response.

OTHER PSYCHOSOMATIC INDICATORS OF MARRIAGE PROBLEMS

Ultimately, it is probably those psychosomatic symptoms not directly related to sexual functions which are the marriage distress signals most often seen by the physician. Such indicators of repressed resentments and tensions as headaches, vague aches and pains, dizziness, heart palpitations, chronic fatigue, tingling of the extremities and so forth, often result from a deteriorating marriage relationship. In turn, they cause further deterioration. It is, therefore, of prime importance that the physician take some action to help in these cases.

The first action, of course, is checking for any possible physical pathologies. Once the physician has assured himself that all of the symptoms are in fact related to functional distress, the next step is to endeavor to ascertain the factors within the individual's life which are responsible for the tensions and emotional problems. Sometimes these will go very deep and referral to the psychopathologist is the only course. But there are many other times when just a little bit of exploration will bring out a whole series of previously well-guarded anxieties. The same encouragement to talk about the problem will lead to relief as well as to diagnosis.

It is not always that the problem is directly related to resentments between the partners. Sometimes the initial cause of a husband's anxiety, for example, might be a poor job situation. But even here, at least a contributory cause to the entire difficulty may be the wife's failure to help her husband rationalize and adjust to his presently unchangable set of circumstances. So, while the physician-counselor may have an important function in helping the husband directly, in getting his problem out where he can reduce his anxiety by symbolically sharing it and talking it over, he may also have a function in counseling with the wife about what she can do to help her husband.

In the course of the marriage problems physical examination, anxiety conditions may be revealed which suggest the use of psychopharmaceuticals. While these may be extremely effective in some cases, they are often not sufficient to do more than "take the edge off" the patient's tension. In fact, in some cases where the patient had expected that the tranquilizers would solve his problem, his disappointment may increase his anxiety. In any psychologic problem, the only real solution is the kind of emotional catharsis and supportive reassurance that can come from successful counseling, or, in some cases, depth psychotherapy.

No one in our culture has quite the opportunity to be of counseling help that the physician has. His status gives his words as well as his pills an enormous placebo effect. He himself needs to add a genuine interest in the patient, an inclination to let the patient talk through his problems and an ability to find those positive aspects of the situation which will allow the patient to look forward to a more successful living experience.

REFERENCES

1. MASTERS, W. H., AND JOHNSON, V. E.: The artificial vagina: anatomic, physiologic psychosexual function. West J. Surg., **69:** 192–212, 1961.

2. KROGER, W. S., AND FREED, S. C.: *Psychosomatic Gynecology: Including Problems of Obstetrical Care*. The Free Press of Glencoe, Illinois, 1956.

3. MASTERS, W. H.: The sexual response cycle of the human female: II. Vaginal lubrication. Ann. New York Acad. Sc., **83:** 301–317, 1959.

chapter nine

Evaluating the Patient's Problem for Counseling or Referral

HERBERT A. OTTO, PhD., *Graduate School of Social Work, University of Utah, Salt Lake City, Utah*

The busy physician often finds himself in a quandary when he detects that a patient may be suffering from a marital problem. Should he ignore the problem and concern himself only with the medical aspect, should he attempt treatment of the problem or should a referral be made? If the latter decision is made, where should the patient be referred? This chapter will provide some guidelines toward a resolution of these questions so that the best interests of the patient as well as the physician may be served through the provision of the most adequate and up-to-date professional services.

EVALUATING THE PATIENT'S PROBLEM

Those patients with marital problems who consult the physician can, for didactic purposes, be divided into two groups: those who admit to having a marital problem or imply that such a problem is present, and those seeking help for a medical condition the physician suspects as resulting from the presence of marital difficulties.

In the former case, the "door is already open" and the patient is usually eager to talk about the problem he recognizes.

The second group, however, faces the counselor—or the physician in the role of counselor—with a very different problem. Modern medical science has increasingly recognized that we cannot separate the psyche from the soma or the person from the interpersonal and social field in which he is operating. If the patient is under tension or if anxiety is generated by his interpersonal environment, *i.e.*, those close to the patient, body function may be significantly affected. Patients can displace disappointments in marriage into a set of symptoms such as backaches, chronic headaches, nervousness and so forth, for which no medical cause can be found but which are, nevertheless, quite real to the patient. But how can the patient be helped to understand this?

In such instances where marital difficulties are suspected to be in the background, tact is required. A "bridge building approach" coupled with an understanding attitude and followed by leading questions often gets surprising results. Some physicians "build a bridge" for the patient by the following or similar remarks: "Often a condition such as yours is aggravated (or recovery and healing is slowed considerably) by worry, anxiety, unhappiness or fears. We know now that these emotional factors have something to do with the way a patient responds to treatment." (At this point the physician should pause to determine if the patient is willing to volunteer information. He may then continue.) "In order to get the best results from your medical treatment, we need to take a look at everything that may be worrying you, bothering you or making you unhappy."

A more directive variation of the bridge building approach follows— "We find that in many instances, medical conditions are aggravated and that, despite treatment, the healing processes are slowed down, if a person is under excessive pressure or worry at home." (The physician pauses to give the patient a chance to speak, then continues.) "I have the impression that some problem with your family or your husband is causing you unhappiness or worry and is placing you under considerable tension."

In the event that the patient denies the presence of any marital problem, the physician should, nevertheless, "keep the door open" by stating in effect that sometimes people find it difficult to admit they have a problem, that "all of us have problems" and that often people think about it and decide to talk over the problems at a later time. It can then be pointed out that the physician would be glad to talk to the patient and spouse whenever they are ready to discuss the problem. At the same time, *the name of an agency or alternate source to which the patient may go for counseling should be interjected, in the event that the patient wishes to have help but for some reason does not wish to discuss the problem with his doctor.*

Even when the patient recognizes that marital difficulties are the basis of his problem, there are often referral difficulties. Almost invariably, marriage problems are complex and the physician-counselor must guard against oversimplified diagnosis. He should be aware that an intricate network of causes has contributed to the formation of the problem and that marital difficulties all too often are of many years standing and have aspects of chronicity. It must also be recognized that *the problem presented by the patient may not be the real problem.* The patient may believe that he has pinpointed the nature of his difficulties only to find after a period of counseling that the real source and locus of his problem is elsewhere.

For example, it is common for patients to insist that the major and only cause of their marital difficulty is to be sought in the marital partner and his objectionable behavior. Later in counseling this type of patient is often surprised to find that the cause of the partner's behavior must be sought in himself.

It is important to arrive at a tentative diagnosis of the marital problem early, but the diagnosis should be kept *tentative*. An open mind should be retained and hasty generalizations and preconceptions about the cause of the difficulty should be avoided.

With the foregoing in mind, the following questions may be helpful in the process of gaining a clearer understanding of the nature of the problem:

1. Has the patient talked about his problem to anyone or sought other professional help?

2. What is the marital history of the patient? (Brief overview)

3. What caused the onset or beginning of the problem, and what are the circumstances leading to the onset, the circumstances surrounding the onset and the history of the problem to date?

4. Is the other marital partner aware of the problem, what is his point of view and what are his proposed remedies?

5. What is the patient's impression of the problem, what are his feelings about it, and how does he think the problem can be worked out?

6. In what ways does the premarital history or background of the patient (and the marital partner) enter into the problem?

It is important that as a part of understanding the problem, an assessment of the personality resources or assets are not neglected during the diagnostic process. What are the personality assets and strengths of the patient and marital partner? What strengths are there in the relationship? These questions should be a routine and integral part of diagnosis.

Oftentimes physician-counselors may have diagnostic or clinical impressions about the causes of a marital difficulty. These impressions may be valuable and can be kept in mind while a detailed diagnostic exploration in the light of the above questions is undertaken. However, initial clinical impressions, although they may be useful for indicating avenues of investigation, should never be substituted for a thorough exploration of the problem configuration. Diagnosis results from the practitioner's patient and often slow-moving pursuit of evidence *as he follows where the evidence will lead him.* As in medical practice, an accurate diagnosis represents a major step toward the completion of successful treatment.

CRITERIA FOR ASSESSMENT: TREATMENT OR REFERRAL?

Whether a patient should be accepted for treatment or whether a referral should be made is often a difficult decision. It is useful in the course of the decision-making process to keep two factors in mind. These are the physician's schedule and the demands on his time which may be incurred with the acceptance of certain cases which need intensive counseling as an emergency measure or on a prolonged basis. The second factor involves the personality and training of the physician. Marriage counselors have found that due to lack of training in specific areas and/or factors in their own personality makeup, they sometimes have difficulty in counseling with certain individuals. In cases where the practitioner finds it hard to develop a helpful and understanding attitude toward the patient and his problem, it may be best to refer.

A number of criteria are considered useful in making an assessment as to whether referral of a patient is indicated.

1. The patient's perceptions of his problem and of the counseling situation. An obvious or extreme distortion in the patient's perception of his problem may be present. There may be an unreasonable insistence on the patient's part that his view of the problem is the only correct one. Presentation of the problem may be in a disorganized or fragmentary manner and the patient may obviously be unclear about the nature of his difficulties. Confusion, incoherence and verbal rambling may be noted while the patient is presenting his problem and also during counseling. The patient may be extremely tense, anxious and fearful, and he may view the counseling situation as threatening. In short, the patient's perception of both his problem and the counseling situation may indicate the presence of moderate or severe emotional disturbance. (See Chapter 4.)

2. Past and current history of family crises. Often a distinct pattern can be recognized in the way the patient deals with the crises which have occurred throughout his life. Some patients marshall their resources and deal with crises in a realistic and organized manner. Others withdraw into passivity or deny the existence of a crisis. Still others seek flight by overindulgence in alcohol or resort to barbiturates, tranquilizers and/or sleep as a refuge. Complete disorganization, sometimes described as "I almost had a nervous breakdown," or "I had a nervous breakdown," is another way of dealing with a crisis. Finally, some patients manage to shift their responsibility to others who will step in and resolve the problem for them. (See Chapter 5.)

3. The self-concept of the patient. Most persons who are confronted with a seemingly insuperable marriage problem which forces them to seek professional help suffer some impairment of their self-image in the process. As a result of being unable to deal with the situation, they think less highly of themselves, feel themselves to be less competent and see themselves as "less of a person." Some of these persons have suffered deep and repeated traumas which have impaired their self-concept. They feel worthless, inferior and incompetent, often to the point of immobilization. A low self-concept may be revealed by carelessness in personal hygiene, dress and grooming.

Related to the self-concept is the presence of a *functioning conscience*. Realistic and appropriate feelings of guilt may be absent, or, conversely the patient's conscience may be excessively active and demanding, leading to self-punitive measures. In some instances, the patient may project his feelings of guilt onto others and take destructive action against them.

4. Chronicity and low motivation. A marital problem may be long standing and chronic and this may make it somewhat more difficult to work with. Similarly, if the patient is in his mid-50's and the problem is of long standing, the prognosis usually is not too encouraging; however, surprising results have been obtained if the patient is sufficiently motivated, is responsive, and has flexibility.

A poor prognosis is also apparent if the patient has low motivation to enter marital counseling. Such patients are often "comfortable with discomfort" or do not believe a problem to be serious. He may be under pressure from his marital partner to seek help while believing the problem to be his spouse's.

5. Ability to relate to the practitioner. Despite all efforts of the counselor in the course of several interviews to be understanding and helpful, some patients are unable to relate to the counselor except in a superficial and distant manner. They appear to have difficulty in forming relationships and, as a consequence, generally do not respond to treatment. A very guarded prognosis is indicated when the patient has a hostile, belligerent or uncooperative attitude, despite the counselor's attempts to be friendly and helpful.

6. Potentially explosive situations. Many marital problems contain explosive seeds or ingredients, but, with the patient's cooperation and the skill of the practitioner, they are usually manageable. In some instances, however, the practitioner is aware that the patient has difficulty in tolerating anxiety or has a low frustration tolerance, and that these elements must be dealt with. There are other situations which have a built-in explosive potential. These include the patient who has a history of mental breakdown, severe depression or psychosis, or who in the past has resorted to suicide as a means of problem solving. Also included is the patient who has a pattern of using assaultive or punitive methods, the patient who has an ineffectively functioning conscience and/or one who is involved in a triangle situation. Finally, there is the ubiquitous, threatening or assaultive "other partner," who sometimes refuses to remain in the background.

The above criteria can serve as an index as to whether referral is advisable. It may be well to keep in mind that if several (or maybe a single one) of the criteria apply to a patient, early referral should be seriously considered. Marriage counselors often take a series of four to five interviews to determine the nature of the problem and to decide whether and where to refer. Inevitably, however, there will be "borderline cases" and the physician-counselor will be perplexed. Perhaps at these moments it may be helpful to recall that the time-honored principle, "When in doubt— refer," is still valid.

Problems for Which Referral Is Routinely Indicated

In a number of instances referral to other sources of help should be routine. This includes the patient who has had an extensive history of depression, mental breakdown or suicidal attempts and the patient who displays paranoid or bizarre behavioral symptoms. (See Chapter 4.) The belligerent or uncooperative patient also may profit from psychiatric help or the services of a clinical psychologist. Patients having long standing or severe sexual problems should be routinely referred to the appropriate medical specialist for a thorough examination before counseling is undertaken.

Potentially explosive situations mentioned previously may be managed by some skillful physicians but are better referred during the initial years of marriage counseling practice. Finally, some patients come to the marriage counselor to seek help with problems which are primarily or predominately of a religious or theologic nature. A minister with a background of training in pastoral counseling who can be of assistance in such cases may often be found.

Making the Referral

Making a referral requires tact and understanding as well as flexibility and firmness. *In marriage counseling referral is a process*, although this process may be completed in one interview. In many instances, however, more than one interview may be needed.

On reaching the decision to make a referral, the practitioner should be clear in his own mind as to why he has made such a decision. He should, as much as possible, recall the patient's words, feelings and behavior which were instrumental in the decision to refer. The patient's own words, examples of his behavior and the types of feelings he has expressed can then be used to illustrate to him that he needs help other than the type that the practitioner is able to offer.

It is always sound practice to prepare the patient for the possibility of referral *beforehand* or as soon as it is suspected that referral may be indicated. This can be done by using the following or similar words: "From what you have told me up to now about the problem, there is a possibility that you may need a different kind of help than I am able to offer you. It may be well for us to think about this." It can then be pointed out that the next two to three interviews might be considered as exploratory with the purpose of determining if referral is the best possible course and to consider who can best help the patient with his problem.

After the physician has reached the decision that a referral should be made, the patient should be helped to express his feelings and attitudes about this decision. This helps to place resistance, anxiety, and, sometimes, anger "out in the open," and the physician can then work with these feelings.

Referrals to psychiatric sources or to a clinical psychologist often pose special problems. In view of this the following principles may be helpful:

1. The practitioner must be quite clear about his own attitude toward psychiatric help. If he feels it is shameful or stigmatizing to see a psychiatrist, he will convey this attitude to the patient.

2. Behavior of the patient in past interviews (using his own words as much as possible) should be used to illustrate the need for referral. For example, it can be pointed out that the patient has repeatedly strayed from the discussion of the marital problem, that he is consistently preoccupied with himself, his feelings, thoughts, fears and anxieties. In this connection, the practitioner may wish to make the following comment: "What you seem to be saying repeatedly is that you are really concerned with your own emotions and feelings and that these need to be worked with first, before work on the marital problem can begin." It can then be mentioned that the practitioner is not equipped to help the patient work through these confusing and disturbed feelings, and that a psychiatrist or clinical psychologist is best equipped to help with this problem.

3. If the patient, despite the practitioner's efforts, vociferously denies that he has a problem, or if he projects his problems onto his marital partner, contending that the spouse is the one in need of help, *it is best not to argue or attempt to cajole*. The patient can be met with firmness, understanding and kindness, and by redirecting his attention to what he has conveyed to the practitioner about his problem. At this point, reasons for the referral could be repeated, using the same as well as added illustrations of the patient's behavior and employing the patient's own words.

In the event of strong resistance to the referral, it is best not to force the issue but to indicate that this can be discussed again during the next interview. The patient should be encouraged to think about the possibility of referral in the interim between interviews.

4. Many patients have misconceptions about psychiatric help and the functions of the psychiatrist or clinical psychologist. He is seen as a "nut

doctor" and a "head shrinker" and is often the object of fear. Patients may be afraid that going to a psychiatrist means that they are "losing their mind." Fears of what family or neighbors may think also are often present and need to be dealt with.

It should be made clear that the bulk of the psychiatrist's practice today consists of patients who have emotional difficulties in some areas of their life, but the vast preponderance are by and large fairly well functioning persons. The seriously mentally ill persons are receiving treatment in hospitals and institutions and not from a psychiatrist in private practice. It is also helpful to point out that findings from modern medical science indicate that emotional disturbance and illness is as common as other illnesses and that most people, at some time in their life, suffer from some form of emotional disorder or disability and need to seek the help of a specialist.

The cost of psychiatric services is also often brought up as a deterrent to treatment. Here the counselor can be of some help in encouraging a realistic assessment of the patient's financial structure. Is he in a position where he can *not* afford psychiatric treatment? It can also be pointed out that community resources such as mental health clinics and outpatient clinics render psychiatric services on a sliding fee scale.

5. Facilitation and follow-through of referral is an essential element of the referral process. It is important that the counselor make the necessary telephone call to the referral source to introduce the patient and to clear the availability of an appointment in the near future. Whenever possible, the patient should be encouraged to make his own appointment following the initial introduction by the practitioner. The practitioner should convey to the referral source the reasons for his referral and the work he has done with the patient. Whenever possible, and especially where there has been prolonged treatment, a short written referral report should be made. Such a report should contain, in summary form, the counselor's impression of the problem, length of treatment and treatment focus, reasons for referral, and other clinical impressions which may be helpful.

At times a patient will be unable to admit that he is suffering from an emotional disturbance. His resistance and defenses will be so strong that despite all the tact and skill which is brought to bear, the patient will not be able to accept referral. In such cases, after all resources to effect a referral have been exhausted, termination of services is indicated. However, an "open door policy" should be maintained by stating that any time the patient wishes to come in for further discussion about referral, the practitioner will be glad to see him and will make the necessary arrangements for referral.

Finally, it should be remembered that professional marriage counselors are available for referral and that in many communities trained and professionally certified social workers are equipped to work with individusals having serious marital problems or suffering from emotional disturbance. Whenever a practitioner has some doubt as to his ability to work with a patient or his particular problem, he should routinely refer as the best possible course under such circumstances.

SOURCES FOR REFERRAL

The location of the physician-counselor determines the number of referral resources available to him. This is readily seen in Tables 9.1 and 9.2 which can be used a guide to pinpoint sources of referral. From the tables, it is evident that a variety of specialists are often available and can be used.

These specialists and their contributions will be briefly discussed:

The Psychiatrist

As previously mentioned, he is a specialist in the treatment of emotional disturbances and is especially equipped to deal with the more severe emotional disorders and illnesses. If the psychiatrist is in private practice,

TABLE 9.1

Possible referral resources in a rural or semi-rural community

Agency or Resource and Staff	Notes
Church Minister	Some ministers have training and experience in pastoral counseling.

County or Regional Mental
  Health Clinic
  Psychiatrist
  Psychologist
  Social Worker
	Necessary to check on referral and intake procedures.

General Hospital (Intensive
  Treatment Unit)
  Psychiatric consultant
	Increasingly, intensive treatment units for mental illness will be found in general hospitals with a psychiatrist as director or consultant.

Psychiatrist Private practice	Getting to know this resource is recommended.
Psychologist Private practice	Getting to know this resource is recommended.
Social Worker Private practice	Getting to know this resource is recommended.

Welfare Department (Child
  Welfare Division)
  Social Worker
	Trained professional help sometimes available to work with marital or family problems.

TABLE 9.2

Possible referral resources in an urban community*

Agency or Resource and Staff	Notes

Child Guidance Clinic
  Psychiatrist
  Psychologist
  Social Worker
	Will usually accept family problems where focus is on helping the child.

Clinic and Outpatient Department
  Psychiatrist
  Psychologist
  Social Worker
	Many hospitals have facilities for the treatment of emotional disturbances.

Community Welfare Council (or Council of Social Agencies) Social Worker	A clearinghouse and excellent source for resources available in the community.
Denominational Agency (Such as Catholic Charities) Social Worker	Trained professional help often available.

Family Service Society
  Psychiatric Consultant
  Social Worker
	A national agency specializing in marital and family problems.

Marriage Counselor
  Interdisciplinary Marriage Counselor
  Psychiatrist
  Psychologist
  Sociologist
	Professionally trained personnel only.

Mental Health Association
  Psychiatrist
  Psychologist
  Social Worker
	Clinical services sometimes available. Otherwise a good source of community resources.

* Resources listed in Table 9.1 are usually available in an urban community.

his fee per interview may be $20 and up or he may have a sliding fee scale arrangement. He often has an extensive waiting list.

The Psychologist

In addition to personality testing, many psychologists are today equipped to work with persons suffering from emotional disturbances. The clinical psychologists usually have a Ph.D., although there are some with a Master's degree and additional training. Fees are usually on a sliding scale, although some practitioners have established fee schedules, especially in reference to testing services. Psychologists are now certified or licensed in most states and a directory may be obtained from the state certification board. In large cities psychologists have local associations which usually can provide referral information.

The Marriage Counselor

Professional marriage counselors are now receiving Ph.D. degrees from a number of large universities throughout the United States, and some are setting up private practice in the larger communities. The University of Pennsylvania, Purdue University, Columbia University (Teachers College), and the Merrill-Palmer School in Detroit offer marriage counseling training. So do the University of Southern California, Brigham Young University, the University of Minnesota, and the Florida State University. There is now pressure for licensing of marriage counselors and California has already passed such legislation. The American Association of Marriage Counselors, 27 Woodcliff Drive, Madison, New Jersey, is taking the leadership in setting standards for marriage counseling practice. This association also provides a referral service which directs inquirers to qualified counselors.

The Social Worker

An increasing number of social workers are entering private practice. The professionally trained social worker has a Master of Social Work degree and usually is a member of the Academy of Certified Social Workers. He has had extensive experience in working with people, especially those having emotional or marital problems, often in a clinic or psychiatric setting, or has worked as a team member with a psychiatrist. The social worker is a specialist in the area of interpersonal relationships and social functioning. Similar to the psychologist, the social worker, in private practice, usually has a sliding fee scale.

The Minister

A steadily growing number of ministers are receiving training in pastoral counseling and are consequently equipped to help persons who have marital problems or who are suffering from the milder emotional disorders. There are some ministers who specialize in pastoral counseling during their ministerial training. The Council of Ministers can be found in many rural and urban communities. The president of the council can usually provide background information on ministers having training in pastoral counseling.

Other Specialists

Included here is the school counselor who often has a Master's degree in counseling, who specializes in testing and, increasingly, in counseling children and sometimes their parents. Also included is the sociologist, educational psychologist and cultural anthropologist who have advanced degrees and, occasionally, additional training in counseling.

Finally, it should be mentioned that there is no substitute for personal contact with your clinical personnel or referral sources. Personal acquaintance with the specialist can result in more accurate referral and is often helpful in obtaining an early appointment which may be needed on an emergency basis. *Consistent use of referrals to community resources assures not only that the patient receives the best of professional care to which he is entitled, but also facilitates the work and effective functioning of the physician-counselor engaged in marriage counseling.*

part two

COUNSELING IN SEXUAL PROBLEMS

chapter ten

Male Sexual Conditioning*

RICHARD H. KLEMER, Ph.D., *Department of Psychiatry, University of Washington School of Medicine, Seattle, Washington*

Men are different from each other in a lot of ways. They come short and tall, fat and lean, tough and gentle, polished and rough, passionate and indifferent.

Some men differ from other men more than they differ from women. This is true not only in things such as muscular strength and mechanical ability; it is also true of what they like and what they like to talk about. But there is one area of variability which causes a great deal of marriage misunderstanding: the differences in sexual desire and responsiveness. For some women, some men appear to have too much; for others, not enough.

Later, Dr. Masters and Mrs. Johnson will discuss the treatment of sexual incompatibility. This chapter deals with the background for some of the incompatibility problems.

How Did the Men Get That Way?

The sex conditioning of the typical American male is a complex and paradoxical process that involves infant conditioning, mother influences, group pressures, social class customs, romantic rhapsodies, dilemmas, contradictions, winked-at behaviors, moral exhortation, blundering experimentation, pornography, sound biologic information and resolute intellectual conviction.

Out of this vast conglomeration, it seems reasonable to speculate that five major nonphysical influences shape and reshape the developing sex consciousness and behavior of the typical middle-class American man: (1) infant love-response patterns, (2) early sex training, (3) intensity of training in social responsibility, (4) the implanted notion of the importance

---

* Much of this material was taken from Chapter 6 of *A Man for Every Woman* by Richard H. Klemer, Ph.D., published by The Macmillan Company. Used by permission.

of women, and (5) gang and man-group influence. Obviously there are, of course, some differences occasioned by differing temperament, physical structure and glandular output.

Those who put more emphasis on the unconscious—and most Freudian psychiatrists in general—might have a longer list of influences, but this one has practical as well as theoretic value. Perhaps you can understand the male patient you are presently counseling in terms of the five influences above. It is questionable if either you or the patient could understand him without months, if not years, of careful probing, if you begin rummaging through all the pathways of his unconscious.

INFANT CONDITIONING

A boy's affectional conditioning (and so, to some extent, his sexual conditioning) begins at birth. If he is warmly cuddled and accepted, if he is fondled and loved, if affection and the demonstration of affection are intimately connected on every occasion with the pleasurable sensations of warmth and satisfaction of biologic tensions, very soon he begins to be a warm, cuddly baby. His so-called "affectionate nature" is more likely to develop. He is probably started on the way to becoming normally marriageable husband material.

But what if he is deprived or neglected? There have been several studies of this. One of the more recent was made by Alice Thompson of about 2,000 college students.

In a paper which she read at the Annual Meeting of the American Psychological Association in 1958, Mrs. Thompson* reported that her study redemonstrated the tendency for those men who were not now in love and who never had been in love to have come from childhood homes in which they had been deprived of affection.

Not every man who is denied affection turns into a celibate recluse, of course. The human capacity to adjust is enormous. Some men will be able to experience very normal love relationships. And there are some others who, because they were denied genuine affection in infancy, may spend the rest of their lives seeking it without surcease. They may wander from sex adventure to sex adventure, hunting satisfaction for their desperate need for affection with one sexual partner after another.

EARLY SEX TRAINING

There are other mother influences as important as affection. Some of these directly affect the developing sexual nature of the boy child. His

* "An Experimental Approach to the Problem of Infatuation," presented at the Annual Meeting of the American Psychological Association in Washington, D. C., August, 1958.

first sex lesson will probably come from a horrified mother who is upset by his natural sensory curiosity and his penis handling. She can—and sometimes does—make the punishment so traumatic that it markedly affects his later sex life. It's difficult to be specific about this one thing though, for often there are so many other possible causes for any later abnormality that few authorities are willing to say for sure what caused what.

Freudian pscychoanalysts are, however, quite clear in their interpretation of the results of this early genital play. During masturbatory activity, the three-, four- or five-year-old boy fantasies that he has an incestuous craving to possess his mother and tries to seduce her by proudly showing her his penis. This brings him into conflict with his father. The little boy develops an intense fear that the bigger and stronger father will retaliate by cutting off the boy's genitals. This is the so-called "castration anxiety," which, it is said, will cause sexual repression and can cause later neurotic behavior.

But whether or not penis handling is the middle-class boy's first introduction to sex repression, it certainly will not be his last. Very soon, at least by the age of three or four, he is given to understand that sex, like death and the excretory functions, is circumscribed by taboos in our culture. He is carefully taught what sexual things he may not do, may not say and may not even think, without guilt. The punishment for violation of any one of these taboos is liable to be more severe than for other misbehaviors. Most middle-class parents, carefully sex-inhibited themselves, have deep-rooted anxieties about *any* childhood sexuality.

And if he is a middle- or upper-class boy who lives in a middle- or upper-class neighborhood, his parent conditioning is only the beginning. The jeers and ridicule of playmates given for a taboo violation are often far, far more effective persuaders that he must not do, say or think that sexual thing again than are the embarrassed silences or the blushing angers of his parent. It may take quite a lot of group reassurance or biologic urging in later years before he mentions sexual thoughts.

Thus, long before a middle-class boy ever learns the real significance of genital stimulation—much less sexual intercourse—social attitudes about these things have been acquired and made a part of his personality. Moreover, as he grows, he will absorb more and more of the middle-class mother's romantic association of sex activity with true love.

This notion, too, will find reinforcement among his age mates. For their mothers also promote the notion that kissing, hugging and every other sexually tinged act that their children are permitted to see are the special prerogatives of those who are married. Or at least they are appropriate only to those who are in love.

By the time the middle-class boy approaches adolescence, the sex-love relationship is deeply ingrained into his emotions. For some boys, the very idea of sex activity with a woman they do not love is as guilt-ridden as betraying a friend, trampling the flag or even blasphemy itself.

But if a boy is born in a lower social level home (clues: father's occupation, economic circumstances, education level the boy reaches), his indoctrination about sex matters will be far different. The clear demonstration of this fact is undoubtedly the major contribution of the otherwise often criticized Kinsey studies. Of course, not *every* boy in any social, occupational or educational class develops according to the sexual customs and traditions of those around him. But most boys either absolutely conform or soon move out of that social stratum.

Usually, the lower social level boys are far less inhibited and far more familiar with all kinds of sexual behavior. Unbelievable as it may seem to middle-class people, such a boy will have observed his parents and other people in intercourse, not once, but often. He will be well aware of the techniques, functions and pleasures of sexual activity at an age when middle-class boys still have no idea that there is such a thing as sexual intercourse. He will come to regard intercourse inside and outside of marriage as normal and usual. Any substitute, such as masturbation or petting, may be looked upon as perversion.

Moreover, many lower social level parents, while urgently condemning masturbation, will advise their boys on how to get sexual outlet through intercourse before marriage, what dangers to avoid and so on.

The outside play group will have its effect on the lower social level boys, too. But in his gangs, sex is discussed far more freely and with far less "moral" restraint than in the middle-class groups. He may learn to want a virgin to marry, but he also learns to take premarital sexual intercourse wherever he can get it.

As such a boy grows toward adolescence, pressure to demonstrate that he is worthy of the group by having intercourse is severe. Kinsey's[1] studies indicate that by the age of 15 almost half the boys from the lower social levels have had sexual intercourse. By the usual marriage age, some 85 per cent have had such a premarital experience, and at the lowest levels, 98 per cent will have had intercourse before they marry.

Few of these men look upon their intercourse experience as anything more than pure physical gratification. Far from loving their casual sex partners, very often these men have only contempt for them. In fact, they regard preliminary lovemaking and petting as a waste of time, if not a little abnormal. On this kind of a "see-how-much-you-can-get" basis Kinsey's report that some lower social level males have intercourse with several hundred or "even a thousand or more" girls before marriage comes close to being at least conceivable.

SOCIAL RESPONSIBILITY

It isn't only because there is more freedom of sexual opportunities and expression among the lower educational and occupational groups that those young men have so many more sexual experiences. Often they have less "socialized anxiety" about doing anything which society defines as bad. There is more stealing among lower social level groups and more homicide. In short, there is less social responsibility about everything—generally less adherence to all codes.

Some young men at the upper end of the social scale also rank among the sexual irresponsibles. Boys of some high income families have a sense of self-esteem and self-importance which often translates itself into a license for greater disregard of social codes. After all, father's money can get them out of scrapes. They have been conditioned to having other people subserve themselves to their pleasures. This very attitude of demanding satisfaction because they are who they are often gets them the sexual satisfactions they desire.

By and large, it is the middle-class boys who are conditioned to be the "good boys." They are the ones who are taught about courtesy, chivalry and honor. They are the ones who go to church, stay in school, obey the rules. Since these boys are taught that lying is not honorable, they probably will not lie to women as readily as other men might. If telling a lie is necessary to seduction, they may then forego sexual intercourse altogether.

Even within this group, though, there seems to be a range in behavior. Some men are more incorruptible than others. Here again, there is evidence of a correlation between general conformity to all rules and laws and sex conformity. There was one important study of 1,300 college students made at a time when college students usually came from middle- or upper-class homes. In this research, the so-called "hot bloods"—those men students who have very much more sexual intercourse than the other males in the college group—were also the ones who appeared to have less sense of responsibility about their other behaviors.[2] They were not the "good boys" in any sense of the word.

IMPORTANCE OF WOMEN

One explanation for at least part of the difference in sexual aggressiveness among even the "nice" young men is the childhood notion of how important women are.

If, while he is growing up, the boy sees that the man is the virtual owner of women and his every whim, sexual or other, is immediately satisfied (as in the Orient and in some old-fashioned homes in this country) he will probably have a different sex life from the man who comes from a modern equalitarian home. If his self-opinion is such that he feels women can and should cater to his sex pleasure, he will be a far different boy in the back seat of a parked automobile than if he were brought up to believe that women are respectable and worthy human individuals.

It is only temporarily surprising to learn that the boy with selfish, sex-demanding attitudes very often is rewarded both in terms of sex opportunities and in terms of respect from the girls he dates. After all, most often the young women are brought up in homes with the same cultural background as the young men and are subject to some of the same attitudes and ideas. Aggressiveness in men is admired in our competitive society. Many girls feel that a boy is acting in his appropriate role when he is sex-demanding and like him better for his appropriateness.

And if the boy who learns sex-selfishness is different from the boy who learns respect for a young woman, he is so much the more different from the boy who is taught by his mother that women are delicate flowers to be cherished and idolized.

In marriage counseling practice it is common to find unhappy and mortified women who blame themselves for their husband's failure in sexual intercourse, feeling that his impotence is the result of their lack of charm. Usually this is not so. Although there are many causes of impotence, in some instances his difficulty can be traced to the attitudes mothers inculcate in their sons. Sometimes this involves establishing a "madonna" image, resulting in a husband's later overromanticized tenderness for the wife who is now beside him, so that he is unable to "defile" her. In other cases, it seems reasonable to believe that many young men have their future sex lives ruined by an overdose of conditioned-in anxiety about what other people think—especially what women think—to the point where the slightest rejection from a woman sends them into emotional panic.

The process by which this conditioning is implanted is often insidious. What it amounts to is this: a mother says to her son, "If you are a good boy, mother will love you." Soon, becoming a good boy is equated with pleasure and being a bad boy is equated with loss of love. It is hardly surprising that many of these young men turn out to be wholly supplicative and timid in their lovemaking. They are so afraid of offending their sex partner that her slightest implication of displeasure or pain is enough to cause the panic to set in. They are hypersensitive to rejection. They not only need the mate's permission to make some sexual advance, they actually need her enthusiastic aggressiveness before they are able to bring themselves to be sexual with her.

Since most women are conditioned to expect and want *male* sexual aggressiveness, very few have the desire or capacity to pamper the emotional system of the more timid male. Consciously or unconsciously they become somewhat contemptuous, a fact that noticably increases the male partner's feeling of rejection and panic. Once this feeling of panic and failure becomes internalized, it often appears without any further stimulus when the time is appropriate for sexual action. This sets up a kind of neurologic confusion within the male that precludes erection or adequate sexual performance.

It has been speculated that some of the very women who neuterize their sons by implanting within them the rapturous virtues of delicate virginity and the oversensitivity to the woman's response are sometimes the very ones who, in their secret sex lives, are consumed with passionate desires for being rapaciously attacked. The conditioning of their sons is a sort of projection, an effort to atone for the guilt feeling they feel in their moments of wild and unbridled desire.

Of course, no one suggests that every mother who distorts the reality of sex in teaching her young son is doing so because of guilty projections. Very often there are other motivations—a desire to keep him with her, a desire that he enter such virtuous professions as the ministry or priesthood, or even a calculated hope that he will not be quite as demanding as his father.

MALE INFLUENCE

Speaking of father, so far his influence has not been specifically mentioned. In the father-directed older homes and in homes where father spent a good deal of time with the children all the way up, father's influence undoubtedly was considerable. Sometimes, especially in the lower social levels, it took the form of a sly wink by father or a "don't-believe-everything-you-hear-you're-only-young-once" attitude which nullified the effect of mother's carefully planned program of indoctrination. Often, though, father initiated the stern moral teaching or, at least, added his weight to the conditioning by reinforcing mother's teachings.

But in our pre-World War II big city middle-class homes where father was away much of the time, mother not only had the advantage of doing the earliest indoctrinating, she also had more time with the boy to answer questions and instill values. Many fathers of today's men really didn't have much idea what their children thought about sex or anything else.

Perhaps it was because they received so little of their early sex conditioning from a man that many of yesterday's middle-class adolescent boys had tremendous readjustments to make when the sexual realities of modern society began to filter through to them. This brings up the fifth major conditioning influence, the outside man-group.

In recent years there has been an increase in the amount of information about reproduction and human biology that is passed along in "sex talks" to young men. This has provided feelings of self-righteousness for the adult who made the talks.

But it is still true that some of the practical sexual training for the realistic world in which he is going to live a middle-class young man gets from some very unrighteous older boys and men. He gets it eavesdropping at the bowling alley or in whispered snatches over by the garage. Particularly since the time when the compulsory school age was raised to 16 and even 18, and more lower social level boys are going on to high school, he has been getting it in boastful exaggerations from the other boys in the locker room.

In this way, the middle-class boy learns—often for the first time—prevailing male attitudes about sexual activities. Here he hears about the techniques of petting and seduction that lower-class boys have grown up knowing. And, usually, he doesn't have to ask any questions, embarrassing or otherwise. Spicy information is freely volunteered in an enticingly dramatic way. All he has to do is listen.

One of the first things he learns is that much of what his mother taught him concerning the universality of continence before marriage is just plain not so, even if she really believed it. He finds that regardless of his values, most other men do have premarital sexual experience.

Of course, he is free to reject this shocking news if his home indoctrination has been strong enough and some men do—completely.

But most of the studies, including those of Kinsey,[1] Burgess and Wallin,[3] and Ehrmann,[4] are in relative agreement that from one-half to over two-thirds of all men—even in the upper educational levels—go on to have premarital sexual intercourse before they are old enough to vote. The Burgess and Wallin study of 580 college men further indicated that less than 20 per cent of all their sample men had intercourse *only* with the girl they later married.

And even if they don't have actual intercourse, Kinsey's figures suggest that over 90 per cent of all men (including those in the highest educational level) will have had some petting experience by the time they reach the usual marriage age.

Many middle-class mothers (and fathers and educators) who grew up in a different age refuse to believe that *their* teen-age boys would seek intercourse or even engage in petting before marriage. LeMasters[5] points out that this may mean that parents emotionally "block" at the thought of their son engaged in any sexual activity.

Some of the middle-class young men take their disillusionment and new understanding of the sexual world in which they live right in stride. It bothers them no more than when they learned there was no Santa Claus.

In fact, it provides an easy rationalization for their increasing biologic urges. Very soon they adopt some of the freer lower social level patterns of behaving and occasionally act as if they were trying to make up for lost time.

There is usually one major difference between these late blooming Don Juans and the lower social level men, however. Most of these young men who change their behavior have a conscience about what they are doing. They are continually aware that they are violating a code. Although they may appear to revel in such violation, they usually never adopt the completely uninhibited and ruthless attitudes of the men who are brought up to believe that premarital intercourse is normal and "right."

The great majority of middle-class men neither immediately reject the idea of some sexual activity of some kind with a woman before marriage, nor do they immediately run out to find an intercourse partner. As with the many other paradoxes and contradictions in our social and ethical concepts, they muddle along trying to find compromises that will let them remain at peace with their consciences, keep up with the rest of the men they respect and still not miss anything.

Some young men make a clear-cut decision before very long as to the ultimate limit of their sexual activity and then stick to it. Contrary to the pleadings of men who are trying to promote intercourse, it is not biologically necessary for any man to have any certain amount or kind of sexual expression. Nor is the tide of social pressure generally so strong that a resolute, think-for-himself middle-class man may not stick to any standard of conduct he genuinely believes in.

Thus, because of an inner conviction, religious or otherwise, some men adopt a definite premarital sexual limit. For some it is kissing. Others vow that their petting will never go so far that they will lose their "virginity." More often, the pledge is that they will never be a party to ending some girl's virginity.

Those who have a limit are probably the most readily marriageable men in our society. For usually these are the well-behaved yet decisive men who will have high standards of ethical behavior throughout life and still have a positiveness that will make them good leaders. These are the men who mentally and emotionally have been conditioned to associate sex, love and marriage in the same way that most woman have. All of their natural sex drive is channeled by their conditioning toward one approved outlet—marriage. They *want* to get married.

There is also, however, some good husband material among the large group of nondeciders—those men who never place any conscious limit on their sexual activity, but just drift with circumstances. For the most part these men play the now-widespread "dating game." The young man sees how far he can go without being so offensive that he is disliked; the young woman is expected to yield as little as possible, yet still give the impression she is enjoying the game and still be seductive enough to keep him coming back for more.

In a very real sense, this puts the control of the sexual destiny of any one of these young men in the hands of the women with whom they associate. If they happen onto more women who are either unskillful at saying "no" or who never intended to say "no" in the first place, these men will have greater sexual experience.

Some investigators, including the Kinsey group, appear to disagree, but I think there is every reason to believe there are some middle-class men who would go into marriage with less sexual experience except for the fact that circumstances, such as military service overseas, made many sexual experiences unusually significant and inescapably easy for them.

For even in this day of easier relationships, sex knowledge and sex desire are a long way from actual sexual experience for the average middle-class boy. Unless his initial experience is to be with a prostitute (less likely for a middle-class young man who stays home these days) there is much for him to learn and emotionally accept before he will be successful in any sexual approach to a "nice" girl. And that goes for petting as well as intercourse.

Scraps of information—and misinformation—concerning how to excite the female, what to say to overcome her objections and what to do to avoid pregnancy must be fitted together and agonizingly reconciled with his early teaching before a boy starts experimenting.

By a process of trial and error in his early dating, a young man furthers this learning. He discovers what happens when he touches her, that she doesn't want him to ask her permission and how far he may go without encountering genuine resistance and hostility.

In this process still another sorting out takes place. The developing man learns what women think about *him* as a sex attraction. Much of his later behavior may well depend on the reflected impression of himself that he gets at this time. Any unsure bumbling may be quickly punished by the girl partner's censure. This creates further inhibitions in the unskillful or unattractive young man. On the other hand, the attractive, "smooth," aggressive individual may be rewarded and encouraged to further experiments.

Some young men, not wholly convinced of the rightness of what they are doing because of their early moral conditioning, make a bad mess of the sexual experimenting. If they have a fairly weak self-opinion anyway, they may conclude from their early failures that women don't want their approaches—ever. Thus, perhaps, some bachelors are made.

There are a good many other properly brought up young men with strong egos and fewer social restraints who begin sexual experimenting almost as soon as they have been disillusioned about universal chastity by the outside man-group. Often, wholly because they are so secure and self-confident, these men will have enormous success. But later they may develop a contempt for both marriage and responsibility toward women. And so, perhaps, another group of bachelors is made.

At least, these men believe, they can have all the sex they want without the usual restrictions. It doesn't take a marriage expert to know that if a woman marries a man like this, she may only increase her problems.

Again, it is probably the young men of the middle group—those who neither abstain from sexual advances nor make sex play a requirement for further dating—who turn out to be the most marriageable. They become the easy to interest men and the ones who are more likely to propose than to proposition.

Regardless of the ultimate limits to premarital sexual behavior that any man accepts, however, his association with the outside man-group usually has an effect on his sex life. In many instances he absorbs some misunderstandings of what women really want. These misunderstandings have their origin in the sexually excited imaginations of a group of not-too-well-informed men.

For example, as a result of the exaggerations and misconceptions they acquired in the locker room, there are many men who seemingly cannot be unconvinced that all women have the same sex appetites they do. These men are likely to approach women sexually the way they would like to be approached—with direct genital stimulation. Some, because such things are deliberately kept from them by well-informed people who know, don't really understand that women usually prefer emotional stimulation in the form of tender exchanges of love talk before any specific sexual contact. Kinsey,[6] in pointing out why some women prefer homosexual relations, suggests that women are likely to understand the anatomy, psychology and responses of their own sex better than they understand the curious approach of the male.

This misunderstanding of the other sex's desires works both ways, of course. Some women find it difficult to believe that some men at times have an intense desire for a sex experience, without necessarily any desire for love play either before or after.

But, again, it should be remembered that there are many men for whom intercourse without tenderness would be impossible. There are some men who want no sex without love just as there are some women who can take the sex experience as casually as some men—if not more so.

There are all shades of the love-sex association resulting from all intensities of conditioning. I have talked with men who, even though initially repulsed by the particular woman with whom they were having intercourse, felt that, at least during the time in which they were actually engaged in the act, they had feelings of tenderness for her.

Impelled by the excitement of an imaginary contact with a nice girl who was clean and beautiful and in keeping with their sexual objective, these men had gone in search of a sexual adventure. Unable to find a sex partner who met their romantic ideals, they turned to a prostitute or a pickup who was a far cry from the beautiful and clean girl they had been dreaming about. Sometimes they were so repulsed in the beginning by reality, that tactile stimulation was necessary in order to make them an effective sex partner.

But once they were actually engaged in the sexual act, all the conditioned patterns of associating love with warmth and closeness to another human being went to work in their emotions. For the period during which there was actual body to body contact, the man felt sensations not unlike those of the individual who is genuinely loving. All the joy, all the tenderness and all the erotic feeling combined for the moment to confuse the feelings within the sexually excited man.

Immediately afterward, however, the befuddling emotions left these men. The conscious and intellectual mind took over again. Because they were not really in love with these women, the men became resentful and were overwhelmed with shame in addition to physical revulsion. That is, they were ashamed for themselves not only for the act itself but also for their feelings during the act.

Human physical variability and conditioning being what it is, it is doubtful if any two men ever wanted the same amount of sex or wanted it in the same way. The range is of course from the weird abnormalities at the one end—homosexuality or complete lack of sex interest—to the weird abnormalities at the other end, the completely promiscuous Don Juan.

There are all manner of side branches and offshoots including the fetishists, the voyeurists and the sodomists (see Chapter 14). Mostly, however, men of the same age group tend to range within a relatively small area of sex appetites and satisfactions.

Even within the normal range, though, there are differences of excitability. A man who has been conditioned to the idea of male superiority and aggressiveness may be greatly excited by violence or a description of violence. For example, some are excited by the male character in a novel who rips the clothing from the woman before him and tears it into tiny shreds in a frenzy of passion before he carries her to another room for forcible intercourse. Some men not only are capable of forcible intercourse, they actually prefer it, just as many women dream of being forcefully embraced and can become even as excited as a man by a description of violent seduction.

But there are other men who are not capable of forcibly taking a woman. Their background conditioning is such that they have built-in inhibitions against any such behavior. Their conditioning has led them to believe—or, at least, to behave as if they believe—that women neither expect nor desire to have intercourse against their will. For them, the role of the man is that of gentle lover.

There is a range in this area, too. It runs downward from the man who, although he could not forcibly penetrate a woman, does desire to be the aggressor once he has reasonable assurance that she desires his advances. It runs through the tender mouselike male who demands constant reassurance from the woman with whom he is having intercourse that he is doing the right thing. And it ends in the absolutely impotent man who has been robbed of his capability by his conditioning.

While the popular stereotype of the sexually incompatible couple is the sexually aggressive male married to the frigid wife, just the opposite situation is frequently encountered in marriage counseling. As was pointed out earlier, most women are conditioned to expect the male to be aggressive, and even though they have married because a man was so kind and considerate and did not make too many sexual advances before marriage, they feel ego injury if he is not capable of persistent lovemaking despite any obstacles they put in his path. Because of their injured feelings they often become even more resistant and thus perpetuate and enlarge the problem. Often the only avenue of approach that leads to a solution of this dilemma is in helping the wife to understand the dynamics of their respective childhood conditionings which caused the problem in the first place. Then, perhaps, she can be encouraged to be more sexually enthusiastic at his first approach and he, in turn, can then approach her more vigorously.

However, it should be carefully noted that this is not an area for generalization and universal rules. Sometimes those men with the greater inhibitions and the less ability to be aggressive are stimulated and excited by the female who takes the aggressive role. But, as we said in the beginning, all men are different. There are those who would be—again, because of their conditioning—revolted by the very same propositions.

This is what makes sexual adjustments between people so difficult—and yet, for most of them, so exciting.

REFERENCES

1. KINSEY, A. C., POMEROY, W. B., AND MARTIN, C. E.: *Sexual Behavior in the Human Male.* W. B. Saunders Company, Philadelphia, 1948.

2. BROMLEY, D., AND BRITTEN, F.: *Youth and Sex, a Study of 1,300 College Students.* Harper & Brothers, New York, 1938.
3. BURGESS, E. W., AND WALLIN, P.: *Engagement and Marriage.* J. B. Lippincott Company, Philadelphia, 1953.
4. EHRMANN, W. W.: Non-conformance of male and female reports on pre-marital coitus. Social Problems, 1: 155–159, 1954.
5. LEMASTERS, E. E.: *Modern Courtship and Marriage*, p. 205. The Macmillan Company, New York, 1957.
6. KINSEY, A. C., POMEROY, W. B., MARTIN, C. E., AND GEBHARD, P. H.: *Sexual Behavior in the Human Female*, p. 468. W. B. Saunders Company, Philadelphia, 1953.

chapter eleven

Female Sexual Conditioning

RICHARD H. KLEMER, Ph.D., *Department of Psychiatry, University of Washington School of Medicine, Seattle, Washington*

Biologically speaking, sexual activity has more permanent meaning for girls and women than it does for boys and men. Margaret Mead makes this point very cogently: "Where for men", she says, "actual sex activity, however insistently it may intrude upon attention, is a matter of a few minutes, for women each of these few minutes is laden with commitment, commitment before and commitment afterwards .... A woman's life is punctuated by a series of specific events: the beginning of physical maturity at menarche, the end of virginity, pregnancy and birth, and finally, the menopause, when her productive period as a woman is definitely over, however zestful she may still be as an individual. Each of these events— because once past they can never be retraced—is momentous for a woman, whereas a man's ability to command an army or discover a new drug is less tied to the way his body functions sexually. So we can say—at least as far as human beings have thus far developed during the course of civilization—that sex in its whole meaning, courtship through parenthood, means more to a woman than it does to a man, although single sexual acts may have more urgency for men than for women." [1]

Despite this greater meaning however, and despite the modern emphasis on orgasms for women in sophisticated circles, it is apparent that in our culture, not only have most young women traditionally been less interested in physical sex than men, but sometimes they have been permanently conditioned to avoid sexual thoughts and sexual activity altogether. This, in itself, is hardly surprising. For the sexual conditioning of young females in western civilization is fraught with paradoxes and perplexities and confusions. In no small measure, it is this confused conditioning which results in many of the sexual problems attributed to women today.

Some of this confusion not only goes back to the very earliest foundations of psychosexual attitudes in a developing girl, it is also implicit in the emotional struggles of her carefully sex-inhibited mother. Often such a parent, having read something of modern psychology, is thrown into disturbed ambivalence when she sees the first evidence of her infant daughter's sexuality in genital play. Usually the mother's resulting behavior makes a poor beginning for the development of sound sexual attitudes and feelings in the child. Later, the child's confusion is enlarged and perpetuated in adolescence and beyond when she begins to understand that traditional sex mores and actual sex behavior in our culture are not necessarily congruent. And this confusion continues even into adulthood when the now-grown woman is perplexed by a new need (if she wants to be a successful woman) to demonstrate enthusiastic sexual response she may not feel. She may even be further perplexed by the contradictions of expert professionals as to where her orgasm must be perceived—clitoris or vagina—if she is to be considered "mature."

In many respects, learning to live contentedly amid paradox and perplexity has, of necessity, become the most practical end goal of female sexual conditioning in our changing society. By the very nature of our space age culture it is no longer practical (even if it were desirable) to condition a young woman to retire in blushing modesty from all the evidences of sexuality in the mainstream of living. On the other hand, there is as yet no well established and universally accepted set of modern standards to replace the sterner taboos of the Victorian era as a guide to proper behavior.

In this dilemma there is a very large need for the physician-counselor to help both the young woman and her parents. The discussion in this chapter is directed toward furthering that help. Before continuing, though, a look at the functional importance of psychosexual conditioning *vis-à-vis* the physical factors in the formation of a woman's sexual personality, would seem to be in order.

The Importance of Psychosexual Conditioning

There seems to be pretty general agreement among those who have studied human physiology and behavior that, except in rare cases, all girls are born with a potential capacity for sexual desire. But it is also very clear that by the time they are adults there are some women who never have any conscious desire for sexual activity and others who have only a very low desire at the age most other women have maximum sexual interest.

The causative factors or lack of sexual motivation are subject to dispute. Some investigators feel very strongly that inhibitions deliberately conditioned into the child as a means of assuring later moral purity are the major factor accounting for low sexual motivation. They point to the fact that more very religious women (a moral conditioning factor) have lower sex interests and often consider sex disgusting.

But there are other very reputable investigators who believe that low sexuality has some physical component. In some cases the relationship between low sex desire and physical abnormality can be demonstrated. Carney Landis[2, 3] reported that psychosexual immaturity in women was associated with immature body form in one study, and that psychosexual immaturity was associated with a history of late onset of menstruation and irregular duration of the menstrual period in another study. However, those who believe in the primacy of conditioning factors could here point out that gonadal function—especially that concerned with menstruation—is sometimes susceptible to psychologic modification and so, therefore, any cause-effect relationship is obscure.

Moreover, even if it be a physical malfunction which causes the delay of sexual interest, it is often a conditioning factor that makes that delay permanent. If a woman in her late teens or early twenties isn't physically or emotionally mature enough to be interested in sex, she may later be prevented from accepting sexuality by autoinhibition. But if later she does become physically mature enough to have desire, she may have by that time so dedicated her life to a cultural pattern of living, religious or secular, that she is psychologically unable to recognize the desires she now could have.

So, whether or not physiologic factors are present, it is obvious that the socialization and conditioning which the female receives as a child plays an enormous part in the development of her sexual desire and in the fulfillment or lack of fulfillment she receives from adult sexual activity.

In a culture so diverse as that in the United States, so varied, so relatively new and so changing, it is inevitable that there will be enormous differences in child conditioning practices and, consequently, enormous differences in the resultant individual desires and behaviors. Some of these differences result from social and economic backgrounds, some from ethnic traditions, some from regional and rural-urban patterns.

But despite all the differences, some common stereotypes are almost universally accepted as the desired expectations for the thoughts and overt expressions of the sexually ideal American girl. Just as we have some relatively close tolerance standards for judging the appearance of Miss America, so we also have certain fairly definite expectations for her attitudes and behavior concerning sex.

To be a successful girl child, the very young American female is expected to be almost completely nonsexual—any indication of sexual knowledge or experience ordinarily earns a severe reaction from her own parents and the neighboring parents as well. But this asexuality is only a brief episode in her lifetime experience. For at the beginning of puberty the expectation changes. Now to be a successful American female adolescent, the girl is expected to know enough about sexual behavior (even though her parents didn't tell her) to say "No" at the appropriate minute. At the same time she is expected to be sexually provocative enough in appearance and manner to keep the boys coming back for more dates. Margaret Mead puts this in terms of the "positive sex response." She says: ". . . in the United States, positive sex responses come to be defined as something women ought to have, like the ability to read. Just as men feel justified in judging a girl by whether or not she keeps her stocking seams straight, because this is a sign that she is the kind of girl who 'pays attention,' so they now feel justified in demanding that she know how to respond positively to sex advances."

"To respond positively," Margaret Mead continues, "includes the ability to say no, to postpone, delay, repulse without offending, during the long years of dating. The whole pattern places heavy demands upon both men and women, not the least of which lies in the contrast of role of play without completion, appropriate to dating, and the shift to complete sex satisfaction in marriage." [4]

This shift, to which Dr. Mead referred, is a second major change in expectation concerning sexual behavior in the life of the typical American woman. As she enters adulthood and marriage (or, often these days, even without marriage) the successfully mature woman is expected to reorient her sexual emotions again. Now she is to be a completely responsive tigress with an invariable ability to achieve complete orgasm, despite whatever inhibitory process her developing emotional system was exposed to. In modern society, it often appears as if cataclysmic orgasm, perceived as taking place in the vagina (where, in fact, all orgasm does take place) is the ultimate test of feminine achievement.

However, it is again Margaret Mead who points out "As experiencing a positive sex climax is probably no more congenial to the whole female sex than was the passive, unemotional role demanded of their great-great-grandmothers, these demands force some women to learn to simulate, as they have always had to learn to simulate through the ages, in order to conform to the current style in sex behavior." [5]

Obviously, these complex and sometimes contradictory goals of modern female sexual conditioning, requiring two major shifts in emphasis, would be difficult enough to achieve with any particular female, even if there were precise agreement on how it should be done. Unhappily, however, it is over just this point that the confusion is greatest. Examining some of the dilemmas faced by both the girls and the parents in the typical conditioning process may further demonstrate the enormity of the problems involved.

SEXUAL CONDITIONING IN A CHANGING SOCIETY

The beginning of sexual conditioning for the infant female, as with the infant male (Chapter 10), is probably the cuddling which she gets while she receives the biologic satisfactions of nourishment at her mother's breast. Learning to associate pleasure with intimate body contacts is a primary source of later acceptance of later sexuality. From here on, the girl child's introduction to sex is liable to vary widely with the kind of home in which she is growing up. Social class differences in toilet training, in opportunity for privacy, and even in the acceptance of talk about sexual activity make for a great diversity in sexual training patterns.

Essentially, lower class girls learn more about sexual activity merely by observing what goes on around them, than middle class girls learn. Moreover, often their toilet training tends to be less rigid and less circumscribed by taboos and feelings of shame and guilt. But even in the lower class homes, the girl child is usually conditioned to believe that saying and doing sexual things is naughty and she will be punished for any infraction of the rules. She, like the middle class girl, is also conditioned to expect that she will be rewarded for her modesty, virginity and fidelity. While these same values are sometimes proposed for boys, most boys discover even as little children that they are actually judged by different standards and that, after all, "boys will be boys" and will be rewarded for it.

As the girl child grows, her preadolescent sexual life is less subject to enlargement and modification by the peer group than the boy's is. She learns that nice girls don't talk about sexual things even with each other. While in the boy gang, boys are rewarded for sexual exploits and tales of sexual exploits to the point where it may pay them to exaggerate sexual experiences, girls often are punished by other girls and by their parents for admitting to sexual thoughts and behavior. Thus are contributions made to building feelings of the "wrong" of sexual activity and feelings of guilt about any form of sexual release—especially masturbation.

The female conspiracy of silence regarding sex not only prevents the growing middle class girl from getting the emotional catharsis of group therapy concerning her sexual thoughts, it also makes inevitable a rude awakening when she comes face to face with the realities of teen-age sex expectations in our American culture.

Only a very small minority of the earth's females are placed by their cultures in the curious situation of those in the English-speaking people of the western world. While girls are told that premarital intercourse is a violation of morality by their parents, those very same parents then dress them up in their provocative best and send them off with a young man on private dates that often end up in panting seclusion. Then only one conscience—hers—stands between the alleged cultural ideal and the fulfillment of two biologic urges. In the other cultures of the world where there is a prohibition against premarital intercourse, there is some external pressure system to help the young woman's conscience—there are chaperones or duennas.

The writer has said elsewhere, "in the United States, there is external pressure, lots of it, but most of it is far from helpful. Movies, magazines, and TV often appear to add their weight to that of the more sophisticated young women in any group. The objective often appears to be to persuade the young woman that at the very least she must have some man who manifests a sexual desire for her if she is to hold up her head as a real woman. From then on the progression is alarmingly simple; woman wants man, man wants sexual experience, and frequently he wants it right now." [6]

But if in her confusion the young woman speedily acquiesces, she may not only damage her future peace of mind by assuming a new guilt load, but she may also destroy the very relationship she sought to enlarge. For, because of their difference in sexual conditioning, if a boy and a girl have sexual intercourse early in their acquaintanceship, ordinarily they do it for very different reasons. Kirkendall[7] has suggested that men who seek sexual intercourse soon after meeting a woman do so primarily for physical pleasure, and/or for prideful demonstration of their manliness, whereas a girl, on the other hand, has basically different motivations for premarital experience. She usually accepts sexual intercourse primarily to please the man or to give her the security of "having a string" on him. With such differing motivations, premarital experiences which occur early in the acquaintanceship between a boy and a girl tend to deteriorate rather than advance their relationship.

But what happens if she does not acquiesce? A good deal depends upon her bargaining position in terms of attractiveness, but often the socially less apt young woman is surprised to find that instead of being rewarded by the contemporary peer group for her virtue, she sometimes appears to be regarded with suspicion as being a prudish type of spoilsport. She may be an unwelcome reminder of guilt to those girls who have already acquiesced. So, it sometimes appears to the chaste girl that the less morally inflexible girls are not only rewarded biologically but socially as well. Small wonder there is confusion!

These days, the confusion in the mind of the teen-ager is often matched—if not outdone—by the confusion in the minds of the parents. Many parents, who have been confused by the rapidity of social changes, have become so afraid of being thought old-fashioned by their daughters that they have not only been hesitant to teach traditional moral values, but they have declined to teach any values at all. The resultant vacuum leaves it up to the child to decide what her sexual conduct will be. Left rudderless by this default, most young people choose the easiest and/or the most popular way. Perhaps, in some ways, those youngsters who receive stern moral guidance are the lucky ones. For at least they have *something* to believe in.

It has been rather widely believed that the severe inhibitions brought about by parental prohibitions against sexual thoughts and activities were responsible for much of the anxiety and neurotic behavior in the adult life of the sternly conditioned child. Now there are many who are beginning to wonder if perhaps a complete lack of parental guidance and its resultant confusions doesn't produce as much anxiety and as much neurosis as the old authoritarian proscriptions. It may very well be that by completely failing to give young females *any* sexual guidance, parents, educators and counselors may perpetuate the very anxiety they had sought to eliminate by their permissiveness.

An integral (but sometimes overlooked) part of the problem of social change is the fact that many people, both young and old, have now arrived at a point where they have accepted change—change in any form—as a value in itself. For them, that which is traditional has become suspect.

Moreover, some of the same social changes which have conditioned our society continually to upgrade the value of change itself, have increasingly caused many people to downgrade the value of premarital chastity. Increased cross-class associations, theoretically better contraceptive devices, supposedly improved venereal disease control, the all-pervasive commercial glorification of sex, prosperity and the general "eat, drink and be merry" philosophy of these times of boom and crisis, have all contributed to the demotion of premarital continence from its former status as a first-class cultural value. One need look no further than some of our marriage relations books which include sections on "positive values of premarital intercourse" to see how far the quasi-official downgrading of chastity has gone. By contrast, it is still almost unthinkable that any American book would have a section on the positive values of blasphemy, trampling the flag or eating human flesh.

But in place of chastity, no widely acceptable "modern" standard of sexual behavior has been offered from any source. "Permissiveness with affection," identified by Ira Reiss[8] as a contemporary observed "standard," actually has very little that is standard about it. There is no standard for the degree of permissiveness to be offered and no standard for the degree of affection to be required. Moreover, the distinction between permissiveness with affection and outright sexual exploitation is dependent upon a knowledge and perception of adult motivation and emotional reaction that is almost unteachable to inexperienced children.

And most of the suggestions from professional counselors and educators—both moralist and antimoralist—in recent years have done little to help parents with their practical problems in moral education, regardless of the theoretic merits of those suggestions. Robert Harper, along with Albert Ellis, has been insistent that parents, in dealing with children, should "stop teaching them that premarital sexual intercourse is bad," and instead ". . . teach them how to exercise their own critical faculties about deciding under what sorts of circumstances and with what sorts of partners it is likely to be functionally desirable for all parties concerned." [9] But even the parent who is emotionally able to adjust to the unconventionality of these directions and who is able to accept their implications both for child and for society, soon finds that the proponents have few practical suggestions to offer as to how such teaching may be effectively accomplished with normal, sexually curious but emotionally immature, children. Moreover, Ellis himself concedes that parents who try to carry out such directions ". . . not only have to explain their view to their own children (which is difficult to do when the children are quite young), but they also have to explain that other people think differently, and that there might be difficulties in presenting their views to these others. Raising children in a nonconformist manner, therefore, is much harder than raising them to conform to the sexual prejudices of their community." [10]

Ultimately, however, perhaps the most insidious of all the confusions impeding more effective moral guidance, is the widely believed allegation that premarital sexual intercourse has become so general that we can no longer hope for *any* real premarital sexual morality on the part of young women. The implication of this is that no fair-minded parent or educator should expect his child to buck the trend and stand up against the alleged majority in defiance of the supposedly steady march toward complete sexual freedom. No one actually knows for sure how far this trend has gone in the mainstream of our society. But many people, fearing the worst, seem to feel that about all they can do now is to help girls protect themselves from unwanted pregnancies by handing out contraceptive advice.

While there may be wide regional and subcultural differences, this complete defeatism concerning young peoples' current sexual morality seems unwarranted for our society as a whole. It seems clear to the writer, after some years of counseling and teaching and after examining the complete returns from his recent study of attitudes toward morality, that individual young women can still be taught to believe in the personal importance of premarital continence to the point where these beliefs are not negative inhibitions, but positive values from which she can gain self-esteem. One 22-year-old woman student in the writer's study told how she thought it should be done. She said:

"Parents must teach their children in such a way that they will not want to go counter to what they believe to be right and just and good. Done this way, taboos become willful self-restraints. They are not set out as things the child must not do or can not do but rather they are things that under the prevailing circumstances the child himself wishes not to become part of him. This has worked for me; I would not want it otherwise."[11]

This young woman was by no means alone in her conviction. In the same study, a very large majority of the college-age women (and men) who were in the sample clearly indicated that they believed that most young people *want* more definitive proscriptions for sexual behavior than most parents now appear willing to give. These young people, though, thought that the sexual direction had best be "sold" on some modern and practical—yet at the same time idealistic—basis and should not be rooted in older metaphysical or theologic concepts which are out of synchronization with present-day reality.

Specific Help the Physician-Counselor Can Give

Implicit in this discussion of female sexual conditioning is the conclusion that there are two periods in the developmental progress of the typical American woman at which the physician-counselor can be of especial help. These two periods coincide with the young woman's two major sexual role transitions—the one from childhood to adolescence and the other from adolescence to mature womanhood—and the concomitant major shifts in sexual attitudes which are required.

In making the first shift from the asexuality of childhood to the knowledgeable sophistication demanded of modern adolescent girls, there may be only a few problems for the attractive, flexible, securely self-confident girl. A little information and direction may be all she needs. But the shy, socially less successful girl will have a very great need for the kind of friendly encouragement and guidance which the physician-counselor is most role-suited to give. While it is relatively easy for the poised and polished young woman who is popular and desirable to maintain any behavior she wishes, the less attractive and less apt girl who doesn't make friends easily often feels she must choose between (1) being promiscuous in order to have the male attention she eagerly craves or (2) rationalizing away her normal needs with "holier than thou" prudery. A few counseling sessions containing reinforcement and/or reassurance from the physician-counselor can sometimes make the crucial difference between success and failure in these difficult sociosexual adjustments.

A second major way in which the physician-counselor can help in the adolescent sex conditioning process is in counseling with confused parents, either in pairs or in groups. He can help them think through their own attitudes and, without violating the value system to which they are committed, to arrive at some convictions which they can then pass along to their offspring who are eagerly looking for just such convictions.

In this process he can help parents not only with their own communications skill but also with their ability to communicate with their children about sex and sexual attitudes. Inability of parents and their children mutually to understand the realistic problems which each faces is often a major inhibitory factor in building better sex understanding between them.

Most important of all, however, perhaps the physician-counselor can help parents to understand the importance of building self-confidence and a skill in human relationships into the personality of their daughters if they expect them to be able to follow whatever pattern of conduct the parents believe in. This does not mean that a girl should be pushed into dating behavior for which she is not ready or encouraged into activities that are prematurely sexually oriented. On the contrary, the principles of human relations which make one girl more popular than another are much more related to the girl's basic self-security and her ability to make genuine friends of both sexes.

The experiments of Solomon Asch[12] and others have shown that most people who have made a judgment that short is short will change that judgment when confronted by a majority which vehemently contends that short is long. But, Asch found, there are always some who will stand up and speak the truth as they see it regardless of the unanimity of opposing judgments. Asch's conclusions indicate that this kind of resolute independence has its basis in the depth of the individual's conviction and the strength of his self-concept.

This suggests that to really help young women to become resolute, secure individuals, it is important to give them definite rules which can provide them with security, stability and self-respect if they abide by them. Yet at the same time they need to be helped to some tempering flexibility and idealistic understanding so as to put sex in its proper perspective as a normal relationship-enriching experience shared by men and women.

THE TRANSITION TO COMPLETE SEXUAL RESPONSE

At the time of the second major sexual transition in the life of the typical American woman, the physician-counselor can also be of considerable influence in helping the normal young wife to readjust to the expectation of sexual freedom in marriage. It isn't *always* necessary that the counseling be directed toward making her sexually ferocious. Sexual behavior is an expression of the individual personalities of the sex partners and there are marriages in which both partners are agreed that gentle tenderness is more passionate than passion itself. Moreover, while orgasm (and more particularly, simultaneous orgasm) may be important, the mutuality of satisfaction for both partners is probably more important. Though many men find it very difficult to understand, some women get satisfaction without orgasm. In Terman's[13] study of marriage adjustment among his gifted group and their wives, he found that almost half of the wives who seldom or never experienced orgasm still claimed to derive either complete or fairly complete satisfaction from the sex act.

Even if orgasm is the desired goal, the physician-counselor should know and point out to both marriage partners that a perfect sexual adjustment, including simultaneous orgasm, is possible but not necessarily probable at the beginning of marriage. Most of the recent studies indicate that a good sexual adjustment is established gradually, and that many of the most responsive women report that their first full orgasm did not occur until weeks, months or even years after their first intercourse experience.

It is usually well for the physician-counselor to help the marriage partners to understand that perfect sexual adjustment involves patience and practice as well as passion. It derives its perfection from the complete emotional acceptance of each partner by the other and not from any set of standardized techniques or social norms.

To promote this kind of acceptance, however, each partner, as well as the physician-counselor, has to know and understand the complexity of sexual conditioning—both male and female—in our culture, and its unique effect on the respondability of the two individuals concerned. Many of the chapters which follow are devoted to that purpose.

REFERENCES

1. MEAD, M.: Introduction. In *Women: The Variety and Meaning of their Sexual Experience*, edited by A. M. Krich. Dell Publishing Company, Inc., New York, 1953.
2. LANDIS, C. et al: *Sex in Development*. Paul B. Hoeber, Inc. New York, 1940.
3. LANDIS, C., AND BOLLES, M. M.: *Personality and Sexuality of the Physically Handicapped Woman*. Paul B. Hoeber, Inc., New York, 1942.
4. MEAD, M.: Introduction. *Women: The Variety and Meaning of their Sexual Experience*, edited by A. M. Kritch, p. 16. Dell Publishing Company, Inc., New York, 1953.
5. MEAD, M.: Introduction. *Women: The Variety and Meaning of their Sexual Experience*, edited by A. M. Kritch, p. 17. Dell Publishing Company, Inc., New York, 1953.
6. KLEMER, R. H.: *A Man for Every Woman*. The Macmillan Company, New York, 1959.

7. KIRKENDALL, L. A.: *Premarital Intercourse and Interpersonal Relationships.* The Julian Press, Inc., New York, 1961.

8. REISS, I. L.: *Premarital Sexual Standards in America.* The Free Press of Glencoe, Illinois, 1960.

9. HARPER, R. A.: Marriage counseling and the mores: a critique. Marriage and Family Living, **21:** 17, 1959.

10. ELLIS, A.: *The American Sexual Tragedy,* p. 248. Twayne Publishers Inc., New York, 1954.

11. KLEMER, R. H.: Student attitudes toward guidance in sexual morality. Marriage and Family Living, **24:** 260–264, 1962.

12. ASCH, S. E.: Effects of group pressure upon the modifications and distortion of judgments. In *Groups, Leadership and Men,* edited by H. Guetzkow, Carnegie Press, Pittsburgh, 1951.

13. TERMAN, L. M.: Correlates of orgasm adequacy in a group of 556 wives. J. Psychol., **32:** 128, 1951.

chapter twelve

Talking with Patients about Sexual Problems

RICHARD H. KLEMER, PH. D., *University of Washington School of Medicine, Seattle, Washington*

Some physicians find it easy to talk with their patients about anything. Others know that there are certain areas from which, usually because of their own conditioning, they ordinarily shy away and in which they are reluctant to become involved. Often, the sexual experience of the patient is one of these areas.

Therefore, before going on to the chapters on counseling in sexual problems, it seems well to review some of the fundamental principles which tend to improve physician-patient communication about sexual matters. It should be remembered, in examining the following suggestions, that no one of them is an axiom in itself. Some can be violated with impunity by some physicians, but all of them may be useful in reevaluating one's own skill.

Easy Self-Confidence is Prerequisite

The first prerequisite for establishing an easy communication with the patient in sexual areas is, obviously, the self-confidence that comes with knowledge and competence on the part of the physician. Relaxed casualness is always the luxury of the person who feels self-assured and has a good background and understanding not only of physiology and sexual psychology, but also of contemporary social values in various subcultural groups. Moreover, some understanding of the feeling and attitudes of the particular patients with whom he is talking is very necessary.

Unfortunately, the typical medical school curriculum today and in years past has contained almost nothing on sexual attitudes and values, very little on the psychologic aspects of such problems as impotence and frigidity, and even less on the practical problems of illegitimacy and adultery. Yet these are the very areas in which many patients have severe difficulties.

It therefore becomes the responsibility of the individual physician to read as widely as possible on his own. It is hoped that this volume will, in its own small way, contribute to this physician need. But, for complete understanding in the sexual area, reading outside the medical literature is often necessary. There is a list of suggested books for the physician-counselor in the Appendix.

But competence (and so self-confidence) in sexual communication requires more than just general library research. It requires knowing your patient, too. It is necessary to have thorough knowledge of his personal value system and his sexual conditioning. Moreover, most sexual problems have psychosocial concomitants, and many times the patient's difficulties have arisen because of the divergence of his own childhood conditioning and that of his mate. For this reason, it is important that the physician take a careful history in order to know something about both partners' subcultural backgrounds, religion and educational status. As Kinsey and his colleagues[1] so clearly demonstrated, sexual values vary considerably in all these particulars.

In addition, the physician will want to know something about the partners' ages, their present anxiety level and the accuracy of their sexual education. Each of these things, and some others, as we shall presently see, have a distinct bearing on the physician-counselor's ability to carry on a skillful sexual conversation.

It should be pointed out here, however, that the physician-counselor's *own* feelings and attitudes are also tremendously important. Rigorous self-analysis (and very possibly some dual evaluation with another person) is a constant requirement for adequately dealing with one's own emotionalized feelings and so one's ability to talk objectively with others. In communication about sexual matters, as in no other area, the counselor's feelings of plain curiosity and titillation can often be disguised as "thorough history taking." It is only the physician-counselor who knows himself thoroughly who can project the necessary attitude of nonemotional, objective interest to the patient.

Most Patients Are Eager To Talk

It is almost axiomatic that the patient will not be embarrassed in talking about sex unless the physician-counselor is. Most patients are ready, within the security of the professional relationship, to discuss any area of human activity which, in the physician-counselor's judgment, has reference to them. Moreover, most of them have read enough in the popular literature so they will almost expect the counselor to want to know something about their sexual experience if their problem even remotely touches that area of living. Indeed, very often patients will want to delve deeper into the sexual aspects of some problems than the counselor had thought to go. Usually they will be reaching for all the sexual information the counselor cares to give and then some. If adequate communication is prevented, it is frequently a result of the counselor's own hesitant uneasiness.

Occasionally, it is true, there are patients who have extreme difficulty in talking about sex. In this case, probably the major counselor effort should be toward a warm permissiveness which will provide the security in which the patient can develop his ability to express himself. This involves the counselor doing a great deal of "encouraging" listening (reassuring nods, understanding smiles, patient pauses), some gentle questioning and some very careful and thoughtful responding.

Sometimes, giving some pertinent information, followed by a deliberately oblique question, can depersonalize the situation and so make the patient more comfortable. For example, instead of asking a patient directly about his masturbatory habits, it is far gentler to say "Almost everyone has masturbated and many people are troubled with guilt feelings. Do such guilt feelings trouble you?" This opens the door, and even if the patient responds with an ambiguous "no", it is far easier for him to answer the second question, "Do you mean you don't feel guilty, or you haven't masturbated?"

Above all else, it is important to be accepting and nonjudgmental. Whatever the patient says and however he says it, the physician-counselor should be neither surprised, amused or alarmed. At times, of course, it is necessary to point out some obvious errors in the patient's approach, but this can be done without any suggestion of ridicule or condemnation by a skillful counselor.

Which Words To Use?

Sometimes, physicians, as all other professionals, have felt that they can enlarge rapport with the patient by responding with the same folksy sexual talk the physician presumes the patient would use. Kinsey[2] felt it was absolutely necessary in his research work to discover the current folk words for sexual activity in the area in which he was doing his research; otherwise he never could be sure that the patient understood the question that he was asking.

It seems clear to me, however, that in the counselor-patient relationship, one can call a spade a spade without calling it a damned old shovel. Ordinarily there is an expectation on the part of the patient that the physician will use accurate medical terminology, even if he has to explain some words. This is something more than a matter of stuffy posturing for propriety's sake; this is a matter of creating confidence by a dignified scientific approach to the problem. A person might well have reason to wonder about the professional competence of a mechanic who talked about the "gizmo" instead of the "carburetor," or a psychiatrist who said he got his training in a "nuthouse."

Moreover, there are other reasons why returning the patient's four-letter folk words is often unwise. Usually these words have a highly emotionalized connotation for the patient, regardless of how glibly he uses them. To hear them returned by the physician-counselor adds to their emotional value at a time when the counselor himself may be wishing to create an unemotional climate in which a better evaluation of behavior can take place. In some cases, the patient hearing the counselor use the folk language is so shocked by the unreality of a professional person talking in these terms that he completely loses empathy, and the whole tone of the communication is destroyed.

In fairness, I should point out that not everyone shares this view. Kirkendall is one of those who appears to lean in an opposite direction. He says:

"Some professional workers feel the need on every occasion to use scientific terminology to create as purposeful and/or dignified attitude toward sex as possible. These persons are often unable to cope with the semantic problems (which really are emotional in nature) involved in the use of four-letter Anglo-Saxon words for sex, as compared with scientific vocabulary. On the one hand, they cannot bear to hear themselves pronounce the folk words. On the other hand, they find it hard to realize that some persons, who have always used four-letter words, are equally ill at ease with the scientific terms—if they know them at all. Thus they are unable to bridge the chasm which the language has created between themselves and the persons they wish to help."[3]

The only resolution of these differing viewpoints seems to lie in the personality of the physician-counselor. If he can project not only meaning, but security as well, by using the four-letter words, perhaps that is what he will wish to do. But for all the reasons outlined above, it often seems to be a needlessly hazardous demonstration of the counselor's ability to be "one of the boys."

PATIENT'S SEXUAL KNOWLEDGE SHOULD BE ADEQUATE

Ultimately, the choice of words is not as important as the communication of meanings. For this reason, it is imperative that the physician be sure that the patient has a real understanding of all the sexual physiology and modes of sexual behavior that is pertinent to his case. This requires accurately gauging the patient's present knowledge. For, while it is important not to talk down to the patient lest you lose his interest, it is also equally important not to assume that the patient knows more than he does. Stone,[4] who tested college students, found that only a minority could be said to be well-informed about sexual physiology.

Even those people who know a great deal about sexual structure and function—and those who think they know a great deal—may be missing the one vital piece of information that is crucial to their sexual adjustment. It is better to review some of the important factors in physiology and function routinely than to run the risk of leaving misunderstanding that could be responsible for a problem.

In this process of information-giving, suggesting books for the patient to read can help. But recommending a book or pamphlet can be a somewhat hazardous practice unless the physician is sure that he knows and approves of the entire contents. At one time in my practice, I thought I had found an excellent book for helping women to understand frigidity. For the most part it was. But I soon found that there were two objections: the first was that the very implication of giving the patient this book sometimes added to her problem by creating in her mind the idea that the counselor thought she was as bad as many of the women whom the author used as illustrations. Masters and Johnson in Chapter 13 will warn of the danger of saying or implying to the patient that she is frigid.

Moreover, the particular author of this book had a Freudian orientation and stated that women who did not regularly experience vaginal orgasm (as opposed to clitoral orgasm) were less mature women. Since all orgasm takes place in the vagina regardless of where it is perceived, for most women, the site of perception of orgasm seems to be of considerably less importance than the experience itself. So this, too, was sometimes a case of adding to a woman's feelings of inadequacy, making her even more ashamed of herself than she already might have felt.

What Sexual Behavior Is Normal?

Frequently the physician-counselor is called upon for reassurance that some specific amount or kind of sexual behavior is "normal." The simple answer that "what is normal for any particular couple is what pleases them" is often not satisfying to the patient who asks the question. In the first place, sometimes the reason he asked was that he cannot agree with his mate about a particular behavior and wants the physician's confirmation that he is "right" and his mate "wrong." Or else, perhaps, he wishes reassurance that other people do what he and his mate have been doing, since mankind has been conditioned from time immemorial to believe that something is right if most—or at least many—other people do it.

While the physician will probably want to avoid taking sides in any controversy over specific behavior, it is true that a great many people are experiencing sexual difficulty because of fears and inhibitions that could easily be dispelled by a physician who did know something of the norms in sexual behavior among married people in our society.

It does help some patients to feel more adequate if they know, for example, that Kinsey[5] reports that the married women in his sample had an intercourse rate of 2.8 times per week in their late teens. This dropped to 2.2 times per week by 30, and 1.5 times per week by 40. By 60, the women were down to once in about every 12 days. It does help sometimes for them to know that men's sexual desire and/or ability reaches its maximum early, around 18, while women's sexual interest and desire, whatever level is ultimately achieved, does not come until later. It does help sometimes for the patients to know that the typical female's sex urge lasts until her death, while the typical male's diminishes slowly over his lifetime. It does help some patients to know that experimentation in married partners in nudity and positions for intercourse and with various sexual techniques is extremely common but that its acceptance varies with the social class levels from which the partners came. It may also help some patients to know that sexual experimenting between married partners of all classes has been increasing in recent times. Kinsey and associates[6] report that manual-genital stimulation has become widespread, especially for highly-educated couples. Even such previously taboo sex practices as oral-genital contact have become more frequent.

However, it should be immediately noted that while there are tendencies in these directions, none of these premises necessarily apply to the particular patients with whom you are counseling. Theirs is their own special case. Some couples are satisfied with intercourse once a month. Some men lose sex interest in their 30's, while others continue to be sexually active into their 70's. And it is interesting to note that in Kephart's[7] study of Philadelphia divorces between 1937 and 1950, wife-initiated divorce suits involving sexual complaints frequently blamed the husband's desire for unusual sex practices such as oral-genital contact. Blood concludes: "In short, while marriage may encourage variety for variety's sake, respect for the partner's scruples is still fundamental."[8]

It should be pointed out that suggesting that "what is acceptable to the partners is right" is something quite different from suggesting that everything the partners conceive of is right. In many cases, the value system or religious belief of either one or both of the partners precludes many forms of sexual behavior which might seem quite right or normal to the physician-counselor. For this very reason, it is advisable for the counselor to know—as was indicated above—not only the religious belief of his patients, but also some of the basic tenets of that belief. Suggesting to a Roman Catholic patient that he manually manipulate his wife so that she achieve orgasm and so solve her sexual problem would hardly be an adequate solution since this might be confused with sinful masturbation by one partner or the other. Nor does it help to suggest to a Mormon that he take a drink to relax his sexual inhibitions, or to an Orthodox Jew that intercourse during menstruation is "normal."*

Margaret Mead, in her introduction to *Women, the Variety and Meaning of Their Sexual Experience*, sums up the "What is Normal?" situation very well. I sometimes read this paragraph directly to my patients:

"Perhaps most of all there is a need to individualize each marriage for both partners, but especially for the woman, who, sitting beside the child's carriage, or scraping the carrots for dinner, has the freest time for reverie, to think more about each other's rhythms, each other's capacities for change and for fulfillment. The kind of sex literature which merely gives statistics on frequency of sex relationships and reported types of satisfaction, so that a man or woman can compare his or her record with some national norm, is the least fitted to inform such reverie. Rather do women —and men—need to know how infinitely varied the sex capacities of human beings are, how complex the patterns which release emotion, how various and wonderful the ways that lead to ecstasy. As they come to realize the extent and depth of sex feelings—in the feeling of the young child and the parent, in the young lover who lives on in the middle aged, and the vision of old age which makes the kisses given by the young already falter in uncertainty—the place of sex in the world, the importance of understanding sex, should take on a new dimension."[9]

In addition to talking *with* the patient about sexual problems, the physician-counselor can and should help the young marriage partners to enlarge their own ability to communicate with each other about sexual relations. Eleanor Hamilton has written on encouraging sexual communication between the partners in Chapter 18. But right here it should be emphasized that in teaching how to create the security necessary to good sexual communication and in encouraging the partners to improve their understanding, the physician can serve as a model. His attitudes of easy permissiveness, his acceptance of what the patient says, without shock or embarrassment, his calm ability to discuss emotionally-loaded topics with both frankness and dignity—all will help the previously fearful patient

---

* The author's original statement implying that manual genital stimulation to orgasm would be sinful has been questioned by several Catholic physicians and laymen who cite ecclesiastical sources in arguing that the sinfulness of the genital stimulation depends both on the intent of the partners and/or the time interval between the manual manipulation and penile penetration. It is contended that manipulation as foreplay which accidentally causes orgasm or manipulation immediately after the husband has achieved orgasm by normal intercourse for the purpose of providing orgasm for the wife, are not sinful. This points up the importance of knowing the fine points of your patients' value systems.

to learn how to communicate with his partner. The physician-counselor can be, and often is, a substitute father figure who openly authorizes and permits the use of sexual words—and thoughts and behaviors—which a real father somewhere in the dim past prohibited and/or inhibited by shock and punishment.

Usually the physician will not know how effective his sexual communication help has been. The typical patients will listen, nod their heads, and perhaps never again discuss their problem with the physician. This is often an indication of important progress, but only the rare patient will return to tell the physician-counselor how much improved their marital relationship has been. It may take a good deal of faith and unprovable belief in the effectiveness of what one is doing in order to be of genuine help to so many young people who need help in sexual communication so badly.

In this context, as well as in general marriage counseling, the confidence of the counselor in himself and in his ability will be a major factor in his counseling success.

There is a reading list of books on sex problems in Section ID of the Appendix. There is also a reading list for patients with sexual problems in Section III of the Appendix and a reading list for sex education in Section VIII.

REFERENCES

1. KINSEY, A. C., POMEROY, W. B., AND MARTIN, C. E.: *Sexual Behavior in the Human Male.* W. B. Saunders Company, Philadelphia, 1948.
2. KINSEY, A. C., POMEROY, W. B., AND MARTIN, C. E.: *Sexual Behavior in the Human Male,* pp. 52 and 61. W. B. Saunders Company, Philadelphia, 1948.
3. KIRKENDALL, L.: Semantics in sexual communication. The Coordinator, **7**: 63–65 1959.
4. STONE, W. L.: Sex ignorance of college students. Family Life, **20**: 1, 1960.
5. KINSEY, A. C., POMEROY, W. B., MARTIN, C. E., AND GEBHARD, P. H.: *Sexual Behavior in the Human Female,* pp. 348 and 349. W. B. Saunders Company, Philadelphia, 1953.
6. KINSEY, A. C., POMEROY, W. B., MARTIN, C. E., AND GEBHARD, P. H.: *Sexual Behavior in the Human Female,* p. 399. W. B. Saunders Company, Philadelphia, 1953.
7. KEPHART, W. M.: Some variables in cases of reported sexual maladjustment. Marriage and Family Living, **16**: 241–243, 1954.
8. BLOOD, R. O.: *Marriage,* p. 367. The Free Press of Glencoe, New York, 1962.
9. MEAD, M.: *Women, the Variety and Meaning of Their Sexual Experience,* Introduction. Dell Publishing Company, Inc., New York, 1953.

chapter thirteen

Counseling with Sexually Incompatible Marriage Partners

WILLIAM H. MASTERS, M.D., AND VIRGINIA E. JOHNSON,
Reproductive Biology Research Foundation, St. Louis, Missouri

At least one result of the cultural relaxation of sexual taboos has been of major consequence. Today, more—many more—marital partners are seeking professional assistance when sexual incompatibility threatens their marriage. Anyone exposed professionally to the emotional anguish and disrupted marriages caused by such clinical problems as impotence and frigidity will look upon this help-seeking trend with considerable satisfaction.

Most of the sexually distressed people are bringing their problems to their family physicians. Although the individual or combined efforts of psychiatrists, psychologists, marriage counselors, social workers and/or clergymen may be needed in addition to those of the chosen physician to solve some problems of sexual inadequacy, it is the family physician, taking advantage of initial rapport and established confidence, who ordinarily overcomes any patient reluctance or embarrassment and builds motivation for further treatment.

Unfortunately, until recently the physician has been hampered in treatment by three major stumbling blocks:

First, there has been a long-standing and widespread medical misconception that a patient will not reveal sex history background with sufficient accuracy and in adequate detail for effective therapy.

Second, in the past the physician has been provided with very little basic information in sexual physiology upon which to develop any effective treatment of sexual inadequacy.

Third, many physicians have been convinced that since most sexual problems are psychogenic in origin, only a specialized psychopathologist can treat them effectively.

Increasingly large numbers of physicians are demonstrating clinically that none of these obstacles now have much substance in fact.

Almost 10 years of investigation in the broad areas of human sexual response has brought conviction to the writers that if the interviewing physician can project sincere interest in the patient's problem and, even more important, exhibit no personal embarrassment in an open sexual discussion, almost any individual's sexual history will be reported with sufficient accuracy and in adequate detail for treatment purposes. Others, such as Eisenbud,[1] who have worked with human sexual problems, also believe that patients are usually very ready to talk freely about their disturbed sexual behavior patterns once they have gathered their courage to a degree sufficient to seek professional guidance.

While it is true that the amount of research in sexual physiology has in the past been meager indeed, this situation is rapidly being corrected.[2-6] Some of this recent material is synthesized in the latter part of this chapter and quite possibly may provide a minimal baseline for the more adequate clinical treatment of frigidity or impotence.

With regard to the third stumbling block—that of requisite referral to the psychopathologist of problems of sexual incompatibility—two things should be noted. First, there is ample clinical evidence for the observation that sexual imbalance or inadequacy is not confined to individuals who have been identified with major psychoses or even severe neuroses. Secondly, long-maintained individually oriented psychotherapy for sexual inadequacy frequently places irreversible strains on the marital state. While the psychopatholgist is working with one marriage partner or the other toward the resolution of his or her individual sexual inadequacy, the marriage itself may be deteriorating. One or two years of therapy directed specifically toward the impotent male or frigid female frequently leaves the unsupported marital partner in a state of severe frustration. Not only are unresolved sexual tensions of the nontreated spouse of major moment, but frequently no significant attempt is made by the therapist to keep the supposedly adequate partner apprised of his or her mate's fundamental problems and/or the specifics of therapeutic progress. Such situations of spouse neglect not only are sure to increase the performance pressures on the sexually inadequate partner, but obviously may lead to many other areas of marital strife and, for that matter, stimulate extramarital interests.

As the result of these observations, the conviction has grown that the most effective treatment of sexual incompatibility involves the technique of working with both members of the family unit. The major factor in effective diagnosis and subsequent productive counseling in sexual problems lies in gaining access to and rapport with both members of the family unit. This community approach not only provides direct therapy for the sexually inadequate partner, but provides something more. An indirect therapeutic gain results from enlisting the complete cooperation and active participation of the adequate spouse (the husband of the frigid woman or the wife of the impotent male). It is virtually impossible for the mate of the sexually distressed partner to remain isolated from or uninvolved in his or her partner's concern for adequate sexual performance. Therefore, most of these individuals can and will be most cooperative in absorbing the necessary material of both physiologic and psychologic background necessary to convert them into active members of the therapy team.

As in so many other areas of medical practice, treating sexual incompatibility involves, first, recognizing the nature of the patient's problem; second, determining the type and degree of the incompatibility and third, developing and activating the therapeutic approaches applicable to the particular clinical involvement.

Recognizing the Sexual Problem

The patient with sexual distress defines the problem directly with increasing frequency during this era of marked change in our cultural attitudes toward sexual material. However, may women initially may discuss such symptoms as fatigue, "nerves," pelvic pain, headaches or any other complaint for which specific pathology cannot be established. The physician-interviewer must anticipate conscious vocal misdirection when Victorian concepts of sexual taboos still exist, or where there is a personal demand to fix blame on the marital partner.

If, for example, the female is the partner experiencing major dissatisfaction with her marriage, for any one of a number of reasons, she purposely may obscure her basic personal antipathies by describing gross sexual irregularities on the part of her marital partner. Sometimes when it is the husband who wishes to end the marriage, he often employs the pressure of partial sexual withdrawal, or even complete sexual refusal. At this point, medical consultation is sought solely to justify condemnation of what is termed the mate's unfair, inadequate or perverted sexual behavior.

Actually, the marital incompatibility which brings the couple to the physician usually is not primarily of sexual origin. Sexual incompatibility may well be the secondary result of marital disagreement over such problems as money, relatives, or child care. Such areas of dispute easily may undermine any poorly established pattern of sexual adjustment. Frequently, withholding of sexual privileges is used as punishment in retaliation for true or fancied misdeeds in other areas. If the preliminary history reveals such a situation of secondary sexual incompatibility, the physician must decide whether he wishes to carry the full, time-consuming burden of total marriage counseling or if referral is in order. In the latter case, he still may wish to retain an active clinical role in the psychosexual aspects of the problems involved.

However, once the problem is established as primarily sexual in nature and as the cause and not the effect of the marital incompatibility, the complaint should be attacked directly and with the same sense of medical urgency with which clinical complaints of either a medical or a surgical background are investigated. Otherwise, permanent impairment of the marital relationship may be inevitable.

THE SEXUAL HISTORY

The need to acquire accurate and detailed sexual histories is basic to determining the type and the degree of the incompatibility of the members of the distressed family unit.

Sex histories must reflect accurately details of early sexual training and experience, family attitudes toward sex, the degree of the family's demonstrated affection, personal attitude toward sex and its significance within the marriage, and the degree of personal regard for the marital partner. While the actual nature of the existing sex difficulty may be revealed during an early stage of history taking, the total history, as it discloses causation and subsequent effect, provides the basis for the most effective means of therapy.

The first step in the team approach to diagnosis and treatment has been to see the husband and wife together as a complaining unit during the initial interview.[7-9] Procedures and philosophies are explained to them. If the family unit desires to continue after the investigative concepts have been outlined, the couple is separated for individual interrogation after both marital partners are assured that similar background material will be covered simultaneously by the two interviewers.

The knowledge that both unit members are undergoing similar interrogative procedures, that essentially the same background material will be investigated, and that all areas of professed concern will be probed in depth, produces an atmosphere that encourages honest reporting and an unusual amount of patient attention to detail.

Finite details of past and present sexual behavior may be obtained during the initial interview with the facility and integrity anticipated for the recording of a detailed medical history. Encouraged by a receptive climate, controlled, brief questioning and a nonjudgmental attitude, the patient is just as free to discuss the multiple facets of, for example, a homosexual background, as he might be to present the specific details of an attack of chronic chololithiasis in a medical history.

It should be noted particularly that in the process of acquiring a detailed sexual history, the usual basic physical and social histories of medical and behavioral significance also are recorded.

For the rapid diagnosis and treatment of sexual incompatibility, a male-female therapy team approach has been developed as reported elsewhere.[9] This approach involves the male marriage partner being interviewed first by the male member of the therapy team. Simultaneously, material from the female partner of the involved marital unit is acquired by the female member of the therapy team. Prior to the second investigative session, members of the therapy team exchange pertinent details of the marital unit's reported sexual distress. During the second session the female partner of the complaining couple is reinterviewed by the male member of the therapy team. Meanwhile, the husband of the distressed unit is evaluated by the female therapist. At the third interview, the therapy team and the distressed family unit meet as a committee of the whole to review the positive features of the prior interrogative sessions and to discuss in detail the active degree of the sexual incompatibility.

While the male-female therapy approach has been found to be eminently satisfactory, obviously this technique usually is not possible in the typical physician's practice. However, the broad general steps toward diagnosis and evaluation which are outlined here can be adapted by the individual physician. For instance, the advantage of honest reporting obtained by simultaneous interviews of members of the marital unit can be retained by interrogating family unit members consecutively.

The Therapeutic Process

Once the background of the individual couple's sexual imbalance has been defined, and the clinical picture delineated and presented to their satisfaction and understanding, a discussion of therapeutic procedure is developed for the family unit.

In general terms, the psychotherapeutic concepts and physiologic techniques employed to attack the problems of frigidity and impotence are explained without reservation. Specific plans are outlined for the therapeutic immediacies and a pattern for long-range support is described. With this specific information available, a decision must be reached as to whether there is sufficient patient need or interest for active participation in the therapeutic program. The decision obviously is based not only on a joint evaluation of the quality of the marriage and the severity of the sexual distress, but also on a review of the individual abilities to cooperate fully with the program. If doubt exists, on the part of either member of the investigative team or either partner of the sexually incompatible family unit, as to real interest in marital unit exposure to remedial techniques or ability to cooperate fully as a unit, the couple is directed toward other sources of clinical support.

Since the two major sexual incompatibilities are frigidity and impotence, treatment for these problems will be discussed in detail.

IMPOTENCE

Three major types of impotence ordinarily are encountered in the human male. They are:

1. *Failed erection.* Penile erection cannot be achieved.

2. *Inadequate erection.* Full penile erection either cannot be achieved or, if accomplished, is maintained fleetingly and lost, usually without ejaculation.

3. *Non-emissive erection.* Full penile erection is achieved, but ejaculation cannot be accomplished with the penis contained within the vagina.

Note. Premature ejaculation, ejaculation before, during or immediately after mounting is accomplished, while not considered a form of impotence, is discussed in this chapter due to the similarity of therapeutic approach.

Impotence is rarely, if ever, the result of lesions of the posterior urethra. Eliminating the possibility of spinal cord disease or certain endocrinopathies, such as hypogonadism or diabetes insipidus, the total history should be scrutinized for the omnipresent signs of psychogenic origin for the specific type of male impotence reported.

In the case of the male with failed or inadequate erection, history-taking should stress the timetable of symptom onset. Has there always been difficulty, or is loss of erective power of recent origin? If recent in origin, what specific events inside or outside the marriage have been associated with onset of symptoms? Are there any masturbatory difficulties? Is there a homosexual background of significance?

Further questioning should define the male's attitude toward his sexual partner. Is there rejection not only of the marriage partner, but also of other women as well? Are the female partner's sexual demands in excess of his levels of sexual interest or ability to comply? Is there a sexual disinterest that may have resulted from the partner's physical or personal traits, such as excessive body odor or chronic alcoholism?

In the case of a patient with premature ejaculation, questions should be concentrated in a different area. Does this rapid ejaculatory pattern date from the beginning of his sexual activity? Has he been exposed to prostitute demand for rapid performance during his teen-age years? Does he come from a level of society where the female sexual role is considered to be purely one of service to male demand?

When working with the male with a non-emissive erection still other questions are more appropriate. Has the male always been unable to ejaculate during intercourse or has this difficulty been confined to exposure to his marital partner? Are nocturnal emissions frequent, especially after heterosexual encounters? Is there an active homosexual history?

Actually, the fundamental therapeutic approach to all problems of impotence is one of creating and sustaining self-confidence in the patient. This factor emphasizes the great advantage in training the wife to be an active member of the therapeutic team. All pertinent details of the anatomy, physiology and psychology of male impotence should be explained to her satisfaction. The rationale of treatment, together with an explanation of the specific stimulative techniques most effective in dealing with the specific type of impotence distressing her husband must be made clear to her.

In the early stages of treating failed or non-erective impotence, it is wise to avoid emphasizing the demand that intercourse be the end of all sexual play. Frequently, the male's inability to meet just such a repetitive female demand is already one of the primary factors in his impotence. Some males find release from fear of performance when they are given to understand that sexual play need not necessarily terminate in intercourse. They are then able to relax, enjoy and participate freely in the sexually stimulative situations created by their clinically oriented wives to a point where erection does occur. After several such occasions of demand-free spontaneous erections, the males may even initiate the mounting procedure and complete the sexual act. This casual mating may well be the beginning of release from their chronic or acute failed or nonerective impotence.

In most cases, manual penile manipulation varying in degree of intensity and duration probably will be necessary. This controlled penile stimulation must be provided by his previously trained female partner. The male with inadequate erection syndrome should be exposed to long and regularly recurrent periods of manual stimulation in a sensitive, sexually restrained, but firmly demanding fashion.

In the opposite vein, the male with the difficult problem of premature ejaculation should be manually stimulated for short, controlled periods with stimulation withheld at his own direction as he feels ejaculation is imminent. The shaft of the penis should be well lubricated to reduce cutaneous sensation. This technique will fail frequently and ejaculation will occur. However, the family unit should be encouraged to return to the technique repetitively until the male's obviously improved control leads to the next therapeutic step. This will be a female superior mounting which can later be converted to a nondemanding lateral resting position. These progressive control techniques emphasize the family unit approach to the problem of sexual inadequacy and from here on psychogenic support and family cooperation certainly will reclaim many of those males who were formerly sexually quite inadequate.

The problem of the male with non-emissive erection is somewhat different. His is largely an infertility problem rather than one of sexual incompatibility. In these cases, reassuring both husband and wife that the problem is of little clinical consequence provides the basic therapy. Sometimes the infertility concern connected with this variant can be overcome by artificially inseminating the wife with her husband's seminal fluid obtained by manipulation. Since psychotherapy has produced so few positive results with this type of impotence, providing clinical reassurance and conceptive information may have to suffice in these cases.

Frigidity

There is a great deal of misunderstanding over the connotation of the word "frigidity." It is often used in a context which presumes an irrevocable lack of sexuality on the part of a female sexual partner. Misconceptions occur too frequently when overdependency is placed on this word as a diagnostic term.

From a therapeutic point of view, the maximal meaning of the word should indicate no more than a prevailing inability or subconscious refusal to respond sexually to effective stimulation. A woman is not necessarily lacking in sexual responsiveness when she does not experience an orgasm. Therefore, the achievement of orgasmic response should not be considered the end-all of sexual gratification for the responding female. Unhappily, many women, unable to achieve an orgasmic level of sexual response in the past, have been labeled frigid not only by their marital partner but also by the physician they may have consulted.

The free use of this term frequently does great psychologic damage. Frigidity is a term that should rarely be employed in the presence of the sexually inadequate female for it may well add shame, and/or fear of inadequate performance to whatever other psychologic problems she may have.

It is true that there are a number of women who experience a persistently high degree of sexual tension, but, for unidentified reasons, are not able to achieve a satisfactory means of tension release. In evaluating this problem, initial exploration should be concentrated in two areas of psychosexual withdrawal. The first is to determine the presence or absence of psychologic inability to respond to effective sexual stimulation. The second is to define the possible existence of sexual incompatibility caused by misunderstandings resulting from a difference in the sex tension demands of the marital partners.

As described elsewhere,[7] three positive indications of female psychosexual inadequacy can be developed by careful history taking:

1. Attitude toward sex and its significance within the marriage.
2. Degree of personal regard for the marital partner.
3. Fear of pregnancy.

In investigating the attitude toward sex, existing negative concepts should be pursued by careful interrogation. Questioning should explore early sexual training and experience, exposure to lack of demonstrated parental affection, history of homosexual experience, if any, and/or any traumatic sex-oriented incidents which might have affected natural sexual responsiveness.

When exploring the area of personal regard for the marital partner, the female partner's disinterest or lack of cooperation with the consulting physician may be an interesting clinical symptom of itself. When essential indifference toward a marital partner has been exposed, the existence of a basically unwanted marriage or marriage undertaken without intelligent preparation or emotional maturity is a real possibility. Perhaps, in these cases, referral to a marriage counselor or undertaking marriage counseling in the more general frame of reference, is in order, rather than concentrating on the sexual aspects of the problem.

When there is any indication of fear of pregnancy the therapeutic approach is obvious to the counseling physician. Actually, satisfactory results are ordinarily more easily achieved in pregnancy phobia situations than in either of the other two areas of psychosexual withdrawal.

After the background of the female's sexual unresponsiveness has been established, and the marital unit has accepted the conclusions presented during the diagnostic sessions, therapy may begin. Female sexual responsiveness may well depend upon the successful orientation to the following framework of therapeutic approach:

1. The possibility of anatomic or physiologic abnormalities that can contribute to varying shades of dyspareunia should be eliminated. Orientation to male and female sexual anatomy, directly if necessary, should be accomplished.

2. Affirmation that sexual expression represents an integral basis for sharing within the marriage should be emphasized.

3. A mutually stimulative sexual pattern should be developed and adapted to the individual psychosocial backgrounds of the marriage partners.

4. Gentleness, sensitivity and technical effectiveness in the male partner's approach to sexual encounter should be encouraged.

5. Emphasis should be placed on the fact that female orgasm is not necessarily the end-all of every sexual encounter.

With regard to pelvic abnormalities, it might be noted that a history indicating actual pain or any other physical displeasure during sex play or coition certainly suggests the need for an adequate physical examination. If physiologic variants, such as pelvic endometriosis, causing severe, recurrent dyspareunia with deep penile penetration, are revealed, subsequent medical and/or surgical adjustments may be indicated. However, it should be noted that sometimes the simple clinical expedient of teaching the family unit proper positioning for coital activity may remove the female partner's distress despite existent pelvic pathology.

A high percentage of psychologically based problems of inadequate female response begin as the result of rejection of, or ignorance of effective sex techniques by either or both marital partners. The physician may also be called upon to provide reassurance as to the propriety of variants of stimulative sexual behavior. Although the number of patients who are sexually incompatible as the result of the wife's or husband's total lack of sexual experience before marriage may well be declining, patients with this type of problem are seen occasionally. Moreover, many women have been taught that only certain specifics of sexual stimulation or certain coital positions are acceptable. These women do not readily accept any deviation from what they consider "right and proper" regardless of the interests of their marital partners. Victorianism, although vanishing from the American social scene, leaves a residual influence that may well require attention for at least another 50 years.

Teaching the sexually inadequate woman and her partner the basic rudiments of sexual anatomy may be extremely important. Many males, however experienced in coition, are unaware of the importance of adequate techniques for clitoral area stimulation. Few are aware that it is the gentle friction of the mons area or of the clitoral shaft rather than the clitoral glans that provides the most effective stimulation for the female partner. Moreover, many females as well as males are not aware of the basic physiology of sexual response and of the fact that physiologic orgasm takes place within the vagina and in the clitoris, regardless of where sensation is perceived by the female or initiated by the male.

In the development of a mutually stimulative sexual pattern it is important that the marital unit's move toward maximal female sexual responsiveness should be accompanied by the female's vocalizing such things as: specific sexual preferences, desired zones of erogenous stimulation, choice of coital positioning and, particularly, the fact of her approaching orgasm. The family unit must be taught to consider moments of individual preference for sexual encounter. Experimentation with varieties of time, place and sexual techniques should be made in order to achieve the necessary mood conducive to the female's successful sexual response. It is well to bear in mind that the two basic deterrents to female sexual responsiveness are *fatigue* and *preoccupation*.

The item in the therapeutic framework emphasizing gentleness and sensitivity needs little elaboration. But it should be noted that the male's approach—his ability to project both security and affection to the female—may be an absolute essential to any improvement in the female's sexual responsiveness. A reevaluation of the male's attitudes toward sex and toward women may be as important to the progress of therapy as the attention paid to his education in specific sexual techniques.

The second major interrogative direction (area two) in the treatment of frigidity is concerned with the possible difference in the degree ot basic sexual tension demonstrated by the wife of the pair as opposed to that indicated by the husband. In analyzing this area of the husband-wife relationship, it should be emphasized that an impression of low level female sexual demand should only be established in relative comparison to a higher tension partner. A lower level of demand does not necessarily connote either inability to respond adequately to effective heterosexual stimulation or homosexual tendency. Yet, when such a divergence in sexual interest is encountered, there are inevitable misunderstandings between the marital partners. In some cases there may be a conscious sexual withdrawing by the lower response partner, developing from a sense of personal inadequacy or from a wish to punish what is considered as excessive demand. Conscious sexual withdrawal also may develop from a deep resentment or a sense of rejection felt by the partner wishing a higher degree of sexual participation.

The marital unit's understanding and acceptance of a difference in sexual tension demand is far more important than its causation and the determination of a specific spouse role-playing. A higher level of demand may well belong to either partner. This is evident in marriages between younger partners as well as in many marriages between older individuals. Feelings of sexual inadequacy, distrust, or withdrawal may be corrected by education of each mate to the other partner's individual, highly personal, sexual requirements. Thereafter, the problem becomes one of adjusting acknowledged differences in sexual tension to a mutually accepted plan for effective release of the higher level of demand. It has been noted frequently that the relief of inhibitions of the lower tension partner (once the family unit problem is understood) may be marked by a more receptive, or even anticipatory participation in family unit sexual activity, even though there is no permanent elevation of the lower level partner's own sexual tensions. [9]

As emphasized many times previously, the individual or combined interests of psychiatrists, psychologists, medical specialists, marriage counselors, social workers and clergymen may be needed to solve severe problems of sexual incompatibility. However, the advice of the initially consulted family physician frequently will be the most important step in relief of marital sexual maladjustments. The physician's forthright guidance and initial reassurance, whether he refers to other professionals or treats the patients himself, provide the best foundation for the solution of problems of sexually incompatible marriages.

REFERENCES

1. EISENBUD, J.: A psychiatrist looks at the report. In *Problems of Social Behavior*, pp. 20–27. Social Hygiene Association, New York 1948.
2. MASTERS, W. H.: The sexual response cycle of the human female: I. Gross anatomic considerations. West. J. Surg., **68:** 57–72, 1960.
3. MASTERS, W. H.: The sexual response cycle of the human female: II. Vaginal lubrication. Ann. New York Acad. Sc., **83:** 301–317, 1959.
4. MASTERS, W. H., AND JOHNSON, V. E.: The physiology of vaginal reproductive function. West. J. Surg., **69:** 105–120, 1961.
5. MASTERS, W. H., AND JOHNSON, V. E.: The sexual response cycle of the human female: III. The clitoris: anatomic and clinical considerations. West. J. Surg., **70:** 248–257, 1962.
6. MASTERS, W. H., AND JOHNSON, V. E.: The sexual response cycle of the human male: I. Gross anatomic considerations. West. J. Surg., **71:** 85–95, 1963.
7. JOHNSON, V. E., AND MASTERS, W. H.: Treatment of the sexually incompatible family unit. Minnesota Med., **44:** 466–471, 1961.
8. JOHNSON, V. E., AND MASTERS, W. H.: Sexual incompatibility: diagnosis and treatment. In *Human Reproduction and Sexual Behavior*, edited by Charles W. Lloyd, pp. 474–489. Lea & Febiger, Philadelphia, 1964.
9. JOHNSON, V. E., AND MASTERS, W. H.: A team approach to the rapid diagnosis and treatment of sexual incompatibility. Pac. Med. & Surg. (formerly West. J. Surg.), **72:** 371–375, 1964.

chapter fourteen

Understanding Sexual Deviations*

JOHN L. HAMPSON, M.D., *Department of Psychiatry, University of Washington School of Medicine, Seattle, Washington*

Almost every physician will sooner or later see many patients who confess (or are accused of) sexual deviation. While the behaviors implied in homosexuality, transvestism, exhibitionism, voyeurism, fetishism, incest and so forth are extremely alarming to the lay public, there is general professional acceptance of the belief that none of these variations should be considered psychopathologic in an isolated, rare and nondramatic occurrence. Only when the atypical behavior is a consistently repetitive pattern in the individual, or his only mode of expression, does it constitute a psychosexual disorder demanding extensive treatment.

In the past, deviant sexual behavior has sometimes been viewed simply as a variant of homosexuality. This is incorrect. The exhibitionist, for example, is often eagerly heterosexual; indeed, his exhibitionism is a part of this eagerness. Some transvestites marry and have families.

Obviously, then, no such easy lumping together of all deviations, together with their causes and effects, is warranted. To understand atypical sexual behavior it is necessary to consider both the erotic components of that behavior and the behavioral and psychologic components as well, and then clearly to distinguish between the two. To do this satisfactorily it seems wise to consider in turn five of the major deviations—voyeurism, incest, pedophilia, homosexuality and transexualism.

VOYEURISM

Although delight in looking at attractive members of the opposite sex is common and usually considered to be normal, certain individuals come to medical and legal attention because they are offensively voyeuristic in

---

* Some of this material is taken from "Deviant Sexual Behavior; Homosexuality; Transvestism" by John L. Hampson, M.D., which appeared as Chapter 28 in *Human Reproduction and Sexual Behavior*, edited by Charles W. Lloyd, published by Lea & Febiger, Philadelphia, 1964. Used by permission.

behavior. Clinically, one defines voyeurism as a compulsive desire to see by stealth a member of the opposite sex in some stage of undress, in the sexual act or in the act of excretion—a desire which is of such intensity that it surpasses and even replaces normal sexual activity. Many explanations have been advanced over the years to explain the voyeuristic impulse.[1] It appears, however, that there is no one explanation, and that voyeuristic behavior is multidetermined. Some voyeuristic individuals seem to obtain frank sexual pleasure in this fashion by identification with one of the persons in the sexual act witnessed, while others seem to obtain their primary gratification from doing that which is prohibited. Indeed there is some similarity between the voyeur's interest in forbidden erotism and the child's excessive sexual curiosity which results when his honest questions are met by silence, evasion or punishment. The case histories of some voyeuristic individuals have documented this early mismanagement of sexual education which seem to find expression in voyeuristic tendencies in adulthood.

Although it has been stated that voyeurism is essentially a benign behavioral abnormality which does not lead to more serious offenses, this is not always the case. Instances are on record of individuals who have progressed from the relatively minor offense of voyeurism to attempted rape, assault and arson, among other crimes. It seems likely, however, that these aggressive impulses had always been present in such individuals, and had been expressed and, for the moment, satisfied by their voyeuristic behavior. Thus, some voyeurs, though by no means all, display an aggressive and even sadistic component in their sexual deviancy, so that it is a mistake to overemphasize the benign and passive nature of voyeurism. The expression of rage through sex is a frequent and important component of the pathologic motivation of many sexual offenders.

As in most of the other types of deviant sexual behavior, case management requires both time and skill and is probably best relegated to the psychiatrist. As our knowledge of such conditions improves, so too will our ability to bring to bear preventive measures during the formative years of youngsters in our society. Yalom[2] has described in some detail the problems and difficulties which the psychiatrist encounters in the therapy of incarcerated sexual offenders. He reported that group therapy with such patients, so often considered untreatable, brought favorable changes in an encouraging number of cases.

FATHER-DAUGHTER INCEST

Of all the deviant sexual activities in which humans engage, incest has seemed to many the most reprehensible. Few people want even to talk about this kind of behavior, much less investigate its origins, so that speculations about cause have generally been accepted without critical examination. "Degeneracy," "low I.Q.," "poverty and overcrowding," and "alcoholism" have been the traditional explanations. In recent years, however, researchers have taken a closer look at the matter and thrown doubt on earlier preconceptions about the incidence of and causal factors in incestuous behavior. For example, studies on incidence suggest that incest occurs as frequently in rural areas as in cities and that overcrowded living conditions is a greatly overrated contributing factor. Moreover, incest is not limited to criminal and sociopathically degenerate groups, but occurs broadly throughout the social structure.

Weinberg,[3] in a sociologic study of incest behavior, found male incest to be of three patterns:

1. Men who were indiscriminately promiscuous and for whom incest was but one of many evidences of their sexual psychopathology.

2. Men who displayed an intense, diffuse, erotic craving for young children (pedophilia) which included (but was not exclusively oriented toward) the daughter as a sexual object.

3. Men who confined their erotic interest and activity exclusively to family members—wife, sister, daughter—and seldom sought extrafamilial sexual contacts.

In this latter group of incestuous fathers, the men are not otherwise criminal, have no pedophilic tendencies and, as a group, have good intelligence and a good work record.[4] It is this group of men who seem most puzzling to doctors and to the community, for the explanation for their behavior is not readily apparent. Typically, these men are in their 30's and 40's. It is in this period of life that some men become increasingly bored and frustrated with a marriage long since gone sour. The presence of an adolescent, erotically appealing daughter takes on special significance in such a setting. These factors in themselves do not explain father-daughter incest, however, for many fathers are faced with similar problems and resolve them in healthy ways. What seems to characterize the father-daughter incestuous relationship is that it represents the outcome of family psychopathology—not merely the father's psychopathology. For example, the wives of such men are not infrequently sexually unresponsive, hostile and unloving women. Still others have been found to be so submissive and passive that they were unable to intervene even when they suspected an incestuous relationship, refusing to see the obvious to the point that they have abdicated their role as wife and mother in the family. Even the sons in such families are often involved, indirectly, for the incestuous father often ignores them or is hostile and indifferent to them in overvaluing his daughters.

The daughters themselves usually claim to have been forced, black-mailed and threatened, though the impression is that this is not always true and that some degree of assent was involved.

One explanation of the father's behavior posits that the daughter has come to replace, in fantasy, the wife—not the wife as she is at present, but as she was during courtship. Even so, one cannot escape the fact that such men function with a markedly unstable personality which permits gross distortions of social judgment to occur.

Following disclosure, the conflicts and emotional pathology within the family are out in the open. The father's pathologic sexual fantasies about his daughter fade and he finds new awareness of himself as a middle-aged man who has mistaken his role. Recidivism is rare and circumspect handling of such cases away from the public scrutiny of publicity offers the greatest chance for rehabilitation and readjustment for the whole family.

PEDOPHILIA

Pedophilia is the term applied to erotic activity involving an adult with a child. The pedophilic adult may be heterosexual, homosexual or even both, so far as his erotic desires are concerned. Needless to say, contemporary society finds such behavior unacceptable and, when pedophilic sexual behavior occurs, the impact on the family and on a marriage are profound.

Although pedophilic behavior is not limited to certain age groups or life periods, there is a tendency for pedophilic behavior to occur at certain times in life rather than at others. *Heterosexual pedophilia in adolescence* commonly occurs in psychologically immature youngsters who have no history of adult sexual experience and often no desire for it. Sexually curious and lacking in social judgment, these adolescents become involved with five- or six-year-old children in activities usually limited to fondling and sexual exploration. With increased personality growth and improvement in social skills, the ultimate prognosis is usually good. *Pedophilia in the middle-aged group* assumes a graver import. Such individuals are often seriously disturbed people psychologically; their history is frequently marked by marital discord and, often, alcoholic abuse. Psychiatric intervention aimed at strengthening healthy personality functioning and restoring supportive family relationships should be the aim in these cases. The *elderly pedophile* constitutes the third largest group. Loneliness, depressions, concern over sexual impotence and judgment impaired by the senile aging process can account for much of the behavior of this group of individuals. However, unless brain damage is severe and judgment grossly impaired, most of these men do not repeat their offense once apprehended.

Fewer than 10 per cent of heterosexual pedophiles relapse following apprehension.

The average homosexual person is no more apt to be sexually interested in children than is the average heterosexual person. However, this kind of double deviancy does sometimes occur, and in roughly the same major age groups as detailed above for heterosexual pedophilia. Many of the same causal dynamics operate in homosexual pedophilia, too, except that the erotic orientation is toward a child of the same biologic sex. Unfortunately, the prognosis for homosexual pedophilia is considerably more guarded and recidivism occurs twice as often as in heterosexual pedophilia.

The social implications of sexual offenses involving children are sufficiently serious that the physician must be prepared at times to be the arbiter in the matter of affording the maximum protection to society, while facilitating the reintegration of the individual into society.

HOMOSEXUALITY

Kinsey's and his colleagues'[5] figures indicate that almost 40 per cent of adult American men and roughly 13 per cent of adult American women have had overt homosexual contact to the point of orgasm. Obviously, since the apparent incidence of exclusive homosexuality among men or women is under five per cent, the difference must consist of homosexual behavior of a more transient sort. Careful study reveals this to be the case, so that it is no more precise to speak of *homosexuality* than it is to speak, say, of *cancer* for in neither case is one dealing with a single entity or condition.

Thus, Rado[6] and others have spoken of the "*situational homosexuality*" of prisoners and sailors, isolated for months or years from heterosexual possibilities; of "*incidental homosexuality*" such as some adolescents or sociopaths get involved in "*for kicks*"; of "*reparative or neurotic homosexuality*" in persons blocked from heterosexual expression by irrational, neurotic fear or rage toward a person of the opposite sex by reason of earlier traumatic life experiences; and of the "*chaotic sexuality*"—which may include homosexual behavior—of certain schizophrenic individuals. An adequate life history will nearly always shed light on the nature of these homosexual problems.

There is still another group of homosexual individuals which has proven somewhat more baffling and perplexing; such individuals display varying degrees of inversion of gender identification (gender role inversion). In common parlance such terms as "effeminate (or passive) male homosexual" or "masculine (or active) female homosexual" have been used to describe these individuals. Perhaps it is better, as Brown[7] pointed out, to regard all such individuals as *inverted homosexuals* and to consider

TABLE 14.1
Relationship of deviant sexual behavior to gender role inversion

Unrelated	Related

"Chaotic" sexuality (including homosexuality) in schizophrenics and mentally defective persons
Compulsive cross-dressing
Exhibitionism
Fetishism
Homosexuality
  Incidental
  Neurotic (reparative)
  Situational
Impotence and frigidity
	Effeminate, "passive" homosexuality in males
	Masculine, "aggressive" homosexuality in females
	Transvestism; transsexualism in males or females

those of the aforementioned groups as *non-inverted homosexuals*. (See Table 14.1.) Seen in this light, the only common denominator in homosexuality *per se* is the use of or preference for a sexual partner of the same somatic sex.

TRANSVESTISM AND TRANSSEXUALISM

Transvestism ("cross-dressing") is the term used to refer broadly to those individuals who dress or intensely desire to dress in the clothes of the opposite biologic sex. Again, like homosexuality, transvestism is not a uniform behavioral disturbance, but occurs in varying degrees and with sundry implications. Certainly, no one would automatically label a person cross-dressed for a masquerade party a transvestite. Only if the individual cross-dresses in search of *psychosexual comfort and satisfaction* is it to be considered transvestism.

At times cross-dressing may be indicative of a sexual neurosis—of fetishism. In this event, the individual feels obliged to wear a feminine garment as a necessary adjuvant to sexual performance. Often, however, a more searching study of such an individual makes it clear that more than simple fetishism is involved. Rather, the situation is one of cautious transvestism involving only minimal cross-dressing (panties, bra). Individuals whose compulsion to cross-dress is on a neurotic basis do not otherwise display inverted psychosexual orientation and are usually not homosexual. The danger of public ostracism obliges many such persons, some of whom may hold excellent and responsible jobs, to defer cross-dressing altogether until they can enjoy complete and unendangered privacy at home.

There are transvestites, however, whose behavior is not, strictly speaking, compulsive in the neurotic sense but rather the expression of inversion of gender role and erotic orientation. The thoroughgoing pervasiveness of the gender role inversion in such individuals can present a bewildering experience even to a professional observer. For example, one 35-year-old lumber-truck driver had for years been accepted by co-workers as one of the men and by several normal girls as a desirable boyfriend; psychologically this person was unequivocally masculine, but biologically a normal female. If life circumstances permit, the psychologically inverted transvestite attempts to live according to his psychologic orientation, *i.e.*, as a member of the opposite sex.

The term "transsexualist" has been used by Benjamin and his colleagues[8] to distinguish the transvestite who earnestly desires and often actively seeks "corrective" genital surgery. It is probably not accurate, however, to consider transsexualism as a basically different phenomenon. Rather, such individuals appear to be transvestites whose ability to repress and deal with their assumed genital incongruity is insufficient to prevent anxious discomfort. It is perhaps understandable that they seek, as a possible solution for their dilemma, surgical removal or "correction" of what they view as inappropriate genital equipment. In any event, these individuals usually seek acceptance as a member of the opposite biologic sex, not for the satisfaction of a successful masquerade, but because it seems to them vastly more natural to talk, behave and think like a member of the opposite biologic sex. One may usefully view such individuals as having established an even more complete and pervasive inverted gender role than the usual inverted homosexual. (See Table 14.1.)

CAUSAL FACTORS IN HOMOSEXUALITY AND TRANSVESTISM

Over the centuries atypical sexual behavior has been viewed in many lights ranging from high social acceptance to indignant social disapproval. It is understandable, therefore, that one concept of causation came to involve elements of morality and willfulness. Even today one hears the term "sex perversions" used to designate these various disorders. Obviously, it is difficult to escape the fact that sometimes atypical sexual behavior may occur as a deliberate, planned flaunting of social mores by a person so disposed by certain deficiencies in social learning; the homosexual behavior of a sociopath who is "out for kicks" may be a case in point. By and large, though, it was early recognized that some sexual deviants were not driven by immoral attitudes so much as by some other influence. Medical speculation as to what this influence might be has resulted in many theories, including Krafft-Ebing's notion that the victory of the "wrong" brain center was responsible; other theories attribute the influence to the result of castration anxiety (Freud), hormonal imbalance, inherited unspecified constitutional factors and irregularities of the sex chromosomes. None of these has withstood the test of time and critical scientific scrutiny. Neuroanatomists and neurophysiologists have been unable to discover brain centers controlling the direction of sexual interest. The original studies purporting to demonstrate an excess of estrogen in androgen-estrogen levels of homosexual men have not been verified and by common consensus the treatment of homosexuals with sex steroids may intensify erotic urges but does not change an individual's basic psychosexual orientation. Lang's[9] report that male homosexuals are genotypically female and Kallman's view that homosexuality is a "gene controlled disarrangement between male and female maturation (hormonal) tendencies," do not stand up to further scientific scrutiny.[10, 11]

In place of these earlier theories of cause which emphasized innate, constitutionally determined mechanisms, an increasingly well documented concept of the origins of homosexuality and related psychosexual disorders has begun to emerge. The evidence for this concept derives from cultural anthropology, sociology, psychology and psychiatry, and points unmistakably to irregularities in *social learning* as the cause of many previously baffling psychosexual deviations. For example, studies by Hess,[12] Lorenz,[13] Tinbergen, Scott and others have described "critical periods" which occur early in the life of certain animals, during which patterns of behavior are established which persist throughout the life of the animal. From cultural anthropology has come evidence of wide variations in the sexual behavior of human societies—from societies where nearly all of the males at times engage in homosexual practices* to instances of societies in which homosexual and other types of deviancy are virtually nonexistent. Still another line of evidence derives from the study of hermaphroditic individuals in whom there exists one or more incongruity between the sexual variables (chromosomal sex, gonadal sex, hormonal sex, internal reproductive structures, external genital morphology and the sex of rearing). These studies[15] have made it abundantly clear once again that the single most important variable affecting gender role (psychosexual orientation) is the sex of assignment and rearing, *i.e.*, the manner in which a child is raised.

It appears, then, beyond any reasonable doubt that humans, like most animals, are markedly influenced throughout their lives by social learning factors; at birth they possess a behavioral plasticity which permits the development of many kinds of permanent patterns of psychosexual behavior.

It would be gratifying to be able to offer a complete and universally accepted account of how deviant psychosexual learning comes about. Only a fragmentary account is possible, however. There are several rea-

---

* Ford and Beach[14] found that over half of their sample of 76 contemporary societies consider homosexuality an acceptable form of sexual outlet.

sons for this, one of which is the unreliability of retrospective accounts given by adults with psychosexual disorders. There is good reason to believe that sex role is gradually and permanently established during the earliest years of life. The experience with hermaphroditic youngsters is that a change in the sex of rearing (*e.g.*, for medical reasons) can be accomplished with children up to the age of about two or two and a half years. Thereafter, one runs increasing risk* of imposing psychologic damage by interfering with the nascent psychologic structure of the child. In fact, this risk is increased manyfold by the time the child is five.[16] In effect, this means that the first five years of life must be of critical importance for the normal individual and, by implication, for the psychosexually inverted person as well.

Basic to these considerations relative to the establishment of gender role is the concept of identification by which is meant the acquisition of the characteristics of another person from, one might say, a human model. Identification is not an all or none process; it can and does vary in strength, and an individual can identify to different degrees and with different aspects of a variety of models. Obviously, the child's selection of a human model will depend upon many factors such as availability, desirability and so on.

In the case of the psychosexually inverted individual the evidence suggests that an early and persistent identification occurs predominantly with an adult model of the *opposite* biologic sex rather than with a model of the *same* biologic sex. The result is a gradual buildup of attitudes, mannerisms and demeanor indicative of a preference for part or all of the role of the opposite sex. Experience shows that frequently, during the formative years of psychosexually inverted male homosexuals and transvestites, the father was: (1) absent or seldom participated in the family and no substitute was available, (2) distant and psychologically ineffectual,† or (3) abusive or cruel so as to preclude his being set up by his son as a model for imitation and identification. Typically, too, the mother (or mother substitute) had become excessively close to the boy, idolized and unconsciously, if not consciously, imitated. Johnson and Robinson[17] have also described parents who actually fostered deviant sexual behavior within the family setting. Concurrently the youngster's sex role rehearsals (play,

---

* This risk apparently is proportional to the quality and pervasiveness of the psychosexual identification which the child has acquired by any given age. Instances are on record where for one reason or another the identification with neither sex was firmly established as late as early teen-age; such instances are, however, rare.

† Such a view is consistent with findings of Mussen and Distler whose studies of the father-son identification process indicated that the significant factor was the father's *salience*—his importance in the child's life—rather than the particular technique he uses in dealing with his child.

fantasy) involve more and more the activities and attitudes characteristic of the opposite sex and less and less the activities characteristic of children of his own sex. The result is *varying degrees* of identification with the opposite sex together with increasing degrees of naturalness and comfort when functioning in the role of the opposite sex.

Although accurate statistics are not available, there is general consensus that inversion occurs less frequently in females than in males. Brown[7] has postulated a reason for this; namely, because all children, boys and girls alike, are reared in a close relationship with the mother, the girl has from the outset an appropriate sex role model, whereas the boy has the more complicated task of shifting from the mother to the father as his model.

This view of the origins of certain types of homosexual behavior and gender role inversion does not automatically answer all the questions that could be raised. Many details remain to be worked out through future research. Hopefully, the possibility of preventing and correcting gender role disorders during the formative years may then be enhanced.

The treatment of homosexuality and transvestism by means of drugs or hormones has not proven useful; such therapies were based on erroneous notions regarding the etiology of such behavior. Psychotherapy has sometimes been helpful in modifying noninverted seuxal patterns involving neurotic or sociopathic behavior. True gender role inversions have proven uniformly resistant to reversal by any of the psychotherapeutic techniques now available, although important changes, it is true, can be effected in the individual's social adjustment and personal comfort. Greater emphasis should be given to the early detection of faulty gender role learning during a child's growing up years, for it is then, if ever, that remedial intervention can take place.

REFERENCES

1. YALOM, I. D.: Aggression and forbiddenness in voyeurism. A. M. A. Arch. Gen. Psychiat., 3: 305–319, 1960.
2. YALOM, I. D.: Group therapy of incarcerated sexual deviants. J. Nerv. & Ment. Dis., 132: 158–170, 1961.
3. WEINBERG, S. K.: *Incest Behavior*. The Citadel Press, New York, 1955.
4. CORMIER, B. M., KENNEDY, M., AND SANGOWICZ, J.: Psychodynamics of father-daughter incest. Canad. Psychiat. A. J., 7: 203–217, 1962.
5. KINSEY, A. C., POMEROY, W. B., MARTIN, C. E., AND GEBHARD, P. H.: *Sexual Behavior in the Human Female*. W. B. Saunders Company, Philadelphia, 1953.
6. RADO, S.: An adaptational view of sexual behavior. In *Psychoanalysis of Behavior*. Grune & Stratton, Inc., New York, 1956.
7. BROWN, D. G.: The development of sex-role inversion and homosexuality. J. Pediat., 50: 613–619, 1957.
8. BENJAMIN, H., GUTHEIL, E. A., DEUTSCH, D., AND SHERWIN, R. V.: Transsexualism and transvestism—a symposium. Am. J. Psychotherapy, 8: 219–244, 1954.

9. LANG, T.: Studies on the genetic determination of homosexuality. J. Nerv. & Ment. Dis., **92:** 55–64, 1940.

10. PARE, C. M. B.: Homosexuality and chromosomal sex. J. Psychosom. Res., **1:** 247–251, 1956.

11. RABOCH, J., AND NEDOMA, K.: Sex chromatin and sexual behavior. Psychosom. Med., **20:** 55–59, 1958.

12. HESS, E. H.: Imprinting, an effect of early experience, imprinting determines later social behavior in animals. Science, **130:** 133–141, 1959.

13. LORENZ, K. Z.: *King Solomon's Ring*. Thomas Y. Crowell Company, New York, 1952.

14. FORD, C. S., AND BEACH, F. A.: *Patterns of Sexual Behavior*. Harper & Brothers, New York, 1951.

15. HAMPSON, J. L., AND HAMPSON, J. G.: The ontogenesis of sexual behavior in man. In *Sex and Internal Secretions*, edited by William C. Young. The Williams & Wilkins Company, Baltimore, 1961.

16. MONEY, J., HAMPSON, J. G., AND HAMPSON, J. L.: An examination of some basic sexual concepts: the evidence of human hermaphroditism. Bull. Johns Hopkins Hosp., **97:** 301–319, 1955.

17. JOHNSON, A. M., AND ROBINSON, D. B.: The sexual deviant (sexual psychopath) — causes, treatment and prevention. J. A. M. A., **164:** 1559–1565, 1957.

chapter fifteen

Counseling in Cases involving Premarital and Extramarital Pregnancies

CLARK E. VINCENT, PH.D., *Department of Obstetrics and Gynecology, Bowman Gray School of Medicine of Wake Forest College, Winston-Salem, North Carolina*

The physician who assumes the counseling role with patients having sexual problems or questions will need to keep in mind the social contexts out of which such problems and questions arise. This is especially true of counseling in cases of extramarital pregnancy, where the physician is quickly confronted with some of the contradictions in social attitudes concerning illicit sexual behavior.

The most persistent of these contradictions is to be found in the social practices and attitudes by which our society *inadvertently encourages, if not implicitly condones, the cause (illicit coition), and explicitly censures and condemns the result (illicit pregnancy)*. I have illustrated this contradiction at length elsewhere,[1] and will only note here in passing that the physician is confronted directly by it in such cases as that of the mother who confidently brings her teen-age daughter in for a diaphragm fitting, but who subsequently and angrily brings that same daughter in with a premarital pregnancy.

The remainder of this chapter is an attempt to balance the physician's knowledge about the anatomic and physiologic aspects of sex with information concerning some of the social and emotional aspects. It is also an attempt to highlight several unique opportunities the physician has for counseling with different categories of unmarried mothers.

CASES INVOLVING UNMARRIED MOTHERS

Physicians, more so than any other professional group, have long been aware that many of the commonly accepted stereotypes of unmarried mothers are erroneous. Prior to the late 1950's the predominant image of unmarried mothers was that they were poor, uneducated, very young and emotionally disturbed females. Such an image had been derived over the years from published accounts of premaritally pregnant females who had come to the attention of therapists and psychiatric social workers and/or who had been attended at a county hospital, maternity home or charity institution. The physician has attended these mothers, but he also has attended in private practice the upper and middle-class females in the older age groups bearing children out of wedlock. Because of his exposure to a broad cross-section of unmarried mothers from all walks of life, the physician has been in a unique position to develop counseling techniques and procedures that are not limited to any one socioeconomic or age group of unmarried mothers.

Counseling with the Young Unwed Mother

If the physician is to be helpful in his counseling relationship with the unmarried mother, particularly the very young one, he will need to be very clear in his own mind and to make it clear to the young girl that *she* is the patient, not the parents who brought her into his office or the couple who may be waiting to adopt the child.

This distinction is undoubtedly not an easy one to make when the parents or the adoptive couple are paying the bill, but it is a crucial one if a bona fide counseling relationship is to be established with the unmarried mother.

The very young unwed mother who is brought to the physician by her parents is already in a very awkward and potentially rebellious position *vis-à-vis* her parents. When the physician fails to explicate to her and to her parents that she is the patient, she will tend to see him as only an extension or tool of her parents and his efforts to be of other than medical help to her will be quite unsuccessful.

The physician's failure to establish and maintain her status as the patient was the most frequently expressed criticism of the several hundred unwed mothers interviewed in my own study several years ago.[2] Many felt the physician had simply been a tool in the hands of the parents or adopting couple. Some indicated this as the reason they never returned to a given physician after the initial visit to ascertain pregnancy. There is a very viable grapevine among single females who become pregnant and who pass the word very quickly concerning the kind of treatment received from given physicians—thus accounting, in part at least, for the fact that over a period of time certain physicians build up quite a clientele of unmarried mothers.

When the single girl comes alone for her initial visit to ascertain pregnancy, the physician has not only a unique opportunity, but also a responsibility, to make sure that she does not become "lost" until the onset of labor pains. For the health and welfare of both the unmarried mother and the child to be, it is important that the physician be able to communicate the importance of regular medical checkups and proper care during pregnancy. Too frequently, young females of inadequate means disappear after the visit to ascertain pregnancy and reappear only when the baby is about to be born. If proper care is to be provided for those females who do not become private patients, the physician will need to have and to impart accurate and up-to-date information about other resources in the community, and to follow through on referrals to such other resources.

Whether she becomes his private patient or never returns, her initial visit is a particularly impressionable experience for her. The very manner in which the physician confirms that she is indeed pregnant may very well be indelibly etched upon her mind and emotions, and thereby, for that moment, assign him the role of counselor—regardless of his desire or intent to have such a role. The manner and the words he uses to convey the information that she is pregnant need to be chosen carefully. Her anxiety and her needs at that moment may be such that an offhand remark or the most casual of comments may be interpreted either as complete approval of her sexual behavior or as utter rejection of both her and her behavior.

Some of the young unwed mothers with whom I have talked manifested all too clearly the failure of their parents to distinguish between the doer and the deed. Some parents reject both in so devastating a manner as to preclude ever being of future help to their daughters. Other parents are so accepting and "understanding" that they encourage their daughters to "con" themselves into believing that no mistake was made, thereby precluding the learning experience and dignity that can accrue from admitting one's mistakes and accepting responsibility for them.

The girls with whom I have talked indicated in a variety of ways their parents' failure to provide them with a learning experience. Some denied any self-responsibility and were quite convinced that their illicit pregnancies were entirely the fault of their male partners, or their parents who were either too rigid or too permissive. Others, who did assume some responsibility for their pregnancies, did not perceive them as mistakes but as inconveniences—inconveniences which were viewed as worthwhile by some girls because they received a parent financed sojourn to another state during the later months of pregnancy, and were able to provide a childless couple with an adopted baby. They were explicit in their belief that they would not have come by such a trip had they not become pregnant. They also reported that their younger sisters thought their parents would provide them a similar "fun" trip when they were older.

COUNSELING WITH THE UNWED'S PARENTS

The confirmation of the young female's pregnancy is also a highly impressionable moment for her parents, and perhaps is the time when they are most likely to express to her those thoughts and judgments they will later regret having expressed with so much destructive hostility and bitterness. The physician can be of considerable help to parents at such a time by encouraging them to vent some of their anger and disappointment before talking with their daughter in the hope that their subsequent discussions with her will be more constructive than destructive. He may also be able to help them examine the degree to which their attitudes toward their daughter involve a projection or displacement of their own feelings of failure as parents.

SHOULD THERE BE A MARRIAGE?

The question of whether the young girl should marry the father of the child-to-be is almost inevitable. The young girl is less likely to ask it in the form of a question; more likely she will try to demonstrate adult status by stating either that she does or she doesn't plan to marry the male involved—hoping, perhaps, that someone will question her statement. In their haste to state their own pro or con position about marriage, the parents may overlook her need to act as if she had already thought through this decision; their arguments with her then influence her to crystalize a decision she really wasn't ready to make. The physician can help the parents to understand the girl's need to act as if everything had been thought of and planned for, and can help both the girl and her parents recognize that the fact of pregnancy is only one of many variables to be considered in reaching a decision about marriage.

DECISIONS CONCERNING THE BABY

Physicians attending unwed mothers in private practice are in a highly strategic position to influence the mother's decisions about whether she keeps or releases her baby, and which channels to use if the baby is to be released for adoption. Such physicians are the primary source of information about adoption for the older, out of state unwed mothers, and are the initial source of such information for many of the younger unwed mothers of middle and high socioeconomic status. Unwed mothers in the latter category usually obtain information initially from their parents who frequently have derived their information from physicians rather than social workers or adoption agency personnel. The strategic position of the physician in influencing the mother's decisions about her baby,[3] imposes a responsibility to be informed and objective about various adoption procedures and agencies.

The following excerpts from three case histories[4] illustrate unwed mothers' differential interpretations and usages of adoption information provided by physicians and social workers.

Unwed Mother "A"

"I'm placing the baby for adoption. . . . Our family doctor recommended a doctor here who could handle it very quietly. . . . I won't even see it, but that's best. It's a closed chapter in my life. Besides, there are more people out here wanting (to adopt) babies than they have, so I know it will get a good home. . . . My parents would never forgive me if I didn't leave it here. They can forgive me as long as no one finds out about why I'm here. . . . To bring the baby home would make liars of them. . . . It would be unfair to the baby to grow up with me and know that it was an illegitimate child. . . . If I kept the baby I'd probably never be able to find a man who would marry me."

Unwed Mother "B"

"I'm not going to lose my baby forever. My aunt and uncle out here will keep it for me until I finish college. . . . I won't marry until I find a man who will accept it as our child, but in the meantime it would only hinder my college work if I kept the child with me and it will be better for the baby in the meantime to be in a home with two people who love children as much as they (aunt and uncle) do. . . . My doctor told me there were lots of opportunities to give my baby to a couple who really wanted one and would give it all the love it needed and the best home imaginable. But I know how I would feel when I grew up if I found out that my own mother gave me up for adoption and didn't want to raise me. . . . This way the baby will always know I did the best thing possible for it. . . . When she gets older I'll be able to explain that I loved her too much to give her away."

Unwed Mother "C"

"I planned when I left home to have the baby adopted, but I can't do it. . . . The social worker explained that it was my decision, but that I should feel they had enough people to choose from to be really able to select a good home. . . . Mother will be furious and Dad will probably disinherit me when I come back with the baby, since they gave clear instructions I was to have it adopted, but I can't do it. . . . What kind of a person would I be if I let someone else have my baby? What would the baby think of me when it grew up if it knew I deserted it for just anyone to have? . . . . I really think that after a while my parents will respect me more for keeping the baby, and what would a future husband think of me as a mother if he knew I gave my child away even if it wasn't his?"

On interpreting these statements, will some girls hate themselves later for giving their babies away? We have no way of knowing, given the paucity of follow-up studies, but such statements do illustrate the unwed mother's need for the most informed and competent counseling possible in making the extremely difficult decision about what to do with her baby and in implementing that decision.

The physician attending the unwed mother may or may not have another responsibility, depending on how he views the professional ethics involved. This possible responsibility pertains to those attitudes and wishes concerning the baby which the mother may express during delivery and/or while partially anesthetized. Should the physician share with other professional personnel who might be involved in helping the unwed mother, the feelings and attitudes expressed during delivery if such feelings and attitudes are strongly and consistently contraindicative of the already announced decision about the baby? Many, if not most, physicians may ignore, or perhaps compartmentalize, such expressions from the patient as being unrelated and irrelevant to their medical role. But does the professional ethic concerning the patient's confidences uttered during periods of extreme stress or while partially anesthetized always supercede consideration of the future welfare of both the mother and the child?

"Unmarried Fathers" *

The concentration upon the female in studies and public concern about illegitimacy tends to obscure the biologic fact that the male is half the cause. The readiness with which they take advantage of the protective anonymity and irresponsibility proffered by society and by unwed mothers may too easily deceive us into believing that unmarried fathers go merrily on their way without remorse or guilt. And although many such fathers are quick to assert either that they had no feelings of guilt and responsibility, or that they quickly resolved such feelings, they just as quickly supply explanations which suggest the contrary.

If he is married, the male may emphasize that the female involved preferred no help or further contact for fear of becoming known as the "other woman"; or he may excuse himself by expressing suspicions that his wife has previously been similarly involved. If single, he may readily cite the advice of the family physician and/or that of the girl's parents to the effect that it is to the advantage of all concerned to sever all ties, including any financial help that might imply future marital obligations. Valid and quasi-soothing as such types of reasons may be, they inwardly distress the male reared in a society where the masculine role is to protect, and not to be protected by, the female.

The fathers who do maintain contact with their illicit sex partners are further demasculinized when unable even to see, much less take pride in, their offspring. And although it might commonly be thought they have no interest in doing so, the comments, questions and implicit wishes expressed to me by unmarried fathers lead me to believe that a sizable proportion of them do. Whether it be called the male ego, the deep-seated

* Adapted from "Spotlight on the Unwed Father" by Clark E. Vincent, Ph.D., in Sexology, Vol. 28, pp. 537–542, March 1962. Used by permission.

desire to create and produce, or the showing of virility, there is something in a man of all walks of life which exacts a price when he is denied identification with that which he has helped to create, even when the denial is of his own choosing.

There is another category of rationale which the unmarried father employs in convincing himself and others that he has no guilt or obligations. This consists of his derogatory evaluations of his sex partner. His mildest portrayal will include such statements as the following taken from case histories: "She was old enough to know what she was doing." "She encouraged it as much as I did." "She went into it with her eyes open." "She could have said no."

A far more disparaging picture is painted by other unmarried fathers, some of whom one suspects are struggling less successfully with their feelings of guilt and/or inadequacy; it is these descriptions which, over the years, have undoubtedly contributed to, and prolonged, the misleading and negative stereotyping of unwed mothers:

"Why should I think it's mine when I know half a dozen guys who've had her?"

"She asked for it, always teasing everybody in the office. If it hadn't been me, it would be someone else sooner or later."

"Why shouldn't she take the consequences? She got paid for it twice over in all the parties, trips, and good times and even clothes I bought her. She has a hell of a lot more now than when I met her."

It is true that the male does not have to endure the physical discomforts of nine months of pregnancy and the labor pains of birth. Nor does he have to face the censorious comments and stares of others and wrestle with the decision about whether to keep or to release the baby for adoption. In fact, the enormity of what the unmarried mother must face is such as to usually make us forget that the physical discomfort of pregnancy and the pain of birth may afford her a form of "punishment," a degree of atonement, unavailable to the unmarried father. Also, for some unmarried mothers there is a feeling of retribution derived from having supported the traditional concepts of motherhood; for example, courageously completing pregnancy even though afraid, away from loved ones and censured. And difficult as the decision may be, many unwed mothers experience a sense of at least partial retribution to society when their illicit pregnancies subsequently make it possible for childless couples to achieve the cherished goal of having a family.

My intent is not to minimize the lopsidedness with which the burdens of stigma, hardships and responsibilities in illegitimacy are borne by females. Rather, it is to illustrate the extent to which we have ignored the counseling needs of the males involved. It is also to suggest that counseling with the unmarried mother may be facilitated when her sexual mate is also seen by the physician.

MARRIED AND DIVORCED "UNWED" MOTHERS

A counseling opportunity available more frequently to physicians than to any other professional group involves the married and the divorced "unwed" mothers. Census data do not differentiate among married, divorced and single unwed mothers; therefore, we have no way of knowing how many of the *estimated* 245,000 illicit births in the United States in 1962 were to divorced women or to married women impregnated by men other than their husbands. In fact, we have no way of knowing how many of the more than 4,000,000 births recorded as ligitimate in 1962 were the result of extramarital intercourse.

We do know from census reports that in the 20 year period from 1940 to 1960, the illegitimacy rate increased five times as much among women aged 25 to 29 (538 per cent), as among those aged 15 to 19 (108 per cent).

The higher rates and greater increases in illegitimacy among older women, as shown in Table 15.1, give us reason to suspect that extra- and postmarital intercourse may be responsible for a considerably greater proportion of illicit births than is commonly assumed. Adulterous illegitimacy is easily concealed from official records, of course, and is probably only reported in the minority of cases. Thus, in the absence of census data breakdowns for *pre-*, *extra-*, and *post*marital pregnancies, we are left with very tentative information from only a few individual studies that have differentiated among these types of illicit pregnancies.

As shown by the following information from 1,062 "unwed" mothers, there was a higher proportion of divorced and married mothers among those attended and reported by physicians in private practice, than among

TABLE 15.1

Increase of illegitimacy rate

Age of Unmarried Mother	Illegitimacy Rate*		Percentage of Increase
	1940	1960	
10–14	0.4	0.6	50%
15–19	7.4	15.3	108%
20–24	9.5	39.3	314%
25–29	7.2	45.9	538%
30–34	5.1	28.0	449%
35–39	3.4	14.4	323%
40–44	1.2	3.6	217%

* Number of illegitimate births per 1,000 unmarried females.

those attended in maternity homes and a county hospital where they were reported by social caseworkers.[5] The fact that few studies are made of "unwed" mothers attended in private practice helps maintain the emphasis on the young, single, never married ones who go to maternity homes and county hospitals where studies are usually conducted.

The minimum attention given to adulterous and postmarital pregnancies is also consistent with society's tendency to emphasize only selected aspects of a given social problem in such a way that perspective is distorted, and other forms of that same social problem are obscured. But the fact remains that each year there are a conservatively estimated 45,000 to 75,000 divorced and married "unwed" mothers who are in potential need of counseling, and that physicians are the major contact with these females.

Perhaps the most striking question concerning adulterous pregnancies is: "Why does a married woman ever reveal that it was not her husband who impregnated her?" The answer in the case of those seeking counseling help is frequently that either the marriage is threatened because the husband knows, or the wife seeks help in resolving her own feelings and course of action without her husband's awareness of the problem. In the case of women who inform their physicians that their pregnancies are adulterous, the answer may be that they need at least one confidant and/or fear they will reveal such information anyway while under the effect of anesthesia during delivery.

In an effort to be of aid to physicians counseling divorced and married women involved in illicit pregnancies, I should like to share a few impressions based on questionnaire data from 256 such women, and on interview and counseling sessions with 35 such women.

TABLE 15.2

Study of 1,062 unwed mothers

Marital Status of "Unwed" Mother	Reported by Physicians in Private Practice*	Reported by Social Caseworkers	
		Maternity Home†	County Hospital††
Single—never married............	65%	82%	76%
Divorced or widowed.............	23%	11%	18%
Married.......................	11%	4%	0%
No answer.....................	1%	3%	6%
	100%	100%	100%

* Total number of cases—425.
† Total number of cases—265.
†† Total number of cases—372.

THE DIVORCED UNMARRIED MOTHER*

The sexual caution of divorced women tends to be reduced by their desire to escape the socially stigmatized category of the divorcee as soon as possible, and by their openness in male-female conversation as learned while married. Not only is the divorcee frequently perceived by men as easy sex prey (as William Goode notes in *After Divorce*[6]), but she herself may unintentionally foster such a view. Previously accompanied by her husband and protected by marriage, she became accustomed to open and frank discussions of sex in mixed groups; now she has to relearn some of the coyness that traditionally accompanies courtship. Without such coyness, and tacitly pressured by society and friends to prove via a successful marriage that it was not she who failed in the first marriage, her involvement with men tends to progress at a much faster and less cautious pace than even she recognizes—until she is pregnant and the man is no longer interested or returns to his wife.

An unknown proportion, perhaps the majority, of divorces involve a period of continued, somewhat sporadic, sexual intercourse between the ex-partners. In the cases of so-called "friendly" divorces, the continuation of coition is frequently regarded as mutually enjoyable, with no love or family obligations expected; and abortion may be a frequent solution when pregnancy occurs. Even when this solution is unavailable or unacceptable to the mother, she is reluctant to affix paternal responsibility on the former husband, in part, perhaps, because of her feeling that others would think her foolish for continuing sex relations with her ex-husband.

In cases where the divorce was not mutually desired, the wife may perceive intercourse as a potential means for reclaiming her husband. She may also, as one stated, "want a memory of him. . . . I hope it's a boy that looks just like him. . . . That way a part of him will always be with me." There is also the case of the ex-husband who desires a reconciliation and who, after considerable effort that often includes the argument of "for old times' sake," impregnates his ex-wife, only to find this makes her even more adamantly opposed to reconciliation.

MAINTAINING THE CONTEXT

One of the counseling needs common to a wide variety of cases involving premarital coition and illicit pregnancy is the need of the counselee to maintain an historical and contextual perspective of their sexual experience. Adult women may unceasingly condemn themselves by imposing adult judgments upon those sexual acts they experienced during adoles-

* Adapted from "Divorced and Married 'Unwed' Mothers" by Clark E. Vincent, Ph.D., in Sexology, Vol. 28, pp. 674–679, May 1962. Used by permission.

cence. Married women may judge too harshly in retrospect their earlier "love" affairs involving coition with other men. Knowing now, at 35, the depth and quality of love they have for their husbands, they may continually reinforce guilt feelings about earlier sex unions with other men with whom they fell in love while single. It is not always easy to maintain the context within which a given event or experience took place years previously, but it is important to try to do so. This does not mean that all early or prior sexual experiences should be lightly excused. It does mean that the woman of 45 should not judge her experiences at 18 as if she at that time had the wisdom, judgment, and values she now has at 45.

The physician may frequently find opportunity to provide both ameliorative and treatment types of counseling in helping his patients maintain perspective concerning the context in which given sexual behavior occurred. The single female who has coition with a male during the time she thinks they are in love and are going to be married, may need help in remembering that at the time of their sex union the context was one of love and planning for marriage. Too often in those cases where the couple later fall apart and decide not to marry, the girl takes the sex experience out of the context in which it occurred and may either feel she has to proceed with the marriage to preserve her self-image as a nice girl, or may regard herself overly harshly as less worthy of her future husband as yet unmet.

The married woman impregnated during an affair with another male may also need help in maintaining the total context within which her affair took place. Her own guilt and self-condemnation may propel her to project too much blame on either herself or her husband and thereby reduce the chances for a strengthening of the marriage. Again, this is not to say she should completely absolve herself of any blame, but that the physician can help her understand the totality of events and circumstances that almost imperceptibly led to the illicit coition.

Physicians are already overworked and spread too thin, but the members of no other professional group have quite the same unique opportunities to become "significant others" in times of sexual crises. Physicians who are genuinely concerned about illegitimacy and the price it exacts from youth will find much to do: (1) in providing the community with a more accurate perspective of illegitimacy, (2) in reaffirming confidence in youth and in not being afraid to point up the adult and community contributions to illegitimacy, (3) in contagiously educating parents to cherish the individual without condoning his mistakes, and (4) in being sensitive to those young men and women who are desperately in need of a significant relationship and identification with at least one adult with whom they can discuss their own sexuality as a mental and physical health entity.

REFERENCES

1. VINCENT, C. E.: *Unmarried Mothers*. The Free Press of Glencoe, New York, 1961.
2. VINCENT, C. E.: *Unmarried Mothers*. The Free Press of Glencoe, New York, 1961.
3. VINCENT, C. E.: *Unmarried Mothers*, Chs. 7–9. The Free Press of Glencoe, New York, 1961.
4. VINCENT, C. E.: *Unmarried Mothers*, Ch. 8, pp. 216 and 217. The Free Press of Glencoe, New York, 1961.
5. VINCENT, C. E.: *Unmarried Mothers*. The Free Press of Glencoe, New York, 1961.
6. GOODE, W.: *After Divorce*. The Free Press of Glencoe, Illinois, 195.

chapter sixteen

Problems of Marital Infidelity

DAVID R. MACE, Ph.D., *Executive Director, American Association of Marriage Counselors, Madison, New Jersey*

The Kinsey research has estimated that half of all married men,[1] and more than a quarter of all married women,[2] have sexual intercourse, during the course of their married life, with a partner other than the spouse.

These acts of infidelity do not always cause problems. Sometimes they are concealed. Sometimes they are condoned. Sometimes they are freely forgiven, and forgotten. But there remain a great many cases where infidelity becomes known to the other partner and creates a crisis in the marriage. Often the injured spouse will seek support, comfort and guidance from a professional person. So, quite frequently, these problems will be brought to the marriage counselor—or the physician serving as marriage counselor—for solution.

Traditionally, adultery was viewed as a grave offense, violating the marriage bond; although in patriarchal societies it was considered much more reprehensible in the wife than in the husband. In England, until the year 1923, adultery was a sufficient ground to enable a husband to divorce his wife, but was only an offense justifying divorce in the husband if there were also further exacerbating circumstances present. Nowadays, the laws have been adjusted, in England and in the United States alike, and adultery is a ground that can be brought equally by husband or wife in support of a divorce suit. It is the one and only ground that can secure a divorce in every state in the United States.

When the counselor is confronted with a complaint of infidelity by one partner against another, he should not be too ready to accept the accusation at its face value. Some deeply disturbed people may convince themselves that their spouses have been unfaithful when this is not the case. The counselor should be on the alert both for deliberate misrepresentation and for unconscious self-deception.

If the facts seem well established, however, the counselor is confronted with two tasks—to find out why the infidelity took place and what it reveals about the unfaithful spouse, and to assess the reaction of the accusing partner and what this reveals about him or her. When these investigations have been carried out, the appropriate course of action will generally become clear.

Subtle differences will be found between male and female patterns of infidelity, but the motivations in both cases are broadly similar. For the sake of clarity I shall assume here an unfaithful husband and an accusing wife. Important differences that arise when the situation is the other way round will be referred to where they are relevant.

Why are husbands unfaithful? Some embittered women would say the explanation is very simple indeed—because husbands are men, and men are by nature licentious and untrustworthy.

Sweeping statements of this kind don't help us much. Making all due allowances for the differences between a man's and a woman's nature, the social attitudes toward infidelity on the part of men and women respectively and the risks of unpleasant consequences in each case, there is no convincing evidence that women are inherently more virtuous than men.

However, it is a fact that husbands are about twice as likely to be unfaithful as wives are. The reasons are the ones I have already mentioned—the temptations are greater, the consequences less serious and the judgments less severe.

As I look back over the many unfaithful husbands I have had to deal with, I can clearly distinguish at least five different types. There are probably more. But in my experience, these five cover most of the situations that are likely to arise.

First, there is *the libertine*. Casanova would be a classic example of this type. A strongly predatory attitude toward women is a basic motivation in the personality patterns of such men. They study feminine psychology so that they may devise techniques of exploitation. Sexual exploits or "conquests" become the grand passion of their lives. They care little for women as individuals. They are like the greedy little boy who sneaks into the dining room before the party and licks the icing off the cakes.

Men of this type don't always marry. Yet sometimes they do, if only to have a secure base from which to make their forays, and to maintain an outward appearance of respectability. In our culture these men are not normal types. Unfortunately, however, the chances of reforming them are very poor, because their exploits are too often successful. Enough flattery, enough guile, enough persistence usually causes the woman who is their latest victim to yield in the end. And since there is no easy way of punishing this kind of behavior, the libertine is seldom disturbed by fear or remorse.

There are promiscuous women whose behavior resembles that of the libertine. A few of them are predatory, with deeply destructive impulses. But most will be found to represent a combination of strong sexual urges and a deep unsatisfied need for acceptance and recognition. Their rehabilitation is best achieved by helping them to outgrow their underlying sense of inadequacy and worthlessness. This generally requires psychotherapy.

The next type of unfaithful husband is *the bored*. This is the man who gets involved with someone else as a result of having a flutter. Usually he has nothing against his wife, and he may be genuinely perplexed or ashamed when he realizes what he has done. The true explanation is that this man, after a long period of dull routine in his marriage, has become highly vulnerable to new and exciting experiences. He may seek such experiences deliberately. But more often, according to my observation, an unplanned opportunity—an absence from home, an encouraging signal from some love-hungry female or a sudden temptation—proves to be too much for him, and, before he has really considered what he is getting into, he is involved.

Most marriages pass through periods of boredom. Sometimes the wife is to blame, sometimes the husband. Sometimes the environment provides no opportunity for new and stimulating experiences. All of us need, from time to time, to make new ventures, to be exposed to the stimulus of change. In a vitally alive and growing relationship, there are infinite possibilities for variety. But when a relationship gets into the doldrums, the craving for variety may seek expression in an adventure with a new partner.

Wives as well as husbands undergo this urge for new experience. When it leads to unfaithfulness, this may involve a really serious threat to the marriage. Where the new relationship proves to be superior to the old one, the person concerned naturally has a strong urge to move forward and an equally strong disinclination to go back.

However, it does not follow that this kind of unfaithfulness means the end of the marriage. The novelty of the new experience may quickly wear off. I have dealt with many cases where infidelity provided the necessary jolt that made husband and wife seriously face the fact that they had allowed their marriage to degenerate into a dull, meaningless routine. In some cases an honest facing of the reasons for unfaithfulness can lead to a better relationship between husband and wife than they had ever known before.

Not far removed from the bored husband is the third type who becomes involved in unfaithfulness—*the curious*. There is, however, an important difference between these two. The bored husband is trying to get *away* from something. The man driven by curiosity is impelled *toward* something.

Sometimes this happens to a man of upright character who has gone straight all his life. Yet he has often wondered what it would be like to do what he knows many others do. He has no thought of forsaking his wife. But he finds himself fascinated by a mischievous urge to try his hand at a little philandering—just to find out what it feels like.

Curiosity is a powerful motivation. It is part of the drive of life itself. According to the Bible story, the desire to taste the fruit of the forbidden tree was the cause of all our human misery. And we are all the children of Adam and Eve. The child ignores our warnings and gets his fingers burned. The older boy climbs too far out along the branch and falls into the river. The staid and proper husband, to his own and everyone else's surprise, breaks out and plays the roué.

This kind of unfaithfulness is occasionally found in middle-aged men who have previously lived exemplary lives. We talk about the "dangerous 40's." At this time a man is aware that he has passed the peak of his masculine vigor. The very fact that he has been all that a husband ought to be may sharpen his curiosity to enjoy the sensation of getting into mischief while he is still acceptable to another woman. The gate is closing, and this may be his last chance. On an impulse, he makes a dash out into forbidden territory.

Men who have been unfaithful in this way sometimes assure their wives that they love them just the same. A wife is usually highly skeptical about such a statement. She may well have reason to be. Yet her husband may be quite sincere, and he may be speaking the truth. A man impelled by curiosity may get into an extramarital sexual adventure without having any real feeling for the woman concerned, and without ceasing to be devoted to his wife. This can happen more easily to a man than it can to a woman, for whom a sexual experience generally means a deeper level of involvement.

It is sound policy to treat an incident of this kind quite lightly. After such an experience, a man usually feels humiliated and foolish, and wants to forget the whole affair and put it behind him. A wife who harps on it and takes it all very seriously may, by her attitude, create a more serious problem in the marriage relationship than existed in the first place.

The fourth kind of unfaithful husband is *the disturbed*. Usually this man is deeply troubled by feelings of insecurity and inadequacy that set up a persistent, gnawing anxiety. The widespread idea that sexual desire is always the main cause of unfaithfulness is not necessarily true. It always plays a part, of course. But quite often it is incidental to the man's (or woman's) real motive, which is to seek comfort or reassurance, or to restore a seriously damaged self-confidence. It is always a flattering experience to be loved, and a man who is deeply unsure of himself will find his self-esteem enormously boosted if an attractive woman is ready or eager to respond to his sexual advances.

Men associate their feelings of personal prestige closely with their sexual powers. It is significant that we use the word "virility" equally to describe the sexual and the nonsexual drive and vigor of the male—as though they necessarily went together. So a man who is struggling with feelings of inner inadequacy or inferiority may try to soothe his frayed emotions by attracting and satisfying a full-blooded woman. He may not reason this out consciously. But often when he later examines, with a counselor, his real motives for infidelity, he realizes that what he was seeking was the experience of being once again, in somebody's eyes, a worthwhile person.

Again, the middle-aged man is very susceptible to this sense of inadequacy. He has reached the time of life when a person has to come to terms with reality; and this often means accepting the fact that he has not achieved, and that he will not now achieve, his major ambitions. Henceforth he must live with himself as he is—a mediocre man, just one of tens of thousands of others who, like him, make up the common herd. This may be a painful realization which he has long tried to evade. There are several ways in which he can still evade it. One is to try to renew his youth, and prove his masculine qualities, by making himself acceptable to a young and attractive woman.

Often a man's emotionally disturbed condition, which impels him into unfaithfulness, is closely linked with his marriage. Maladjustment in the marriage itself may have given him a feeling of frustration, discouragement and worthlessness. Or it may just be that he looked to his wife for understanding and healing that she could not, or would not, give him. Either way, the wife has played some part, even without knowing it, in bringing about the situation that now upsets her so much. If she can recognize and accept this, instead of pointing a self-righteous and accusing finger at her man, it can make a big difference to the chances of getting the relationship restored.

The fifth and last type of unfaithful husband is the most logical of all—*the sexually frustrated*. To some people this is the *only* motivation for infidelity. I have deliberately put it last to show clearly that there are many other causes.

Despite all our frank, down-to-earth talk about sex in these days, there are still some wives obtuse enough not to understand that a sexually starved man is highly vulnerable to any temptation that comes his way—and that our modern world has become a veritable hotbed of sexual temptation.

Even Saint Paul, who has been much maligned on account of his supposedly straightlaced views on sex and marriage, knew human nature well enough to warn married couples against keeping each other in a flammable state of unsatisfied desire. This is one of the simple and elementary duties of marriage. If we neglect it, accusations of unfaithfulness against our marriage partners have a hollow ring about them. A man who commits adultery is indeed culpable, whatever the circumstances; but if his wife has helped to drive him to it, the justice of heaven, if not that of the courts, demands that she accept her share of responsibility for what has happened.

There are many ways in which a wife may drive her husband into sexual frustration, apart from a downright refusal to respond to his advances. She can do it by coldness, by evasiveness, by ridicule, even by declining to seek help about her sex relationship with her husband, in these days when help is so readily available.

Marital infidelity is not at all a simple matter. It may be very complex. There can be no clear, overall judgment that applies to every case. That tragic mistake has been encouraged by our legal system. In fact, each individual situation needs to be carefully examined on its merits.

This is what the experienced marriage counselor tries to do. His approach is entirely different from that of the courts. Their aim is to establish whether or not adultery has taken place. The counselor's aim is to understand just what has happened, and why; and then to help husband and wife to find the best and most constructive way to handle the resulting situation, using the techniques described elsewhere in this book.

REFERENCES

1. KINSEY, A. C., POMEROY, W. B., AND MARTIN, C. E.: *Sexual Behavior in the Human Male.* W. B. Saunders Company, Philadelphia, 1948.
2. KINSEY, A. C., POMEROY, W. B., MARTIN, C. E., AND GEBHARD, P. H.: *Sexual Behavior in the Human Female.* W. B. Saunders Company, Philadelphia, 1953.

chapter seventeen

Counseling the Marital and Sexual Problems of Older Patients

NADINA R. KAVINOKY, M.D., *Newport Beach, California*

Marital and sexual problems of older patients may have many causes. They may be physical and physiologic, or they may be psychogenic. Or they may be caused by problems or malfunctions of all three systems. These problems may be brought on by social and economic pressures, by poor interpersonal relationships or by conflict in cultural backgrounds.

But whatever the cause of older patients' problems, their diagnosis and treatment will require not only the best of the physician's medical skill, but probably the best of his counseling ability as well. For usually life's frustrations and insults, as well as basic economic insecurity, have left older patients in need of something more than an impersonal examination. Only when the physician has, through his permissive understanding and thoughtful listening, opened a two-way avenue of communication with these patients, can any real therapy—physical or psychic—take place.

In this chapter, it will be possible to consider only a few of the marital and sexual problems of older patients that will be presented to the physician in active practice. But there are some general principles which are applicable in almost every case. The first of these is that the opening of an avenue of communication between the physician and the patient is the starting point toward therapy. The history taking and the examination usually form the beginning of that communication.

THE MARITAL HISTORY OF OLDER PATIENTS WITH MARRIAGE PROBLEMS

In recording the history of the patient, the marital history of both partners must be covered. This should include the number of marriages, at what ages, the preparation or lack of preparation for marriage and attitudes toward marital responsibilities and toward sexual behavior.

The need for all of this history can be easily demonstrated. For example, a difference of many years in the ages of the marriage partners can cause

serious problems of sexual adjustment during the later years. The older
husband may be waning sexually while his younger wife may be just awakening. This difference in sexual interest and capacity may create suspicion and jealousy as well as a feeling of inadequacy and frustration.

The medical history is not only essential for its classic purpose, but also
—in older patients with marital and sexual problems—for providing
special insights. For instance, a chronic illness of either husband or wife
can affect the sexual need and capacity. Patients having diabetes or
hypothyroid activity may be below normal sexually. Sexual activity may
be too much physical strain in patients having cardiac or chest problems.
Intercourse may be deemed inadvisable, yet the desire may be normal.
Some physically handicapped patients must spend hours, days or months
in bed. They may have normal desires for sexual contact. During such
periods, loneliness and anxiety create a greater need for affectionate
caresses and the nearness of a loved one often stimulates the sexual need.

For the genuinely interested practitioner, the following checklist form
may be used to obtain a thorough marital history for treating the older
patient.

1. Number of marriages
   a. Duration of each
   b. Terminated by death or divorce
   c. Reasons for failure of marriage
2. Ages of marriage partners
   a. If late marriage—why
   b. Health of mate
3. Preparation for marriage
   a. Positive
      (1) home preparation, attitudes
      (2) church
      (3) reading materials
      (4) courses in college or high school
      (5) professional counseling
   b. Negative—traumatic experiences during adolescence or early
      childhood
      (1) personal
      (2) family
      (3) home or neighborhood
4. Early sexual relationship
   a. Satisfactory—happy
   b. Difficult—traumatic—much bleeding—delayed orgasm response
   c. Emphasis on unrealistic satisfactions such as a simultaneous
      orgasm

5. Pregnancies
   a. Premarital pregnancy
   b. Number of pregnancies
   c. Number of children (live births)
   d. Health of children
   e. Planned pregnancies
   f. Unplanned pregnancies
   g. Complications, if any
   h. Abortions
      (1) spontaneous
      (2) therapeutic
      (3) criminal
   i. Spontaneous miscarriages
6. Deliveries—easy, normal—prolonged—complicated
   a. Names of obstetricians
   b. Names of hospitals
7. Duration of presenting problem in this marriage
   a. Personal
   b. Interrelationships
   c. Sexual
   d. Other
8. Marital problems
   a. Sexual adjustment or maladjustment
   b. Dyspareunia
   c. Frigidity
   d. Impotence
   e. Sterility
9. Attitude toward parenthood
   a. Of husband
   b. Of wife
10. Adjustment to
   a. marriage
   b. in-laws
   c. friends
   d. money
   e. religion
   f. recreation
   g. environment
   h. work, tensions, competition, insecurity, job relationships

THE PHYSICAL EXAMINATION

Since many chronic diseases are asymptomatic in their early stages, it almost goes without saying that every older patient should have a thorough physical examination, complete with laboratory tests. However, usually by the physician's very training and experience, pathology becomes the objective of such an examination. This should not be. Physiology and the ability to function normally are fully as essential as pathology, especially in marital and sexual problems.

The very thoroughness of the examination has in itself therapeutic value. It builds confidence and thus releases tension and anxiety. Most patients beyond the middle years are apprehensive and fearful of what the physician might find. They have suffered the shock of being exposed to friends and relatives of their own or older age bracket, who have had inoperable carcinoma or other serious illnesses. A kind, gentle, unhurried approach to the physical examination is of inestimable help.

In examining the woman patient, a carefully done pelvic examination can often reveal the cause of both sexual and marital problems. But the pelvic examination may be an ordeal which most older patients dread. Their first reaction is embarrassment and their second is fear of pain, as well as fear of the diagnosis. Some quiet reassurance is necessary, as well as careful attention to the patient's psychologic preparation for the examination. The patient should be asked to bear down as the physician explains that this relaxes the sphincter muscle, thus increasing the diameter of the introitus. This increase makes the examination more comfortable and more accurate. An electric light over the tray of specula should be provided to keep the instruments warm. Specula should be kept covered, as their very appearance sometimes frightens the patient. The proper size of the speculum must be chosen to avoid pain. One with a narrow ¾-inch blade is available and adequate.

Local pelvic pathology which affects the sexual interest and capacity are easily recognized in the wife. For example, dyspareunia localized at the entry can result from:

1. Atrophy, lack of lubrication or senile vaginitis which decreases the elasticity and size of the vaginal canal.

2. Vulvitis due to bacterial or mycotic infections.

3. Fear instilled years before might have caused vaginismus and persisted, with a resulting traumatic consummation of marriage.

4. A husband who is inept, clumsy or inconsiderate, or who does not understand the change in the physical condition of his wife due to the above pathology.

Pain after entry of the penis deep in the vaginal canal may be due to:

1. Scars from clumsy efforts at vaginal repair.

2. Senile vaginitis, vaginal atresia or pelvic inflammatory disease.

3. Endometriosis, especially in the vaginal-rectal septum.

4. A fixed retroplaced uterus which followed previous pelvic inflammatory disease.

5. Urethritis.
6. Cystitis.
7. Proctitis.

In addition, sexual inadequacy may also be due to cystoceles, rectoceles, prolapse, overlubrication caused by cervical erosions, mycotic vaginitis and genital relaxation.

A complete examination will help the physician to determine the physical condition of the patient. Thoughtful, relaxed communication will allow him to understand the patient's emotional condition. Both are essential to therapy. The opportunity for the patient to talk should be a mandatory part of a well-done examination.

EVALUATING THE PROBLEM

Taking a good medical and marital history, carefully examining the patient, and then perceptively listening are all essential to evaluating the problem and making an accurate diagnosis.

It should be constantly kept in mind in assessing the marital and sexual relationship of older patients that there is no universal reason for their having difficulty. Many older couples have even richer sexual experiences than they did in their younger years. Most women, free of some of their earlier inhibitions and their fears of pregnancy, are capable of far greater responsiveness than ever before. And some men, despite any statistical trend, not only retain complete potency, but actually are even more stimulated by their wives' newfound sexual freedom. For some people the so-called "declining years" can actually be a time of increasing sexual harmony, more affectionate attention and comradeship. However, the physician is less likely to see these men and women as patients. The ones he will more likely see will be:

1. Those for whom aging has magnified earlier marriage and sexual difficulties.

2. Those for whom advancing years have brought marital and sexual problems for the first time.

3. Those with chronic degenerative diseases which affected their sexual capacity and interest.

It is important for the physician to make an early distinction between those patients who have never had any real sexual harmony in marriage and those for whom marital and sexual problems are relatively new. In the latter case, there is probably much that can be done, both physiologically and psychologically. But almost any treatment may well be too little and too late for those who have not been able to adjust over all of their years of marriage. Frustration and disappointment for the physician-counselor might be avoided by the simple expedient of finding out *when* the problems began and how deeply they were rooted.

Regardless, however, of the duration of the difficulties, most older patients who have sexual complaints present a complex picture of interwoven physical and psychogenetic causes. Identifying physical symptoms of sexual difficulties in older people is relatively easy; identifying the emotional causes is often more difficult. A woman's worry over her loss of youthful appearance or a man's loss of self-esteem because he has been retired may be important causes of marital and sexual dysfunction, even though they are not as apparent as pelvic relaxation and impotence.

Moreover, the problem of evaluating any sexual difficulty of an older married pair is complicated not only by the various physiologic and psychologic components of the *individual* which interplay upon each other, but also by the effect of the *mate's* physiologic and psychologic problems. For example, a man may have less sexual desire because of:

1. Pain (angina) during intercourse.
2. Worry over financial problems.
3. Fatigue brought on by emotional tension.
4. All of these things.

At the same time he may be affected by his wife's irritability or pain caused by her arthritis. He may find less tactile stimulation due to lack of adequate contact during intercourse because of his wife's pelvic relaxation. At the same time he may be esthetically repulsed by the transitory urinary incontinence which this pelvic relaxation may have produced. Perhaps any or all of these factors are interrelated, producing the unhappy sexual situation which the patient or patients have brought to you for help.

Despite the complexity of the problem, however, if the partners have enjoyed a good marriage relationship over the years, and if they are eager to help each other find a solution, the physician can help them. If, on the other hand, all these interrelated difficulties are superimposed upon a marriage relationship which has been resentment filled and barely tolerable over many years, the prognosis for finding a renewed sexual life together is poor. Long smoldering resentments often are intensified by the problems of aging.

The first step toward planning treatment involves evaluating to what extent the patient's problems are due to physiologic difficulties, to what extent to psychologic problems, and to what extent the interrelationship between the two is at fault. Treatment, to be adequate and successful, must include all three approaches.

TREATMENT

Therapy in sexual problems and marital problems of older individuals should include:

1. Medical treatment for the physical problems which may be the cause of the marital and sexual maladjustment and for the psychosomatic complaints which may be the result of tensions and anxieties related to those problems. Physical problems need to be treated, whether they are primary or secondary.

2. Counseling help for the psychologic and relationship aspects of the patient's problem should be given simultaneously. This kind of help includes teaching, interpreting and developing understanding through communication.

Treating the physical aspects of the older patient's sexual difficulty is, in the case of the woman at least, relatively well documented. Diagnostic aids such as Papanicolaou vaginal smear tests not only reveal malignancy, but also determine the adequacy of the estrogen level and suggest the amount of estrogenic substance to be prescribed.

In the last decade there has been more general acceptance of estrogens and androgens to compensate for the deficiencies of aging. The estrogens are of utmost importance in keeping the vaginal tract normal and so providing for adequate sexual functioning of the female. Androgens are useful for increasing sexual interest and capacity.

In senile vaginitis, estrogenic substance, both as tablets and locally applied as estrogenic creams, can often return the vaginal mucosa to normal histologic structure within three to four weeks. The addition of lanolin-plus, a liquid lanolin used as a lubricant, is a help, as is any vitamin A cream, in healing the vaginal mucosa. Contraindications to the use of estrogen include fibroids, endometriosis and/or a strong history of malignancy.

Methyl testosterone sometimes increases the patient's libidinal interests and gives a feeling of well-being and energy. The androgens also have an effect on nitrogen balance and increase the sexual capacity of both sexes. Virilizing effect on the woman rarely occurs with small doses.

Dyspareunia due to atrophic urethritis and cystitis also responds to estrogen treatment. Occasionally, more specific treatment for stenosis, such as dilating the urethra, may be necessary. Dyspareunia due to endometriosis also sometimes responds to androgens.

The patient with genital relaxation often has a contrasting problem to the patient with senile vaginitis. Instead of atrophy, atresia and a dry, inelastic canal, the large, relaxed vagina is often overlubricated by seeping erosions of the cervix. Frequently, a cystocele, bladder incontinence, a rectocele or a prolapse of the uterus are a part of this condition. Such a syndrome causes obvious difficulties during sexual intercourse.

An effective treatment of this condition is the one suggested by Arnold Kegel.[1, 2] This consists of repetitive exercises to develop the pubococcygeus muscle. This technique was first used for treating bladder incontinence and soon proved to be effective in relieving associated menorrhagia. Greater sexual adequacy for women in their postmenopausal years also resulted in many women.

In older patients, aches and pains in the back and lower limbs are often interpreted as due to coitus. Actually, these symptoms are usually due to musculoskeletal pathology. The pain may be due to postural defects because of a relatively sedentary way of life in the later years, or it may be pain reflected from osteoporosis, osteoarthritis or disc problems. For this reason, a careful diagnostic study should be made. Once the cause is established, a great deal of relief can be given the patient by a program of skillful muscular reeducation, regardless of the seriousness of the bony pathology found. Muscle relaxants and analgesics can give much comfort, as well as enable the patient to spontaneously relax the spastic muscles. Vitamin B complex relieves much of the neuritis which triggers the muscle spasms.

Prescribing additional sex hormone, appropriate to the sex of the patient, often can be helpful in preventing further development of osteoporosis. This is very important, for the brittleness of the bones contributes to fractures and hospitalization just at a time when many older couples are experiencing economic problems along with their other difficulties.

Fatigue and Emotional Problems

In considering the older patient's sexual problems, the management of the patient's feelings of fatigue provides a transition from dealing with the patient's physiologic problems to dealing with his emotional ones. Fatigue is the great enemy of sexual activity in both men and women.

Fatigue may be due to physical causes such as anemia, glandular dysfunction or malnutrition. Fatigue which has such a physical cause is relatively easy to prescribe for and the patients who can thus be treated are fortunate.

Often fatigue is the result of nervous exhaustion and tension. Medical therapy such as the tranquilizers must be associated with counseling to prevent such fatigue. Tensions created by the lack of understanding in marital and sexual relationships, by worry over financial difficulties or by the lack of self-esteem because of retirement from a cherished role, need to be treated by the understanding counseling help which the physician can give.

The actual techniques of counseling with older people about sexual problems are similar to those which have already been discussed in other chapters and need not be further elaborated here. For, if real communication can be established between older partners, the resultant enhancement of sexual activity can motivate comradeship between them. Then, in the very closeness of the sexual act, the partners can gain reassurance for their insecurities about their own attractiveness and grow in mutual understanding of the problems that aging is causing each of them. Ultimately, this understanding is the one thing that can help each of the partners to accept the process of growing older.

Unhappily, however, older patients are often prevented from achieving this comradeship through sexual activity because sex has become a major cause of misunderstanding between them.

Sometimes this misunderstanding has developed over a long period as a result of earlier inhibitions, fear of pregnancy, feeling of guilt and rejections. It is not impossible that these inhibitions, possibly resulting from a fear of pregnancy, are now no longer based on any real fear and may well have worn themselves out. However, sometimes the partners have become so conditioned by earlier experiences that they are unwilling to make any real effort to restore sexual harmony. Very often this difficult state of affairs is perpetuated because the partners have developed habits of not talking to each other. They feel they know the other's attitude so well and the earlier rejections are so painful that they have no desire to communicate about them.

Here is one place where the physician can help considerably. If he can get the partners to reexamine their present sexual interest in each other in the light of their present relationship, rather than bringing in the mutual recriminations of the past, some useful progress can be made toward bringing the partners closer together. In talking it over with the physician-counselor, sometimes the older married partners find for the first time that they are able to communicate with each other about their long pent-up sexual attitudes. It is important, however, to keep the communication on a positive level and to avoid rehashing old painful, unsuccessful experiences.

There are other partners who suddenly find that their sexual relationship, which had been at least adequate if not spectacular, has deteriorated to almost nothing. Often the older wife will feel rejected and inadequate because her husband no longer appears to desire her.

It is too bad that—just as many men cannot understand the physical and emotional needs of the woman who is going through the menopause—so many women cannot understand the physical and emotional needs of the male who is experiencing a loss of potency. Very few physical insults are more traumatic to the human emotional system than this.

Here again the physician can be especially helpful. He can give the male calm reassurance that not everything worth living for is lost. At the same time, he can help the female to understand her husband's difficulty.

He can help her to accept, regardless of her previous conditioning, the need for taking a more aggressive role in sexual activity and for varying her techniques of sexual arousal to compensate for her husband's slow loss of excitability. Helping the woman understand that coitus has physically beneficial effects on the circulation and musculature of the vaginal canal motivates her cooperation. Here again, communication and understanding are the key to the problem. The doctor-patient communication can also establish a pattern which will improve the patients' ability to talk to each other.

Just as the lack of communication causes many problems to start with, so can the reestablishment of communication open the road to some solutions to the problems.

There is a reading list of books on aging in Section IH of the Appendix.

REFERENCES

1. KEGEL, A. H.: Sexual functions of the pubococcygeus muscle. West. J. Surg., **60**: 521–524, 1952.
2. KEGEL, A. H.: Stress incontinence of urine in women: physiologic treatment. J. Internat. Coll. Surgeons, **25**: 487–499, 1956.

chapter eighteen

Encouraging Sexual Communication*

ELEANOR HAMILTON, PH.D., *New York, New York*

When two young people first fall in love, they think it will be easy to communicate with each other on every level. Particularly is this true in the area of sex.

But most young people, despite their optimistic self-assurance, are not really ready for sexual sharing. Some quickly become frightened by self-exposure—either physical or emotional—so that the slightest questionable word or circumstance sends them into emotional panic. Then they come to you—the physician-counselor—for help.

Many of these patients are very afraid of emotional expression. This is understandable, of course, for since earliest infancy they were probably punished for the expression of a true feeling. In adult life, with enriching sexual communication as the goal, they must be encouraged to venture without fear into a world they have been conditioned to believe is fearful.

How can you help them?

It certainly would be well to point out to them (and to reiterate to yourself) right at the start that sexual communication is one of the most sensitive arts that man knows anything about. As such it demands positive knowledge and practiced skill. Though we are born sexual beings, we are not born artists in the use of sex, any more than we are born artists of speech. Healthy, free-flowing sexual communication, which sometimes seems so effortless, is actually the result of practiced skill.

Communication of any kind between any two people, especially between lovers, is stimulated and encouraged when carried on in an atmosphere of approval and mutual involvement in each other's well-being. It is in such an atmosphere that lovers become married partners in the first place, and it is only in such an atmosphere that sexual communication between them can deepen. The husband whose eyes scan the dust

* Parts of this chapter were adapted from ideas originally presented in *Partners In Love* by Eleanor Hamilton, Ph.D., published by the Ziff-Davis Publishing Company in 1961.

on the furniture before seeking out the welcoming smile on his wife's face is limiting, if not actually preventing, sexual communication between them.

One of the commonest complaints that both men and women will bring you is that the partner hurls verbal darts, if not blasts, and then, cleansed of his own poison, proposes that they make love.

It will help to make clear to these partners that this won't work; not unless the one receiving the attack thoroughly understands that he is not the real target of his partner's wrath. Such an enlightened person can receive tirades like a game of catch, knowing that when the partner's shots are all fired, his accumulated tension spent, he will once again be free to move lovingly. However, since few people have reached this level of maturity, it is wiser to proceed on the theory that love and anger don't mix, especially when the expression of anger takes the form of destructive criticism.

One disturbed wife said to me "My husband is such an idiot! He accuses me of frigidity and even of not being interested in sex. Yet his idea of lovemaking is to needle me about my imperfections. Then, when I am at the point of slinging a plate at him, when I literally feel like murdering him, he wants me to go to bed with him. I could no more make love to him in that mood than I could fly. And I tell him so. But he says that he likes the fire in my eyes when I am mad."

Unfortunately, this husband has learned only part of an interesting phenomenon; that while anger does indeed stimulate some of the same physiologic responses as does sex, this is true only up to a point. Then the ways drastically part. If a man proceeds hell-bent along anger's trail, he is likely to miss the turning and find himself in the land of hate, not love. The focus has to be on love from the beginning.

Some men seem to find it difficult to say the things that their wives need to hear—appreciative things, heartwarming words affirming her goodness and worth. Some women also suffer from the inability to be generous with praise. Yet mutual appreciation is always a key to communication of any kind, and is absolutely necessary in opening the door to a love partner's readiness for sexual communication.

Perhaps you can give your patients a little practical exercise in the giving and receiving of praise. Suggest that they respond to some compliment a friend pays them so that their response brings the friend pleasure. This is not as easy as it sounds, but if they can learn this one lesson alone, they will have been helped.

What the partners say to each other, and how they say it, is tremendously important. But how it is received is also important. There are large discrepancies between what we mean by the words we say and their impact upon those we love. Words may have emotional meanings to one person that are not shared by another, some words being so emotionally charged that their use sets off surprising reactions. Sometimes they seem to place one partner at the opposite pole from his mate.

It is important that the patient be helped to understand that words are learned; they are conditioned by the environment in which one grows up. Words are symbols attached to experiences. If a patient's experience was pleasant, the word associated with that experience will be for him a pleasant word. But if his partner's association with the word was painful, the use of that word may trigger a pain-giving reaction.

This is especially true in the sexual area, where so many words are associated with embarrassment. Some women have been so rigorously conditioned against sex in their premarital lives that even upon hearing someone say the word "penis," an emotional shock is set up within them.

Outside the sexual area there are also problems with word associations. For example, saying the word "yellow" may set up a series of beautiful thoughts in the female partner's mind—a new gown, a field of waving daffodils. But the same word may trigger off a whole series of unpleasant and threatening thoughts in the mind of the male partner—cowardice, shame and so forth.

Following Dr. Calderone's suggestion,[1] I believe that we should encourage marital partners to explore their own feelings about words and to trace down the associations with any that are troublesome. Often an offended person can be greatly helped in this proceeding if his partner will ask questions about word associations without being critical, judgmental or evaluative. In other words, if he is able to say "What do you think of when I say 'penis'?"; and if the questioning partner can hear, receive and encourage whatever associations are returned without trying to tell his mate what they mean, that mate will make her own discoveries and experience a growing relief as she divests herself of an unsuspected load of useless embarrassment and emotional confusion.

This is not to say that it isn't permissible and even wise for the young couple to develop a language of their own to replace emotional words. Many married couples form substitute words which they use instead. Once the physician has assured himself that there is understanding of the physiology involved, perhaps it is better to encourage this love language than to attempt to change it, if improving sexual communication is the desired aim.

There is one more important thing about verbal communication. The patient should be helped to understand that in addition to the danger of using words with negative connotations, there is also a danger of *not* using words that convey positive thoughts. Caressing words are powerful sexual stimulants. These tend to bring about the very responses they suggest. This is especially so with words that express appreciative enjoyment of the sexual organs themselves. Many a husband has told me of the transforming effect it had had upon him when his wife mentioned how much she delighted in his penis, of her excitement at its movement in response to her, of how she came to life at its touch upon her body, of her sense of fulfillment in intercourse.

Such attitudes—cultivated, believed in and reciprocated—lead to sexual communication and sexual harmony. The partners move closer to each other in trust because, in the deepest sense, they *know* each other.

A verbal caress is the touch of love, expressed verbally. The man who says "Your eyes warm me in a bath of love," or the woman who says "Your courage gives me strength," are giving each other verbal caresses. In our culture, where loved beings are physically separated from each other for so many hours of every day, we need singing words to affirm the reality of psychic closeness, even body closeness. Especially for women are these phrases tremendously important. For them they are often more precious than money or material things. In fact, they are treasured so highly that whenever a woman comes across one in literature, she may cling to it hungrily, pretending it was for her.

Nonverbal Sexual Communication

Nonverbal sexual communication is enormously important, too. The wiser a person becomes, the more he pays attention to what people say without words, to what they say with their eyes, their gestures, their habitual ways of moving and the quality of their touch.

Without words, people can communicate much with their eyes. Some husbands and wives are acutely aware of these messages and are especially sensitive to those with sexual overtones. I have known of occasional partners so responsive to active eye encounters that their sexual excitation from this stimulus alone resulted in full orgastic release. I have known others who were sexually "frozen" by a glance.

People also communicate with each other in body movement. As Dr. Reich[2] points out, one important clue to understanding body language is the recognition that emotion itself is simply *feeling-in-movement*. Free-flowing emotional expression involves freedom of the muscles to *move*, while repression of feeling *imprisons* those same muscles as surely as if they were under lock and key. What we experience then is muscular tension, which is often described as pain or muscular spasm.

It follows, of course, that freedom to move affects sexual communication. A person can no more lose himself in orgastic delight while his jaw is set and his pelvis rigid, than he can hope to relax into blissful sleep while holding a tiger by the tail. Repressing desired movement of any kind requires fantastic amounts of energy and leaves a person chronically fatigued. Furthermore, repression of movements connected with anger, fear and sorrow stops the flow of movements connected with ecstatic love.

It is important for young lovers to understand this. If they don't, they are in danger of approaching each other with residual muscular tensions that bear no resemblance to the expression of love and, as such, these will be rejected. The hand that wants to punch, for example, is not going to feel the same, nor carry the same message in lovemaking, as the hand that has previously released its anger and now is free to express tenderness.

In helping marital partners to understand each other, get them to imitiate each other's expressive movements. Children do this intuitively. It is one reason why they leap language barriers so easily. Help each to find in his own musculature what is being enacted in the other's, and presently the feelings of the other will become clear.

What each does with these "true messages" is another story. At first, you teach him to simply acknowledge them to himself. Then later, as he learns to trust the accuracy of his perceptions and the authenticity of nonverbal communications, he can learn to gauge his actions by the true messages he "hears" and not be misguided by spoken ones that often mask, rather than reveal. As he learns to make his responses reflect his understanding of the unspoken, as well as the spoken, he will achieve a deeper and more mature communication with those with whom he deals. I might add that he will also encourage verbal honesty as well if he is able to refrain from judgmental or critical reactions to the revelations of others, especially to those of his mate.

TOUCH AS COMMUNICATION

In the language of the body, the act of touch, when freed of all destructive tensions, says to the other person "You are liked." Everyone knows that people reach out to touch that which pleases them and recoil from that which displeases them. Most people are hungrily searching for evidence from others that they are likable, so when someone gives them the simple gift of touch approval, it comes like healing balm.

Touch for the specific arousal of sexual response accomplishes its goal to the degree that the toucher is sensitively aware of what and how he touches. His hand, after all, is his bridge of communication over which and through which passes his devotion. This is true for men and for women. A sensitive man, like a sensitive woman, derives little pleasure from limp, rigid or mechanical approaches.

Many young couples find it hard to keep two organisms in focus at once; in other words, to be fully aware both of themself and of their partner in the sexual act. Yet this is almost exactly what accomplished sexual communicants learn to do.

In the recent past, to overcome the notion that men were unfeeling brutes who thoughtlessly raped their wives in selfish satisfaction of their personal lust, counselors have been urged to emphasize to each partner, and to the man in particular, that he consider the other's feelings from the outset. In some cases this may be good advice. But for many others in today's world, the physician-counselor might do well to suggest that each partner focus upon himself until he is able to remain alert to his own sensations and to control the level of his own responses. Then he may reverse the process, and focus upon those of the other. This is much like the problem faced by dancing partners. Each practices his part and then, and only then, are they able to blend together in harmonious movement. Mutual orgasm is the ideal climax for such a pair.

In my own counseling, I have come to respect the role of touch and body contact during sleep in enriching a marriage. Sleep consciousness is not unconsciousness. It is an altered form of consciousness. In sleep, people reach a level of awareness, characterized by deep relaxation. In this state, inhibitions drop away and the healthy, loving core of the person emerges unarmored. Perhaps one partner awakens in the night, to find his body moving rhythmically in response to the movements of the other, in an act of love so spontaneous, so unplanned as to seem without any conscious direction. Such episodes as these are almost unforgettable. They reach the deepest and most refreshing levels of communication known to man.

It is my feeling that a woman hardly knows a man at all (or vice versa) until she knows him in sleep consciousness. His anxieties, his joys, his terrors, his longings, his ecstasies come across to her unmistakably and unmasked, as he lets down his daytime defenses. Some wives (and some husbands) lament that their bed partner simply "isn't there" in sleep; that he "conks out" or becomes "like a log", or that "his spirit leaves me and I feel desolate and alone." These persons enjoy sex, to be sure, but they rarely experience the ecstasy of dreamy-eyed, half-awake sexual love that is entered spontaneously and with no premeditation.

Such persons are usually unable deeply to trust anyone in a sexually exposed situation. Often they are the same ones whose mothers treated them punitively in childhood when found masturbating in bed. My files are full of tales told by grown men who suffered horrendous humiliation, fear and anxiety at the hands of an adult female who, because of her own sexual anxiety, reacted violently to evidences of childhood sexuality. No wonder that such men shut themselves off from women in sleep, even from the woman they now wish to trust.

When mothers can begin to relax about their sons' childhood sexual exploration, wives will benefit in trust from the men they marry. Here the physician has an especially important role in his work with young mothers—helping them to understand the relationship between their positive attitudes toward their sons' sexuality and the ultimate sexual happiness of those same sons.

If a man is among those who have been badly conditioned, there is no reason for his remaining so. Little by little, the physician-counselor can teach the patient's wife how to help him to rebuild respect for his own sexuality. The physician can help her to understand how to let him know that his sexual responses are good and that they always have been good. Moreover, they are one of the most hopeful signs of his healthy creativity. He can help her to convey to him that she is glad and grateful for every good sensation he has in every part of his body. Deep down, she must realize that in their sexual relationship whatever makes him *feel* good, tends to make him *be* good.

By now, you have surely gathered that the more that you, as a physician-counselor, can help your patients to successfully send and receive messages that say to each other, in essence, "I love you; I revere you; I want psychic and physical health for you," the more will you insure happiness in their lives and in their marriages. In assisting them to achieve a deep and satisfying level of sexual communication, you are giving them the greatest gift that your profession can give to those it serves.

REFERENCES

1. CALDERONE, M. S.: *Release from Sexual Tension*. Random House, Inc., New York. 1960.
2. REICH, W.: *Selected Writings*. Farrar, Straus & Company, New York, 1960.

part three

OTHER MARRIAGE PROBLEMS

chapter nineteen

Counseling in Parent-Child Problems

HERBERT C. WIMBERGER, M.D., *Director, Child Psychiatric Clinic, University of Washington School of Medicine, Seattle, Washington*

The physician who concerns himself with more than just the physical complaints of his patients, and takes time to discuss their mental difficulties, will frequently uncover emotional problems involving their children. The child may show this problem in ways which are disturbing mainly to himself, as in an inability to function at the level of his potential in school, or ways disturbing to others, as in temper tantrums or juvenile delinquency.

There are, of course, innumerable sources of childhood disturbances and parent-child conflicts. Three of these appear to be especially important in the contemporary American culture. These are:

    1. Lack of emotional contact between parents and the child.

    2. Devaluating attitudes of the parents.

    3. Lack of defined limits by which the child can guide his behavior.

An evaluation of these three problems, together with the discussion of what can be done by the physician-counselor to help with these and other parent-child conflict problems, forms the major part of this paper. However, for any real understanding of parent-child difficulties, it is necessary to begin with a few paragraphs about recent developments in our understanding of family dynamics and parent-child relationships in recent years.

The New Concept of Family Interaction

The last decade has seen very significant changes in our view of the emotionally disturbed child. In times past, the feelings of children received little attention and abnormal behavior was either attributed to organic factors or considered in moral terms, such as laziness or badness. Over the years, investigations into the causes of normal and abnormal behavior of children resulted in recognition of the effect which the environment has on the child, and attention was consequently focused on the attitude of his parents and the atmosphere of the home in general. However, for many more years the child was still seen as the passive recipient of parental influences which were either healthy or disturbing, and, frequently, the parents were seen in a very critical light if they had the misfortune of having a child whose behavior appeared disturbed. Adjectives such as "anxious" or "rejecting" were used freely by many workers in the field of child guidance, and to this day many parents of disturbed children wonder what they have done wrong, as if they were accused of wittingly doing harm to their children.

Presently this concept is being revised and the child is seen not as the passive victim of his environment but rather as an active participant in a small group, his family. Investigators are continuing to study the intense interaction of the members of this group, the way they affect each other and the roles they assume. Each member of a family is an important actor whose presence codetermines the total performance of this family group. And while the child does reflect in his behavior the way he was raised by his parents, he also affects the feelings of his parents and siblings, thereby often changing their behavior in very significant ways.

A short illustration may be helpful. An anxious and insecure young mother gives birth to her first child. She has prepared herself well for her job and looks forward to the experience of taking care of her infant. The baby turns out to be tense and fussy, however, and makes it difficult for mother to cuddle him because he tends to stretch in her arms when she holds him. Mother, who had dreamed of a cuddly infant, becomes insecure feeling that she has failed in her job. As a result she withdraws from her role as much as circumstances will permit, thus giving less comfort to the baby, who becomes even more fussy. Father, annoyed by her withdrawal and the baby's consequent fussiness, becomes angry, completely overlooking his wife's need for support. This example could be spun out almost *ad infinitum* in all its cause and effect relationships, but by this time it should have illustrated the involvement of all members of a family.

Understanding present day concepts of family interaction requires some knowledge of the concepts of communication and family homeostasis. It is well known that communication refers to more than verbal interaction and that messages can be conveyed in many different ways. The world which the child is construing in his mind, and in which he will live for the years to come, depends in many ways on the amount and the clarity of the messages which he receives. Inability of the parents to give clear directions and information will make the child uncertain about himself and the limits and expectations which are set for him. Only recently has it been shown how disturbing confused and contradictory messages can be to a child. A characteristic example of multiple simultaneous messages is the case of the mother who tells her young child to go to school, at the same time holding him tightly embraced. Here the mother's verbal behavior tells the child that he should go, while she simultaneously conveys to him that she does not want him to leave her. The unconscious message —stay with me—is the one which the child will obey, thus getting into difficulties with his parents and the school authorities. It appears well established that different forms of disturbed communications within a family can be at the root of many forms of pathology.

Family homeostasis refers to the equilibrium which is established between the various members of the family. A physician commonly sees how a change in the physical or psychologic condition of one family member may seriously affect others. As illustration serves the youngest child, who is assigned the role of the baby. His growing up, with such consequences as a move to college, will deprive mother of her role as his caretaker. If this role cannot be replaced by other functions, anxiety and possibly a depression may be the result for mother. The members of a family complement each other, gratifying each other's needs in various ways. Because of the importance of the homeostasis in a family, most child guidance clinics include both parents in their therapeutic efforts. This decreases the likelihood of merely shifting symptoms to another person and makes it possible to deal with the pathology of the whole family.

It should be clear from the discussion that a child influences the functioning of a family in different and very significant ways. He can be the cause of disturbance or he can function as a stabilizer. In general, his influence will depend to a great extent on the adjustment of his parents, their ability to see the child and his needs in a realistic light and on their ability to be flexible and to meet the varying demands which are part of normal family life. There is no end to the number of ways in which the child can evoke disturbed feelings in his parents. A common finding here is the conflict created in a family when one member with strong infantile needs, strong wishes to be taken care of by his partner, is unable to yield to the needs of the child. The resulting rivalry between parent and child is very much like the competition between siblings. In this instance, the child threatens a parent whose needs are not appropriate to his situation. In another common situation, a parent uses the child for the gratification of his needs, much to the child's disadvantage. This occurs when a parent unwittingly uses the child to fill a role which is different from what the child's role should be, e.g., when a child is expected to reach a level of success which was never reached by the parent. While a child never disturbs a solid marriage of mature and well-adjusted people, these examples have shown the problems he can cause to a neurotic marriage. Some adults have needs not congruent with their age and position, needs which are gratified to some degree, however, by neurotic interaction with their partner. The more inappropriate and infantile these needs, the greater is the danger of a child's disturbing their marriage.

COMMON PROBLEMS IN THE PARENT-CHILD RELATIONSHIP
Lack of Contact

The complete absence of emotional interaction between mother and child, as it was found in the orphanages of the past, is very rare in our society. However, milder forms of emotional distance are not at all uncommon, and in fact are seen quite often in professional families. In these homes, either feelings are not shown, or their demonstration, especially in physical terms, is discouraged. The adults in such families are not skilled in the perception, let alone the communication, of their own feelings, frequently because they were themselves products of intellectually oriented, emotionally distant parents. An educational philosophy which prevailed some 30 years ago contributed to this attitude. The show of any warmth and affection was seen as mawkish and unnecessary, if not harmful.

But recent studies in emotional deprivation of children and primates amply demonstrate the child's absolute need for love and emotional warmth. Absence of these ingredients during the growth of the child usually results in a tendency to be withdrawn, to avoid close contact with other people. In the severest forms the child will not talk, will not play with anybody and will not participate in any shared activity, as is demanded of him, certainly, when he enters kindergarten. In his thoughts he lives in his own world. His high performance in some such circumscribed area as spelling may show that he is not mentally retarded. However, his knowledge is isolated from his life experiences and cannot be integrated to enable him to function at a level commensurate with his age.

Another feature of these emotionally deprived children is their inability to stand any frustrations; everything in life just has to go exactly their way. Since this condition can never be achieved, withdrawal or tantrums of a severe nature are the result. In milder forms, this disorder manifests itself in the child's tendency to establish only superficial relationships and in a detached attitude toward the world, possibly with a strong element of suspicion and distrust. As long as these children do not encounter stressful situations, they may appear to be quite well adjusted. In difficult circumstances, however, their limited ability to adapt often results in serious disturbances of their functioning.

The parents of these children are, at times, seen as rejecting. Although there may be factors operating outside their awareness, which make them resent the child, it is more practical to see them as persons who have never learned that feelings are part of life and who need assistance to overcome this lack.

Devaluating Attitudes of the Parents

It is natural for parents to have certain expectations of their child and to show approval or disapproval of his actions. Although the level of these expectations naturally varies, it can be too high, especially if the parent feels the need to do well by his own parents' standards. Or, someone with strong feelings about another person, usually a member of his own family, may want his child to be different. In any case, the parents see the child not in his own right, but merely as being like or unlike somebody else. Unwittingly, they push their child into a mold, often by being very critical of him. If their disapproval is expressed frankly, the child often takes a stand and rebels. Such a parent is often insecure in his attitude, however, and is likely to take a different course. Resorting to more subtle means of disapproval, he may nag the child, praise him very little and carp at him a great deal. The child discovers the lack of firmness in all of this and learns to challenge the parent by starting arguments or simply by contradicting. The outcome is a series of endless harangues, terminated at last either by mutual exhaustion or by angry outbursts; rationality is suspended and the child feels that he is treated unfairly.

Although the child does receive some pseudogratification from these battles, it is not sufficient to raise his decreased self-esteem. A variety of other symptoms such as school underachievement and some forms of depression may also be the result of decreased self-esteem.

Lack of Limits

The growing child needs to understand his own role, which means that he should know the expected "do's" and "don't's" by noticing his parents' clear and consistent approvals and disapprovals. Although he should have sufficient opportunity to gain experience and to test his abilities and limitations, he also needs understanding guidance in his encounters with the world.

Two common problems can be seen in connection with behavior limits—one concerning the child who is controlled too much, and the other the child whose limits are not clear enough. The establishment of unrealistically strict limits can result either in open defiance and rebellion or in an unfortunate constriction of the personality. The opposite problem comes to the attention of a physician more frequently, however, since lack of limits may result in an overt behavior disorder which is bound to get the child into trouble with various authorities.

It has been shown that unruly or delinquent behavior often is not only the result of the parents' failure to set limits. It also can be traced back to parental attitudes which in subtle ways condone or even encourage delinquent behavior. A typical example of this are the parents whose children fail to respect the property of others and who at the same time boast about their ability to cheat the government on their taxes. Some parents appear quite pleased, more or less openly, about the wrongdoings of their offspring. This usually happens when the child actually acts out their own hidden desires. Overtly this may manifest itself in a "boys will be boys" attitude, and smiles can be seen on the faces of fathers or mothers who report their child's misbehavior.

Parents also can show very divergent attitudes and one partner will set stricter limits for the child than the other is willing to enforce. By and large, many men are brought up to believe that severe discipline makes men and they treat their boys accordingly. Women, conditioned to a softer kind of approach in human relationships, disagree strongly with their husbands' approaches. The converse of this is the family in which father is passive, an attitude which is despised by mother who compensates for her husband's lack and is very definite and firm. Many marital conflicts have arisen from these differences. The real victim, however, is the child, who may end up being utterly confused or playing one parent against the other for a pyrrhic victory.

Helping parents to find the right balance between firmness, understanding, and sometimes condoning may require a great deal of patience and sensitivity on the part of the physician who is helping them. The right mixture of these ingredients, however, may be crucial in the child's development.

In this discussion we have concerned ourselves primarily with some attitudes of parents and their consequences for the child. Not much has been said about the child's reaction to these attitudes. Behavior is determined by many factors and our understanding of them is sketchy at best. One important shaper of the behavior of a child is the precept which is established by his parents. Everybody is well aware of the ways in which children imitate and emulate their father or mother. The traits which the child assumes from his parents, however, are not always the most desirable ones, and disturbed behavior in a child is often a replication of his parents' conduct. In this, the child may simply repeat what a parent is doing, or he may display patterns which are an exaggeration or caricature of the examples set for him.

In many instances, however, the child's behavior appears very much unlike anything his parents are doing. Take the case of the savage youngster who is untamed and is a cause of trouble wherever he goes, and whose parents are model citizens, never losing control of themselves. Chances are that these parents fail to set adequate limits for the child, as we have discussed earlier. This alone still fails to explain the child's aggressiveness. The whole problem usually becomes less puzzling when the thoughts and feelings of these parents are explored. An interview in such a case often reveals strong feelings of anger or resentment, feelings which, however, are rigidly controlled and never shown. Children have an uncanny talent for perceiving the feelings of their parents, and all too often act out the very same ones which the parents push out of their own minds.

Aggressiveness is not the only behavior which is transmitted from parent to child. Another common example concerns passivity and underachievement in school. Again, an inquiry into the family often reveals the very same pattern in one parent, such as the father, and, in contrast to this, a mother who is always bustling with activity and is overtly critical towards the passive members of the family. Passivity here becomes a family issue, a focal point for much of the interaction within the family group.

One other disturbing behavior pattern in a child concerns manipulation as a way to establish control. Particularly, adolescents of high intelligence at times can resort to ingenious ways of wielding their power over their parents, making it difficult or impossible for them to exert any control. Practically speaking, they may refuse to attend school or defy their parents' efforts to set limits. Manipulation as a pattern of interaction ceases to be functional in a family if the child becomes a better manipulator than his parents.

Because of its clinical importance in medical practice, the refusal of a child to attend school has been used twice to illustrate certain points. This entity, usually termed "school phobia," is an acute disorder which demands immediate attention if prolonged absence from school is to be avoided. Etiologically, it stems from a child's inability to separate from home, usually from mother, and not from a fear of school or a teacher, although these factors may be cited as causal. The anxiety caused by separation can become very strong and is frequently expressed in physical symptoms, such as abdominal pain or nausea, without detectable organic causes. The child deals with his anxiety by refusing to separate from home and, in order to accomplish this, uses all his skills to involve his parents in his disability.

A common way the child uses to get the parents to agree to his need to avoid school is the use of manipulation. This maneuver—if successful—provides the child with a great deal of gratification, and the matter of outwitting the parents can become a major factor perpetuating his phobia.

The practicing physician should be aware of the entity of school phobia and avoid becoming another participant in the usual power struggle, another adversary who needs to be defeated by the child. Immediate understanding intervention is essential and can be rendered by the family physician or a child psychiatrist.

After this short discussion of family problems and their relationship to the behavior of parents and children, some considerations concerning the treatment of disturbed families will be presented.

THERAPEUTIC ASPECTS

Behavior therapy differs from other forms of medical treatment in some very significant ways. First and foremost, emotional problems and disturbances do not come into existence suddenly, but usually develop over a long period of time. In certain cases a particular symptom may make its appearance all of a sudden, but the precondition, a readiness for this symptom to appear, has usually been present over a long period of time.

Furthermore, in the psychologic sphere, pathology represents not the intrusion of a sick element into a person's normal behavior, but rather an unsuccessful adaptation of his ways to meet the demands of the environment. Treating a behavior problem, therefore, is more like rechanneling a river into more appropriate territory than stemming a sudden overflow which may have appeared. Because of this, the development of better, more adaptable patterns of behavior usually requires considerable time. Anybody who wants to help a disturbed child or family has to be prepared to spend many hours in this endeavor.

Another important consideration pertains to the need for a personal relationship. People do not live in a vacuum and their behavior constitutes to a large extent their reaction to the environment. This is even true for such autistic behavior as depressions and hallucinations. Many disturbed patterns of behavior are perpetuated by the particular reactions which they cause in other persons. For this reason, treatment can be conducted only in an intensive interaction between at least two persons, and never in an emotional vacuum. Anybody who undertakes treatment of emotional disorders has to be willing to enter into a relationship with people, to concern himself with the causes and effects of the other person's behavior, and has to control his own emotional needs during this process. Like all people, the physician has developed certain patterns for the gratification of his own needs; his power over the patient may be very important to him. The disturbed child usually needs to individuate himself, to free himself from the powers which his environment exerts. The physician-counselor with an unresolved need to be powerful will not be able to help the patient in this effort to change the image of himself and others.

To help a child with his disturbance, which creates difficulties in the life of the family, it is important to arrive at an agreement concerning the problem. Therapists have wasted many hours trying to impress on a family the existence of a problem, which was disturbing to others, such as the teachers of the child, but which really was not seen as a matter of concern by the child and his parents. Younger children—that is, preschool and lower grade school children—are rarely concerned about the problems which bring them into the office of the physician. They come because the parents take the initiative. Even in these instances, however, it has to be determined whether the parents really feel that a problem exists or whether they come because of pressures exerted by the school or other agencies.

The older child, preadolescent and adolescent, often knows that something is troubling him and causing him to be disturbed in his behavior. This does not necessarily mean that he is willing to admit it. Many a teen-ager is brought in by his parents against his own will. For him the trip to the doctor's office is just one of the many incidents in which his own wishes are not considered and he is forced to submit to a decision which he feels not to be in his best interest. Such a setting is certainly not conducive to the development of a trusting relationship. The contract with the parents and the patient—if the age permits it—should contain an understanding of which symptoms are to be the focus of treatment, as well as an agreement concerning the family's willingness to cooperate in interview situations. The family should understand that their cooperation not only will involve sacrifices of time and money, but may result in the experiencing and recognition of uncomfortable feelings and memories.

The choice of treatment approaches in helping a family will depend on a number of factors. The physician who becomes aware of a problem in a child must first choose whether to involve himself in the situation. The limitations of his own time or the availability of alternative therapeutic facilities may make a referral mandatory. If he can help the family and the child, he must decide on the setting for treatment. Family group discussions are used with increasing frequency as an effective procedure for resolving conflicts between parents and child. Two main factors determine whether this method is appropriate to the case. First, the age of the child will have to be considered. Usually a youngster below the age of 9 or 10 years will not be able to participate meaningfully in the exploration of the family's problems. The second consideration is the type of conflict which exists. Often when parental control is the source of conflict, the child will not be able to ventilate his feelings in front of the parents, or at least not until the parents prove to him that they are willing to change their attitudes. There is no need to maintain rigidly a particular setting. During the course of group interviews it may appear that one or two individual sessions with a member may be conducive to the progress of the family group discussions. An exploration of a particular personal problem may be more productive in a one to one situation. The therapist should, however, be aware that a request for individual interviews may be the result of this person's need for special attention. In this case continuation of individual sessions will not help to integrate this member into the family group, but rather will be disruptive.

Serious individual psychopathology can disable a member to a degree which makes his participation in a group discussion impossible. The material which is uncovered, the feelings which are revealed, can simply be too threatening to a person who barely manages to control himself. Flexibility in the arrangements is therefore necessary and temporary or permanent separation with the institution of individual interviews may have to be made.

Family interviews have diagnostic and therapeutic value. The physician observing the interaction can form an opinion about the roles of the various family members and about the types of interaction which are characteristic for the persons involved. The roles can be assessed along different dimensions such as involved-detached, dominant-submissive, active-passive, masculine-feminine and many more. The interaction can be seen in such terms as verbal, nonverbal, impulsive, controlled, warm, cold, dictatorial, considerate, encouraging, critical—an almost endless list could be compiled here. The roles and usual ways of interacting have their roots in the childhood experiences of this person. They may be learned or they may be the expression of a neurotic conflict, usually both. The interviewer can observe the dynamics of the family and relate this to the presenting problems for a diagnostic formulation.

The intervention of the physician can be therapeutic in a number of ways. Most basic is the opportunity which it affords the patients to talk about their problems to someone. Having an interested listener can be helpful to any troubled person. It permits the patient to see the situation in a different light and gives him the feeling that he does not have to face his problem alone and unaided. Furthermore, letting off steam often decreases the pressure which is caused by usually unexpressed feelings.

Having formed an opinion about the cause of the problem, the physician can point out behavior patterns which lead to conflict. It may, for instance, be possible to show a mother her tendency to answer for the child in the interview and to take over for him, with the effect of keeping the child from becoming self-sufficient. Interpreting characteristic ways of interacting in this manner can be very effective, particularly with the more intelligent parent. It requires a positive attitude on the part of the patient toward his physician.

Directive counseling is another effective tool in the hands of the physician-counselor. Many patients perpetuate their own, their spouse's or their child's problems, mainly because they have never learned behavior patterns which would be less traumatic to the victim. This makes it possible in many instances to teach new or alternate approaches to particular situations. An illustration of this could be the mother who simply does not know how to play with a small child. She may be very willing to learn new ways of being with the child, ways which will be beneficial for both of them. Also amenable to this treatment approach is parental encouragement of undesirable behavior in the child. A mother who responds with anger to the temper tantrums of her child may provide him with more closeness during her outbursts than he ever experiences. Finding better ways for giving the needed contact with her and ending the unwitting encouragement for the tantrums can be very therapeutic.

Of main importance in helping the patient and his family is the establishing of a trusting and understanding relationship between doctor and patient. This may be a simple procedure or it may turn out to be a very difficult one. The patient will relate to the physician in the same ways which, in his experience, are most effective to provide him with safe and gratifying forms of interaction with other people. This means that he can present himself as infantile-dependent, for example, or as suspicious-defensive, or as openly hostile and challenging. The healthy reaction of the therapist now should be different from the reactions the patient has encountered in the past. If the therapist succeeds in establishing the proper relationship, the patient will be helped—first, because he has found an understanding person who can lend him strength and secondly, because the therapeutic relationship affords him a different life experience, a situation in which he can develop new and better patterns of behavior.

The physician who is willing to concern himself with emotional aspects of family life and with problems of parents and children can be an important helper for those who encounter problems. His natural role as a person with great authority and expertness in matters of health and disease, immediately provides a relationship which facilitates further therapeutic efforts. His judgment can be used directly by his patients to remedy disturbing conditions, and if he is interested in their emotional life, he can offer them with the understanding, corrective, supportive or interpreting type of relationship which they need.

The majority of all people, children and adults, have significant conflicts, many of which can be improved by the physician-counselor without the intervention of the trained psychotherapist. A serious lack of trained professionals exists and it is hoped that in the future this gap between supply and demand will be filled to some degree by the physician.

Obviously, however, the deeper aspects of psychotherapy as well as special techniques such as play therapy for children need considerable experience for their successful application and should be left to the psychotherapist.

There is a reading list of books on parent-child relations in Section IE of the Appendix. There are also reading lists for parents and for teen-agers in Sections VI and VII, respectively.

chapter twenty

Counseling with Alcoholics and Their Families

RAYMOND D. FOWLER, JR., PH.D., *Director, Psychological Clinic, University of Alabama, University, Alabama*

Alcoholism, a major public health problem, has claimed four and one-half million victims in this country. For each of these alcoholics, an average of four other people, members of the immediate family, are affected. The incidence of broken homes in families affected by alcoholism is over seven times as high as for the general population.[1]

It would appear that the physician is the first line of defense in problems of alcoholism. Certainly, he is the community resource most likely to be consulted by the wife of the alcoholic for assistance in dealing with the family problems associated with alcoholism. Over two-thirds of a group of wives interviewed in one sampling indicated that they had gone to a physician for help with their problem.[2]

The purpose of this chapter is to examine the alcoholic, his effect on the family and the role of the physician in counseling with the family. Because of the greater incidence of alcoholism among men, the focus will be upon the alcoholic husband. A later section will consider some special problems of the alcoholic wife.

STAGES IN FAMILY ADJUSTMENT TO THE ALCOHOLIC HUSBAND

Alcoholism does not "strike" a family in the manner of an accident or an acute disease. However, both the onset of alcoholism and the adjustment of the family to the alcoholism may be viewed as a series of loosely defined stages.[3] The developing alcoholic takes drinking more seriously than other people do, and drinks to make himself feel more adequate, socially acceptable and relaxed. As excessive drinking increases, the husband, approaching the borderline between controlled and uncontrolled drinking, is less able to handle job and family responsibilities. His drinking episodes place a strain on the husband-wife relationship. Arguments and disagreements increase and the wife feels hurt, rejected and angry.

The first stage of family adjustment coincides with the first stage of alcoholism. The husband shows a lack of control, and his life is increasingly oriented around drinking. He experiences blackouts, and his hangovers become so intense that he requires a morning drink to start the day. He is aware of his loss of control, but he believes that he can regain it. During this period, the wife gradually recognizes that her husband is an alcoholic. Her chief concern is to *conceal* and to *control* the drinking, and her activities are oriented toward that goal.

The second stage of alcoholism is characterized by physical, social and economic deterioration of the drinker. As jobs, friends and health slip away, the alcoholic loses all hope for himself. The family becomes increasingly isolated and preoccupied with drinking. The wife may decide to leave. If she stays, the family assumes a new organization with the wife as head, and the husband is excluded from the family ranks.

In the third stage, the alcoholic has reached a point of apparent hopelessness. He has been hospitalized and institutionalized repeatedly. He is violent or even psychotic when intoxicated. He has had delirium tremens and suffers from permanent physical and mental damage. This gloomy picture represents the course of alcoholism in a family when no professional help is obtained. At any stage, the course might have been interrupted and perhaps reversed. The physician has a unique opportunity and responsibility to help the family affected by alcoholism because he is likely to see the family at a relatively early point in the development of the illness.

Treating the Alcoholic Husband

The male alcoholic may be from any social, racial, religious or occupational group. He may be rich or poor, old or young, successful or unsuccessful. *Essentially, an alcoholic is a person who can no longer control his drinking and whose drinking causes a continuing problem in one or more aspects of his life.*

Despite efforts to demonstrate the existence of an "alcoholic personality," [4-9] the overwhelming evidence from clinical research and observation shows no such consistent personality pattern. It seems clear that alcoholism is often associated with disorders of personality, but, as Syme concludes, ". . . it is rather clear that, on the basis of the evidence (all available relevant literature published from 1936 to 1956) there is no warrant for concluding that persons of one type are more likely to become alcoholic than persons of another type." [10] We may conclude that efforts to describe the alcoholic as a particular type of person are, at best, misleading. Alcoholics, like other people, exhibit immense variability, and each may present unique problems in treatment.

In many larger communities a variety of specialized resources for treating the alcoholic exists. The best known is Alcoholics Anonymous, an association of recovered alcoholics who are dedicated to maintaining their own sobriety by helping other alcoholics attain theirs. Other resources include private and public sanitoria and hospitals, alcoholism clinics, mental health clinics and psychotherapists in private practice. Where such facilities exist, the physician will usually desire to work toward a referral of his patient to one or another of them. But, where they are not available, or when the patient is not ready to accept a referral, it may be necessary for the physician to provide psychologic as well as medical treatment. According to Fox, "In order to develop a constructive or healing attitude toward alcoholics, the physician must do two basic things: (1) learn about the illness and the treatment available, and (2) reorganize on a realistic level his self expectations regarding these patients." [11]

Fox points out that the physician should regard alcoholism as a chronic disease rather than as an acute one, since "viewing alcoholism as a chronic illness helps relieve the frustration we feel if and when the alcoholic resumes drinking."

The physician, Fox says, has three areas of responsibility to the alcoholic:

1. The management of the acute withdrawal syndrome. Depending on the severity, this may be done in the office, clinic or hospital. Ataraxic drugs have simplified this process.

2. The diagnosis and appropriate treatment of all concomitant and resulting physical disabilities of the patient.

3. The long range management of the alcoholism. This requires the assistance of the physician for several years, while the patient, after having regained abstinence and physical health, struggles to attain emotional, social and economic stability.

"The most powerful medicine the physician has to offer the alcoholic," says Fox, "is himself and his attitude toward his patient." For many alcoholics the physician may be the first person who has been willing or able to look at him objectively and without moral judgement. Often, the discovery that a respected member of the community can view him as a worthwhile person is strong medicine indeed. It will not result in a dramatic recovery, but it may help the alcoholic to regain hope for himself.

Because he is respected by the alcoholic and his family and because he is a neutral party with respect to the family problems associated with the alcoholism, the physician is in an ideal position to "mediate" marital problems, and will often be called upon in this capacity. Joint interviews with the alcoholic and his spouse have been found particularly useful. Often this permits the reestablishment of almost nonexistent communication. The physician serves as a buffer to prevent the too violent expression of feeling and thus may facilitate the frank discussion of mutual problems between the two people.

TREATING THE ALCOHOLIC THROUGH HIS WIFE

The popular and professional views of the alcoholic's wife have ranged from that of a martyred near-saint to that of an emotional cripple who drives her husband into alcoholism, assumes his role as head of the house, resists his efforts at recovery and, if he recovers, regresses into psychosis or depression.[12]

Where lies truth? Certainly, a large portion of the confusion must lie in the fallacy of trying to develop a "personality type" which would fit so diverse a group of women who marry men who are, or will become, alcoholics. Since the evidence reveals no typical "alcoholic personality," the search for an "alcoholic's wife's personality" seems doomed at the outset.

The available information concerning the wives of alcoholics may be summarized as follows:

1. Wives of alcoholics show no typical personality types.[3, 13]

2. Similarities among wives of alcoholics exist because they are faced with a common life situation.[3]

3. Wives of alcoholics appear more "disturbed" on personality tests than wives in general.[18] However, when compared with other women with marital problems, wives of alcoholics appear *less* disturbed than wives of nonalcoholics.[14]

4. The "behavior of the wife and the personal traits inferred from this behavior is a reaction to a cumulative crisis in which the wife experiences progressively more stress."[3]

We may conclude from the above that the emotional disturbance of the wife is, at least in part, a result of the stresses inherent in living with an alcoholic. The counselor's efforts, therefore, should be directed toward enabling the wife to adapt to the stress with less anxiety and hostility. Many wives respond favorably to this approach, will be able to function more comfortably, may eventually motivate their husbands to seek help and can become the major therapeutic agent for treating their husbands with the physician's help.

The counselor should avoid extensive history taking with the wife. She is more likely to become involved with treatment if the initial focus is upon the husband's condition. Counseling is not likely to be successful

when the focus is entirely upon the personality of the wife. It is also unlikely to be successful when the focus is entirely upon the husband's alcoholism.[15]

The counselor should help the wife see that alcoholism is a family
problem and that her behavior influences her husband just as his behavior
influences her. She should be encouraged to examine her aims and then
to assess the appropriateness of her behavior for achieving these aims.
For example, she may intend to compensate for the family pressures by
creating a warm and pleasant home environment, but she may find that
she is spending much of her time crying, nagging or complaining. The
counselor's task is to accept the aims of the wife and to assist her in finding
ways to accomplish them.

Two general observations should be made initially. First, the counselor
must see the wife realistically. He must avoid the extreme of seeing the
wife as the helpless and nonparticipating victim of a marriage situation
which is "all bad." The counselor must also avoid accepting at face value
the alcoholic's claims that his nagging wife has "driven him to drink."
The counselor should recognize the wife as a person who has a difficult
life situation with which she is attempting to cope, with whatever abilities
and liabilities she possesses and with varying degrees of success and failure.
She is not the cause of her husband's alcoholism, but she cannot avoid
being a part of it. She can neither cause his recovery nor prevent it, although her behavior may have an influence in either direction. The
marriage is not "all bad" or she probably would not have continued in
it. There are things about her husband she likes as well as things she does
not like.

Second, the counselor needs information. Unless he has had specific
training in the field of alcoholism, he may know relatively little about the
condition. A physician is familiar with the medical treatment of acute
alcoholism but may have little information about the nature of the illness, its etiology and its prognosis. In addition to the material contained
in this chapter, the suggested readings in Section *IF* of the Appendix may
assist the counselor in increasing his own knowledge about alcoholism.

The problems brought into the counseling situation by the wife of an
alcoholic vary with the individuals involved. Certain problems recur so
frequently, however, that a separate discussion seems justified. The following section contains information from the published literature and from
clinical experience which may be useful to the counselor in dealing with
these recurrent problem areas.

Learning about Alcoholism

The wife is a part of a larger society which has strongly negative feelings
toward the alcoholic but relatively little information about alcoholism as

a disease. More than anyone else, the wife needs information in order to clarify her understanding of the condition and to help her make rational decisions with her alcoholic husband. Information written at a level she can understand should be available to her. A list of the available material may be found in Section *IF* of the Appendix. It is the task of the counselor to help the wife to understand the facts as they apply to her specific situation and to help her adjust her attitude and behavior to the facts as she understands them.

Facing the Situation Realistically

The wife has adapted to her increasingly painful life situation by utilizing a variety of defense mechanisms, particularly repression and denial. In her efforts to "cover" for her husband she has lied to others and to herself. She must admit to herself, without minimizing or exaggerating, the extent of her husband's drinking. She must avoid the superficial view that "it will all blow over." She must be helped to see that failing to get help now because she fears to "stir things up" will only delay the eventual solution of her problems. She should take an objective inventory of her current situation, personal, social and economic, as a first step toward making intelligent decisions and plans.

Motivating the Alcoholic to Seek Help

The alcoholic may resent his wife's insistence that he obtain treatment. He may resist this as another effort of his wife to control him. If an issue is made, he may be inhibited from seeking help on his own later. The wife has made a large step toward her husband's recovery by accepting help for herself. By doing so, she increases the probability that her husband will obtain help and will profit by it.

Avoiding "Home Treatment" Methods

"Home treatment" methods are those techniques by which the wife attempts to control her husband's drinking by direct or indirect means. She may utilize nagging, preaching and lecturing, threats of separation or divorce, hiding or pouring out his liquor or restricting his money. The counselor should know about the futility of these methods, should be able to recognize them when they are applied and should help the wife to understand their futility. The wife can usually recognize this readily, since they have been uniformly unsuccessful. The only effect of the home treatment method is to make the alcoholic angry and resentful. *The counselor must convey to the wife that she cannot control her husband's drinking, that the control must come from the alcoholic himself. The counselor must also recognize that he cannot control the drinking, either directly or indirectly.* The wife should understand that she did not make her husband an alcoholic, and that she cannot make him cease to be an alcoholic. By discontinuing the home treatment, she returns the responsibility to her husband, where it belongs.

Letting the Alcoholic Face the Consequences of His Drinking

The wife must come to recognize that she cannot protect her husband from the consequences of his drinking. When the wife covers up for her husband, it increases his illusion that he can "get away with it." Most wives have become very proficient in shielding and protecting the husband from the results of his drinking episodes by lying to employers, inventing imaginary illnesses and so forth. All of these actions help the alcoholic to deny his problems and his need for help. The wife must permit the consequences of the drinking to occur. This requires perhaps even more encouragement from the counselor, since the wife feels guilt and bitter self-recrimination when losses occur which she could have prevented by taking over. By not protecting him, she may find that he loses jobs and that neighbors and friends become aware of the family's humiliation. She will need help in continuing the course of action which leads to such problems. Allowing the drinking and permitting its consequences may make the wife's problem and life situation more difficult. She must hold to the belief that the eventual outcome is worth the temporary consequence. The willingness of the wife to permit the drinking and to discontinue the nagging may even cause the husband to be more willing to accompany her to seek professional help.

Maintaining a Stable Home Atmosphere

In her anger and frustration, the wife may feel justified in resorting to the same behavior as her husband. Feelings such as, "Why should I work to keep the family going when he takes no responsibility?" and, "Why bother? Nothing seems to help" are likely to be expressed. The counselor must help the wife see that: (1) her husband's illness does not reduce her own responsibility to her children, her home and herself, and (2) her husband is more likely to recover from his alcoholism if there is something left. By neglect and irresponsibility, the wife can only make her own situation more acute. By contributing to the chaos of the home, she compounds the damage to the family and reduces the possibilities of salvaging something from the wreckage.

Adjusting to the Alcoholic's Improvement

As the alcoholic begins on the path to recovery, a new set of suggestions to the wife becomes relevant. The counselor can be helpful to the wife in her painful process of readjustment. He is aware that she has many reasons to mistrust her husband's intentions and his assurances that things are going to be different. She has established a mode of adjustment to her husband's condition. This adjustment, perhaps necessary for the family's survival during the more severe stages of the husband's illness, may now be a handicap to his recovery. The councelor will encourage her to develop a new, more flexible adjustment to her husband's improving condition. She must be prepared to relinquish, although perhaps gradually, those aspects of her husband's family role which she has, of necessity, assumed. She may have come to enjoy the role of head of the house and may be hesitant to give it up. The counselor will help her see the important advantages to the family of the balanced distribution of roles.

Maintaining Realistic Expectations

The physician views alcoholism as a chronic disease and, as such, he anticipates periodic flare-ups and regressions during the recovery period. He must share this point of view with the wife and help her to tolerate the inevitable "slip." The wife must guard against shifting her expectations too suddenly. Over the years, she has lost hope for her husband and expects nothing from him. When his recovery begins, she must not suddenly shift to impossible expectations of total permanent sobriety and responsibility. She must, on the other hand, be willing to recognize positive gains as her husband makes them. She must avoid discouraging his good intentions. To the extent that she can do so, she should share his hopes and optimism, while accepting the reality that recovery is a noncontinuous process.

Accepting the Alcoholic's Means of Recovery

The wife who has done much to assist in her husband's recovery may feel hurt and resentful when he assigns the entire credit elsewhere, whether it be to Alcoholics Anonymous, the physician, the clinic or some other resource. She may also feel that she has gained little in terms of support and encouragement from her husband because his life is now as devoted to his *treatment* as it once was to his disease. The counselor can be of assistance at this juncture by preparing the wife for these feelings. Her husband, now recovering from a painful and seemingly hopeless disease, is intensely grateful to the external source of his recovery. As he becomes more confident of his sobriety, he will look increasingly to his family as a source of gratification. The wife should encourage the development of new interests and family activities which will help to bring him back into the family as an important participant.

Letting the Alcoholic Retain Responsibility

The wife, having learned the futility of home treatment controls during the period of her husband's active drinking, must now avoid the temptation of protecting her husband from temptation. Efforts on her part to keep him away from alcohol will diminish the feelings of self-confidence and personal responsibility which are essential to his continued sobriety. Avoiding restaurants which serve liquor, asking friends to eliminate before dinner cocktails or wine when he is present or pouring out the remains of bottles found around the house are viewed by the recovered alcoholic as votes of "no confidence." The responsibility is *his* and the wife should leave it with him.

Recognizing that Mistakes Are Inevitable

The counselor must realize, and help the wife to realize, that mistakes are inevitable. In the turmoil and anxiety associated with her husband's alcoholism and with his recovery, she will not always make the right decisions, nor will she always consistently carry through with the decisions she has made. It is here that the counselor may help with support, encouragement and reassurance. The knowledge that she can discuss her mistakes in a noncritical and nonjudgmental atmosphere will be, in itself, supportive to the wife. Helping her to recognize that she, like her husband, is a person with problems and human frailties may be, in the end, the counselor's most valuable contribution.

THE ALCOHOLIC'S CHILDREN

The physician may be called upon to help children understand an alcoholic parent. Occasionally, he may discuss the matter directly with the children. More often, he will encourage the nonalcoholic parent to do this, perhaps suggesting concepts the parent might wish to convey. The explanation, whether by the physician or by the parent, should include: (1) the effects of alcohol on thinking and behavior, (2) the nature of alcoholism—loss of control and the power of choice, and (3) the present family circumstances and future plans.

Parents should be encouraged to be aware of the child's feelings about the problem and to give emotional support. Since the child feels uncertain and insecure, consistency on the part of the nonalcoholic parent is particularly important. The nonalcoholic parent must refrain from using the children to increase the alcoholic's guilt and must avoid turning the children against the alcoholic. Such a stratagem inevitably leads to increased distress of the children, intrafamily strife, and greater feeling of rejection and consequent withdrawal of the alcoholic parent. It also reduces the possibility of reestablishing normal family relations when the alcoholic attains sobriety.

THE ALCOHOLIC WOMAN

Of the estimated 4,500,000 alcoholics in this country, about three-fourths of a million are women[16]—a ratio of one in six. In contrast to the male alcoholic, relatively little is known about the female alcoholic. Alcoholism in the male is a public problem. The male alcoholic may drink publicly, lose his job, get into difficulties with the police and create public disturbances. Alcoholism in the female is much more likely to remain a private family problem. She is shielded from public view by an unspoken conspiracy of her family, friends and even law enforcement agencies.

Usually, women alcoholics begin problem drinking at a later age than men, but the development of alcoholism is more rapid for them. The entire period from moderate drinking to alcoholism appears to be telescoped.[16] Also, women alcoholics appear to be more severely emotionally disturbed than males.[17]

From a study of women who have come into outpatient alcoholism clinics for help,[16] some facts have emerged which make it possible to describe the patterns of development which are characteristic of at least this special group of female alcoholics. Typically, she is a married woman with children. At the time she comes for help she is about 40 years of age. She has had a drinking problem for 10 years; for 10 years before that she drank moderately but with increasing regularity. During the past 10 years her drinking has become more nearly continuous, with episodes of more intensive drinking on weekends or during periods of heightened emotional stress. She has come to view her regular drinking as almost a necessity to control her tension and discomfort. Her occasional binges are viewed by her and by others as a much more serious problem. They are followed by remorse, guilt and depression.

Alcoholic women attribute their drinking episodes to a variety of personal and situational factors. When 200 women alcoholics were questioned,[18] four principal causes of drinking emerged: (1) marital conflict, (2) tensions, (3) loneliness, and (4) problems with children. All four of the above are closely related to the marriage relationship. Although these women tended to isolate specific causes for their drinking, most seemed to be symptomatic of the marriage relationship itself. This, in turn, appeared to reflect problems in their early backgrounds which were marked by difficulties.

Much less is known about the adjustment of the family to the alcoholic wife than to the alcoholic husband. Alcoholic wives are seen in most clinics in small numbers. Their husbands are often unwilling to come to give information.

Counseling the Husband of an Alcoholic

The typical response of the husband to his wife's excessive drinking is denial. He may behave in an angry, punitive manner toward his wife in private, but he is often the last person to admit that his wife's drinking may be excessive. Since society condemns excessive drinking in women so strongly, and since the husband may feel that he should be able to "control" his wife, there are strong forces which act to prevent his admitting his wife's condition, even to his family doctor. Typically, he will minimize the seriousness of his wife's drinking as long as possible. When this is no longer possible he seeks divorce, especially where there are no children. Even when the husband does not leave, he seems to be much less able to recognize his wife's condition as an illness. He is reluctant to seek or use help, often preferring to "suffer in silence" rather than face the possible embarrassment of seeking help outside the family.

The principles already suggested for counseling with wives are equally applicable in counseling the nonalcoholic husband of an alcoholic. Special emphasis should be placed on: (1) recognition, by the husband, of alcoholism as an illness, and (2) the avoidance of attempts at direct control, rationing and the like. Through counseling, the husband may be helped to find ways to support his wife in her efforts to attain sobriety. These would indicate an avoidance of direct control and the judgmental approach, an effort to assume some family responsibilities and a reassurance to the wife of continued affection and need for her.

There is a reading list of books on alcoholism in Section IF of the Appendix.

REFERENCES

1. HEWLETT, A. H.: Family adjustment to the crisis of alcoholism (press release). Alabama Commission on Alcoholism, December 1, 1963.
2. BAILEY, M. B.: The family agency and social casework in treatment of the spouse and family of the alcoholic. In *What Family Agencies Can Do to Help Alcoholics and Their Families*, edited by A. J. Kuhn. Illinois Division of Alcoholism, 1962.
3. JACKSON, J. K.: The adjustment of the family to the crisis of alcoholism. Quart. J. Stud. Alcohol, **15**: 562–586, 1954.
4. FENICHEL. O.: *The Psychoanalytic Theory of Neuroses*. W. W. Norton & Company, Inc., New York, 1945.
5. FORIZS, L.: A closer look at the alcoholic. North Carolina M. J., **15**: 81–84, 1954.
6. HEWITT, C. C.: A personality study of alcohol addiction. Quart. J. Stud. Alcohol, **4**: 368–386, 1943.
7. SELIGER, R. V., AND ROSENBERG, S. J.: Personality of the alcoholic. M. Rec. New York, **154**: 418–421, 1941.
8. SILLMAN, L. R.: Chronic alcoholism. J. Nerv. & Ment. Dis., **107**: 127–149, 1948.
9. WELLMAN, M.: Towards an etiology of alcoholism: why young men drink too much. Canad. M. A. J., **73**: 717–725, 1955.
10. SYME, L.: Personality characteristics and the alcoholic. A critique of current studies. Quart. J. Stud. Alcohol, **18**: 288–302, 1957.

11. Fox, V.: Medical management of the alcoholic. In *Basic Papers: The First South-eastern School of Alcohol Studies*, edited by A. L. Vreeland. Millsaps College, 1961.
12. Futterman, S.: Personality trends in wives of alcoholics. J. Psychiat. Social Work, 23: 37–41, 1953.
13. Kogan, K. L., and Jackson, J. K.: Role perceptions in wives of alcoholics and non-alcoholics. Quart. J. Stud. Alcohol, 24: 627–639, 1963.
14. Ballard, R. G.: The interrelatedness of alcoholism and marital conflict: symposium, 1958. 3. The interaction between marital conflict and alcoholism as seen through MMPI's of marriage partners. Am. J. Orthopsychiat., 29: 528–546, 1959.
15. Hunter, G.: Alcoholism and the family agency with particular reference to early phase and hidden types. Quart. J. Stud. Alcohol, 24: 61–79, 1963.
16. Lisanski, E. S.: alcoholism in women: social and psychological concomitants. I. Social history data. Quart. J. Stud. Alcohol, 18: 588–623, 1957.
17. Karpman, B.: Quoted in *Alcoholism in Missouri*. Committee on Alcoholism, Missouri State Medical Association, 1958.
18. Rosenbaum, B.: Married women alcoholics at the Washingtonian Hospital. Quart. J. Stud. Alcohol, 19: 79–89, 1958.

chapter twenty-one

Counseling with Widowed, Divorced and Unmarried Women

RICHARD H. KLEMER, PH.D., *Departmemt of Psychiatry, University of Washington School of Medicine, Seattle, Washington*

Until recently, it would have been almost unthinkable to include widowed, divorced and unmarried women all in a single chapter on counseling. For, in the past, society made important distinctions between women in each of these statuses, and consequently created differing problems for the women themselves. Divorce was looked upon as an unexpected and undesired perversion of morality, therefore the legally divorced woman was to be shunned and ostracized. On the other hand, the widow, victim of a natural and inevitable result of mortality, was accepted, but often was treated with pity. The never married woman was thought of as being somewhat odd, and was subjected to derision or veiled ridicule.

Now, however, there is a new willingness to recognize that separation and aloneness, for whatever cause, is a social problem, and not necessarily a moral, a natural or a humorous one. There is a new willingness to place more emphasis on the consequences of the unfortuante accident which led to loneliness and frustration than upon the cause.

Three major factors have contributed to this new atmosphere. The first is the changed attitude toward divorce and toward women providing their own support. The second is the recognition that there may be wider differences among divorcees, among widows and among single women, than between them. There are reluctant divorcees and delighted divorcees. There are reluctant widows and delighted widows. There are reluctant single women and delighted single women.

The third major factor contributing to the new attitude regarding the woman who is alone is the understanding that regardless of the cause of the separation or aloneness, those who are disturbed by it face a similarity of experience. While perhaps only the widows and divorcees experience the sudden shock of a separation, all of the reluctant women alone have experienced (1) frustrated resentment in asking themselves why it happened to *them;* (2) anger at a former husband or man friend for having left (even if he had no choice); (3) guilt, in terms of what could the woman herself have done to have prevented it; and, finally, (4) fear or panic over what will happen in the future.

All of these specific feelings may be counseling needs for any particular patient. But ordinarily, the counselor, or the physician serving as counselor, will have to deal with three much larger, more general problems when he is counseling with the older unmarried woman. The first is to help her to adjust to her present situation, whatever is involved. The second (applicable to the widows and divorcees) is to help her to help her children adjust and the third is to help her to build new social relationships.

The problem of helping the brand-new reluctant widows and divorcees (the delighted ones rarely come for counseling) to work through their initial grief, bitterness, confusion and insecurity, sometimes seems almost hopeless. Often the shock of the actual departure of the mate has been so sudden and so devastating that psychologic depression is evident. Sometimes there are those physical symptoms which accompany severe emotional disturbance, from stomach cramps to hysteria, which can be treated with tranquilizers and sedatives.

But even after these symptoms have been successfully treated, there remain the emotional emptiness, the hostility, the self-punishment and the bitterness. As was noted above, the patient may be angry at the rest of the world because fate singled her out to be the one to be deprived. Or she may be filled with self-recrimination for having done this or that which might have contributed to her mate's going. This happens to widows as well as divorcees. Some women in their grief over the death of a mate blame the deceased with such irrational accusations as "How could he have done this to me?"

In counseling these women toward self-adjustment, the counselor's greatest ally is time. But keeping the emphasis upon the positive remaining values in the woman's life is also helpful, regardless of how she came to be alone. This should be done, however, while remembering that it is especially important for a person who is grieving or resentful to have an opportunity to express that grief or resentment. She should voice her feelings, rather than repress them. If, for some reason, she is expected to be strong all the time and has no one to whom she can admit her resentments and anxieties, she will become a first-class prospect for later emotional disturbances or psychosomatic illnesses.

In some cases, particularly those involving widows, referral to a clergyman will be indicated even if, initially, the woman seems reluctant to go. Sometimes the reawakening of latent religious feelings can be a powerful source of tension reduction.

But when all has been said and done, there is nothing that helps in the readjustment to an emotional shock as much as the passage of time. This is equally as true for the reluctant divorcee as it is for the widow. It is probably wise that she be helped to understand this. However, it is also necessary that she be helped to see that time in itself is no excuse for perpetuating patterns of mourning or resentment beyond the period when they are functionally useful shock absorbers. Mourning and martyred criticalness can become a habit.

Many of those older women alone who appeal to the physician-counselor for help are going to have financial problems of one kind or another. While usually these are too complex and time-consuming for the counselor himself to handle, there are almost always community resources that can be counted on for help—from the bank's investment counselor to the high school home economics teacher. The experienced counselor will keep a list of these helping specialists in his top desk drawer. There are some good printed materials, too; for example, the Department of Agriculture booklet *Helping Families Manage Their Finances.*[1]

The problem of adjustment or readjustment for the never married woman is somewhat different, albeit similar and no less difficult. As she approaches middle life, the single woman may see for the first time that the marriage relationship which she had always casually assumed would be inevitable is not inevitable at all. Or she may see that her fear of being left, about which she worried some, is now about to become a reality. In either case, it often amounts to a real tragedy, for some of these women are the best educated, best behaving, and in a real sense, the most deserving women in our society. Few physicians—indeed few men—have ever had to face such an awful feeling of complete rejection or despair.

The writer is the author of a book, *A Man for Every Woman,*[2] which has as its major thesis the strong conviction that many of these women should be encouraged to reexamine themselves, to relearn social skills and to renew their efforts rather than to give up altogether the notion of being married. While it is true that there are some women who, for one reason or another, have such a remote probability of ever being married that they should probably be helped to work through their feelings of frustration to arrive at some satisfactory goal other than marriage, this should be a reluctant conclusion, arrived at only when the facts make it inescapable. There will be more about this in a later section of this chapter.

Usually, the lack of marriage itself isn't the only problem which brings the older single woman to the doctor's office. It is unhappily true that many of these women arrive with so many problems that it is difficult to sort out which is causing them the most trouble. It may be that their feelings of frustration at not marrying have caused various psychosomatic complaints. It also may be that just at this time when their marriage lack has become acute they face the onset of premenopausal symptoms, or the general loss of vitality and youthful attractiveness that would be affecting them even if they were married. Often the counseling with the unmarried woman becomes multifaceted before it has gone very far. Patience, reassurance and complete acceptance can do wonders.

HELPING THE WOMAN TO HELP HER CHILDREN

Some of the most difficult problems in counseling the widow or divorcee come in helping her to help her children. Perhaps the first problem is to help her stop imposing on her children by using them—perhaps even exploiting them—for companionship and emotional release. Very often the woman will turn to her teen-age daughters for sympathy, or to her teen-age sons for the security and reassurance that she used to get from her husband. Ordinarily this is extremely unfair to the children, who have problems of their own they are trying to work through.

After separation from one parent, the child often feels the loss more keenly than is recognized by the remaining parent. There is sometimes confusion and anxiety in the child's mind as to whether he might have been the cause of the marital breakup or even the death. *He* needs the calm reassurance and security that must come from the remaining parent. Here again the important aspect of the counseling is to keep the focus on the positive aspects of the situation, however gloomy that situation may appear to be to the patient. Sometimes it is necessary to help the patient to understand that her grief has been selfish. She has a responsibility to provide *at least* a feeling of hopefulness for the children, even if satisfaction of their other desires is temporarily impossible.

There will be other problems which the remaining parent faces in addition to providing security. These will include such things as establishing new patterns of family discipline and authority, providing some father figure for the male child's sex-role identification (this has come in for much attention recently) and, of course, providing some sort of day care for the children so that mother can go to work. Here again the wise physician-counselor will probably have a supply of suggestions in the form of referral sources, books for the parent to read and groups for her to attend.

In many communities, there are regular meetings of such groups as Parents without Partners, designed for the heads of one parent families. The counselor can also help the patient select schools or summer camps where the child can get the kind of sex-role identification he needs from a teacher or camp counselor. In large communities the school system operates parent education classes and has other helpful resources for the worried parent. It isn't hard, either, to get to know the telephone number of the social work and group work agencies in the community which provide some kind of day care and/or character building help for the children of employed mothers.

REBUILDING SOCIAL RELATIONSHIPS

Of all the problems which will face the counselor who is working with the widowed, divorced and unmarried woman, none will be more difficult than helping her build new social relationships. And nothing is more important. Some of the women want this above all other help. Others may demur. But whether they know it or not, for most mature women, divorced, widowed or never married, finding new companionship (especially male companionship) is the only thing which is ultimately going to lead to renewed feelings of self-worth and emotional health.

But helping in this area is more difficult than it might first appear. The reasons why this is difficult lie among our social customs, the circumstances which provide an uneven sex ratio, and within the women themselves.

First of all, our society insists that many of the places a respectable woman might go to meet a man she must go escorted, and, therefore, she is stopped even before she can get started. Moreover, until recently we have insisted the male do all of the contact making. Since many of the eligible males in middle life, either by selection or by deterioration, are incapable of being aggressive enough to make social contacts easily, the woman was placed in almost an impossible position. In *A Man for Every Woman*, after several pages of qualifications and safeguards, I propose that more mature women make greater use of the informal meetings they have with men in everyday situations, to encourage further companionship. To do this just right, however, requires the building of considerable self-confidence. It also requires much practice. Some women have trouble getting both the self-confidence and the practice.

There are many other social problems which face the woman alone. Her married friends don't invite her now, even if they did before, because now she supposedly has different interests as an unmarried woman. Furthermore, she is a tacit threat to the wives in these married couples, even though she may have no present eyes for the husbands involved.

There are also many circumstance factors which diminish the possibility of the unmarried woman finding the companionship she would like. Some women find it hard to believe that there are actually more marriage-eligible men in the United States in their 30's and early 40's than marriage-eligible women.[3] What appears to them—quite correctly, probably—is that the men who are available to them often are more inhibited, more problem-filled, and less interesting, than the men they knew at 18. Moreover, the available men are more likely to be selfish and sex-demanding. It comes as a great shock to some women who thought they might be returning to the kind of dating they did when they were teen-agers to find that more mature men who are available either aren't interested in sex at all, or else assume that they are doing the women a great service to bestow their sexual favors upon her. The utter candor with which some men suggest sexual relationships to the divorcee or widow often sends her rushing to the counselor in high indignation.

As a matter of fact, many women will define this as their number one social problem. They feel outraged that the men they meet expect at least a *quid pro quo* in the form of sexual intercourse for an evening's entertainment. What many of them don't understand is that the men who are aggressive enough to ask for dates are also aggressive enough to expect sex. There are literally millions of male "lambs" hidden in libraries and behind drawing boards, but many of these men wouldn't have the courage to ask for a date and the women might not go out with them if they did. They wouldn't be "smooth" enough to be bothered with.

There are other circumstance factors which trouble the woman who is trying to reorganize her social life, too. For many widows and divorcees, there is a problem of finding time for any social activity in between the necessary job and the homemaking and child care chores. Sometimes the children themselves inhibit the woman's social activity, either because of their need for care, or else because of their very presence. Many women think men don't want women with children. And I have had a number of women tell me that they were surprised at themselves for developing feelings of resentment against the children because they did interfere with their social lives. Here is an obvious need for counseling help.

It is probable that of all the problems of building new social relationships, none is more difficult than overcoming the obstacles raised by the woman's own feelings. In the case of the divorced or widowed woman, these problems may center around the fact that she is still emotionally tied to the previous mate. This can lead a sentimental widow to reject all prospective companions and suitors as being unworthy and inadequate as compared to the idealized image of her former mate. Or, it may lead a resentful divorcee to jump at the first man who comes along because she is going to show her ex-mate (to whom she is still emotionally tied) that even if he didn't love her, she is still desired by other men. In neither one of these instances does the woman provide any kind of solution to her problem. The counselor may have a role in helping her see this.

THE NEVER MARRIED WOMAN

As the writer has pointed out above and elsewhere,[4] successful counseling with more mature unmarried women can be directed toward one of two results: (1) helping the patient to readjust and to accept the probability and desirability of remaining unmarried and still having a successful living experience, or (2) helping the patient to so improve her interpersonal relationships and her motivation to seek male companionship that she really does have a good chance of finding a marriage mate.

The first alternative often appears to be the simpler and safer. Yet adopting it would ignore the statistical fact that even at age 35 a never married woman still has a fifty-fifty chance of being married, at 40 a 20 per cent chance and at 45 a 12 per cent chance.[5] Remarriage rates are much higher. A widow has a 67 per cent chance at 35, 50 per cent at 40, and 34 per cent at 45. The rates for divorcees are 94 per cent, 84 per cent, and 69 per cent, respectively.

Adopting the first alternative also ignores the fact that helping an unmarried woman to improve her interpersonal skills will enrich her life even if she does not ever marry. So the counselor or the physician serving as counselor may well be of far greater ultimate value if he has the time, energy and confidence to encourage the unmarried woman to try to improve her relationship skills, rather than to encourage her to adjust to her present inadequate situation. Naturally, however, the individual woman's initial motivation to improve her relationship skills, her ability to do it and her personality, will play an important part in the decision as to what is a realistic goal for her. It should be noted with emphasis that many of the women who do not have relationship skills are lacking in persistent motivation to get them, whether they know it or not.

The process of helping a particular woman to increase her relationship skills is basically helping her to more completely evaluate herself, helping her to increase her self-confidence and her feeling of self-worth, helping her to practice and perfect (in a protected situation) the skills she needs and, finally, providing her with the reassurance that the goal is attainable for her.

Helping the mature woman to genuine self-evaluation may be a rather slow and painstaking task. Many of these women have adopted rationalizations for their present situations and they have convinced themselves, at least, that these rationalizations are the real reasons why they have never married. Some say they have had too many obligations to help aged relatives. Others say they didn't have enough opportunity to meet men.

There are undoubtedly a number of women who really do have such strong obligations to care for parents or relatives that they couldn't possibly have considered marriage. It has sometimes been overlooked that there has been a general change in the status of the older, unmarried daughter from a dependent to a supporter of dependents. But many of the women who talk about their obligations don't bother to add that they were emotionally dependent upon their father and mother even before those parents became their dependents. They just *couldn't* leave emotionally when they could have left financially.

And it is true that there are a few women who have lived such isolated lives that they didn't really have a fair opportunity to meet other men. But most modern women come within meeting distance of enough eligible males in a week's time to provide them with all the dates and love affairs they might need, if they could only meet and relate to those men.

While there are many reasons that they don't take advantage of the opportunities they do have, probably the most important one is their own feeling of self-worth—their own self-definitions. Many of these women have very low self-esteem and upon meeting someone else, they figure in advance that he won't like them. Consequently, they are so standoffish, so quiet or so obviously eager to impress, that he *doesn't* like them. Thereupon they say to themselves, "See, I told you so, he didn't like you." And they are even less able to relate to the next person they meet.

On the other hand, women who do have self-confidence don't have to spend all their time thinking "What is he thinking now?" or "I wonder if I look all right?" Instead, they can think about what they could be doing to help the man to be more comfortable in the situation. Consequently, he likes them and they are even better at relating to the next person.

It should be noted that in working with older women, it is not only necessary to bring the feeling of self-worth up to what it might have been for the normal teen-age girl, it is probably necessary to help the woman to achieve something more. For, in our youth conscious society, even many women who had self-confidence which was adequate when they were younger, begin to lose it as they approach middle age. They are made to feel so inferior by our colossal commercial promotion of the attractiveness of the college-age girls that their self-confidence begins to waver. Once this happens, they are in fact less attractive.

Thus, helping the woman to a feeling of self-worth—self-love in its finest sense—is probably the number one objective of any counseling that is going to help her to improve her relations with others. It is this self-confidence which is the epitome of the good first impression which she will have to make if she is going to improve her relationships with other people. Naturally, helping her to provide a better first glance impression through improving her grooming, her appearance and her smile, is going to help. (Parenthetically, you might point out that the smile is tremendously important. Several studies have indicated that this is all-controlling to the good first impression and the consequent opportunities that any individual has in human relationships.) But the first glance isn't enough. Ultimately, it is the woman's persistent feelings of self-confidence that will provide the total good first impression.

As a part of improving self-confidence, it is, of course, necessary that the woman counselee learn skills in conversation and in social behavior which are in keeping with her personality. Those people who are popular learned to be popular. Mostly they learned it by a slow process of trial-and-error experimentation in childhood. While the middle-aged person can relearn these things, it is often difficult, especially if she has been used to sheltering her ego and hiding from others. Here, as elsewhere, she is going to need the counselor's encouragement. By starting her in a protected situation, however, and by encouraging her to take just one small step at a time and practice that until she internalizes it and can do it automatically, sometimes remarkable things can be accomplished. One good first step, for some women, might be learning to say "hello" first at a church group meeting. Simple though it may be for the normally self-confident individual, this might represent a tremendous accomplishment for some of those who have had relationships difficulty in the past. Once this step is accomplished and polished to the point of being automatic, then the woman is ready to take another step—and then another, and so on. It will be tremendously rewarding both to the woman and to her counselor to see how much can be accomplished in this manner.

There are some further suggestions for improving social self-confidence in *A Man for Every Woman*, which is designed for the single woman herself to read.

Ultimately, however, the most important step in creating a deeper love relationship with another person will be in helping the woman to become emotionally indispensable to that person. There is a curious fallacy held by many people, including many older unmarried people, that they can get someone to fall in love with them by being so irresistibly fascinating that the other person cannot help himself. Obviously this is nonsense. People fall in love, and stay in love, because they have an emotional need for the other person. The wise course, therefore, for any woman, is to recognize and meet the emotional needs of the person to whom she wishes to relate.

In some cases this will mean helping the women to know and understand what the emotional needs of men are. In other instances it will mean helping the women to put their own emotional needs aside long enough so that they can meet the emotional needs of the men to whom they wish to relate. For example, many women can see that some of the men who brag have a tremendous need for recognition. What they can't see is that because they are shy and backward they are expressing an even greater need. They are insisting that the man meet their need for security before they will even talk with him. Sometimes it will require quite a self-struggle before the woman gets an insight into this kind of problem, and an even greater self-struggle before she is able to be self-sacrificing enough to put her own needs aside while she reaches out to meet his need.

But difficult as it may be, the counselor (or the physician who is serving as counselor) who is willing to take the time and risk the disappointments that inevitably go along with this kind of counseling, will occasionally find himself amply rewarded. In my own practice, I find no greater satisfaction than in getting a wedding announcement from some woman who had all but given up when she came to see me. And as I said before, even in those cases where a marriage doesn't eventuate, there is an almost equal sense of satisfaction in seeing the improved relationships and general life enrichment which come to the woman who has increased her interpersonal skills.

There is a reading list of books for unmarried women in Section IV of the Appendix.

REFERENCES

1. U. S. Department of Agriculture. Consumer and Food Economics Research Division. *Helping Families Manage Their Finances.* U. S. Government Printing Office, Washington, D. C., 1963.
2. KLEMER, R. H.: *A Man for Every Woman.* The Macmillan Company, New York, 1959.
3. U. S. Bureau of the Census. *Current Population Reports,* Series P-20, No. 81. U. S. Government Printing Office, Washington, D. C., 1958.
4. RUTHERFORD, R. N., KLEMER, R. H., AND RUTHERFORD, J. J.: The unmarried woman. In *Marriage Counseling in Medical Practice,* edited by E. M. Nash, L. Jessner, and D. W. Abse. University of North Carolina Press, Chapel Hill, 1964.
5. JACOBSON, P. H.: *American Marriage and Divorce,* Tables 37, 38, and 40. Rinehart & Company, Inc., New York, 1959.

chapter twenty-two

The Climacteric Years in the Woman, Man and Family

ROBERT N. RUTHERFORD, M.D., *Department of Obstetrics and Gynecology, University of Washington School of Medicine, Seattle, Washington,* AND JEAN J. RUTHERFORD, *Seattle, Washington*

The 40's are a time when men and women seem to be thrust into pre-formed molds which few desire. There are certain physical facts of aging which must be accepted, albeit reluctantly. The physician-counselor can occupy a vitally important role, if he will but accept it, in helping these mid-life folk to seek positive attitudes rather than to look at their "liver spots," to worry over their failure as parents, or to contemplate upon which barren shore their old carcasses, with spirits dwindling, will be left to wither and die.

And these days there is much for the physician and the patient to be positive about. Away back at the turn of the century—some 60-odd years ago—the life-span of the typical woman ended in her mid-40's. Often she died of overwork and overbabies as if she were a spent skyrocket. Today she has an average life expectancy lasting into her mid-70's, because of the many things which can help her mentally, emotionally and physically.

Not so dramatic, but equally encouraging, has been the increased longevity for men.

Just living longer, though, is not enough. Unless mid-life patients can be helped to make creative adjustments to the menopausal and post-menopausal years, they may not have really gained anything. Fortunately, both hormone therapy and counseling skills are now available to help the physician help his patients. Both are important and both will be discussed herewith, in their relation to women, to men and to family living.

THE FEMALE CLIMACTERIC (MENOPAUSE)

Our earlier concepts of the menopause often made it a wastebasket into which could be consigned many female "megrims and miasms" of difficult classification. The writers have seen this diagnosis pinned upon patients as early as age 17 and as late as age 73. It has been as useful and as acceptable as the diagnosis of "hypochondriasis" or "functional illness" or "problems of unknown etiology" or even "psychiatric problems."

What goes on within the female body and psyche at this time? A number of things can be documented:

1. Osteoporosis—a loss of protein and calcium from the bones resulting in a thinning and weakening of the bones. Even if this fails to progress to the point of causing loss of height, "dowager's hump," backache or collapse fracture of the vertebrae, it can never be considered a "normal" or "good" change. The 80-year-old woman who suffers a fractured hip in a minor fall may blame it on the fact that her ovaries ceased functioning 30 years before and substitution treatment was never given.

2. A loss of the normal female protection against atherosclerosis.

3. A tendency to gain weight and to develop diabetes in those who have the hereditary potential.

4. A withdrawal of protein from the skin, thinning it and giving the fine wrinkles usually blamed on aging.

5. An increased irritability and vasomotor instability leading to such symptoms as hot flashes.

6. The atrophy and drying of mucous membranes. This includes drying of the lining of the nose and throat, eyes and tear ducts, and of the neck of the urinary bladder and vagina. Individuals vary widely as to the degree of symptoms that result, but many times the local irritation or itching is a cause of serious discomfort.

7. An increased tendency for the kidneys to waste salt in the urine, leading to a decreased volume of blood which may cause weakness and dizziness.

8. An increased incidence of cancer of the breast and uterus.[1]

What are the subjective, emotional, difficult to measure things which may be far more important than changes in lipid metabolism?

From its beginning in marriage, the first major strain the family unit will have is the advent of the first baby. This requires mutuality in every sense of the word. Interestingly enough, the second major strain is the last child's leaving the parental home.

Then, the middle-aged couple turn toward each other for strength and reassurance, comfort and inspiration for further living. But, what if this partnership has foundered long since—foundered by reason of the wife who has given herself completely to "her" children at the expense of a husband's love. The husband now has compensated for his wife's inattention toward him with his job, his hobbies and his community responsibilities. She turns to him only to find that he has little more than a basic simple courtesy toward her. Usually he wants no other woman. He is just busy with other things now.

It is unfortunate that events are timed so that in the mid-40's a series of family shaking changes converge on the family unit all at once:

1. The children physically leaving home for the great wide wonderful world, whether to jobs, higher education, the armed forces, marriage or what you will. No longer is the mother in her erstwhile role of past great significance.

2. Even though the mother may have called her menstruation "the curse" for many years, when it suddenly stops she may realize that this means she cannot have another baby to make her of paramount importance again to some dependent person. Of course, there is the sorry substitute of grandmotherhood, but this usually is of little consolation.

3. Father is just reaching his stride, even though he may be balding. His importance is still on the upgrade, his community efforts and increasing recognition keep him busy—almost too busy—and importantly happy.

The mother looks about at a wasteland which can be most heartbreaking. She may be troubled by easy emotional upsets which even a Phi Beta Kappa mind cannot seem to control. The body she has lived in and controlled over the last 45 years is changing and shifting in its responses. Her feelings of attractiveness may falter, and consequently her sex urge may be disrupted, even though she consciously wishes no basic change in her other relationships with her husband.

Treatment for Women

In this day and age, a great deal can be done for a menopausal woman, probably more for her than for her husband.

In the realm of medications which can be prescribed we have the estrogens. Excellent work emerging from geriatricians has shown that *every* woman should be given positive medication at this time. Prior to this last decade, an occasional lonely medical prophet such as Dr. Fuller Albright advised routine use of estrogens whether the patient was having menopausal symptoms or not.[2] The bulk of medical thinking then felt that menopause was a normal and natural physiologic phase completed within a few months or a few years by every normal female and it should not be interfered with. But, evidence has continued to pile up that certain basic benefits can be given to all aging women by judicious use of estrogens.

In the majority of women, the ovarian source of estrogens withers in the late 40's. However, the adrenal sources of estrogens continue until roughly age 60. From this age on, it appears that women share about the same incidence of vascular problems as men, *i.e.*, coronary occlusions, cerebral vascular accidents and the like.

In any event, increasing support is given to the concept that women who show estrogen deficiency by Papanicolaou smear will be benefited by supplementary administration of estrogens. Specifically:

1. There is less loss of elasticity of the skin (*i.e.*, "wrinkling," to our patients).

2. There is less atherosclerosis.

3. There is less osteoporosis.

4. There is less shrinking and drying of the vagina, less cervical stenosis, less shrinking of the bladder capacity and urethral problems, less anal stenosis.

5. Lipid and lipoprotein metabolism remains unchanged, with less of the "dowager's hump" and thickening of the midriff.

If there is loss of libido (this is reported in some 10 per cent of menopausal women) androgen can be added with benefit, should estrogen alone not be an adequate stimulus. If androgens are combined with estrogen, side effects of masculinization are minimal, particularly if treatment is interrupted from time to time. Usually, explanation of the slowing cycle of sex interest in the wife and reassurance that this often is shared by the husband will help a great deal, with or without hormone aid.

In the realm of psychologic treatment, the promotion of positive attitudes is tremendously important. It is a matter of simple arithmetic to show the menopausal woman that the children have been her concern for only 20 years, and that now she faces what can be a promising vista of 30 years with her husband. Usually income is less encumbered as is leisure time. This can be made to sound like an insurance brochure hailing the delights of retirement insurance. The suggestion from the physician that there is no loss of femininity—courtesy of estrogens—is of no less value to every female patient.

Reassurance that life still can hold a great deal of rich, creative living is an important therapeutic procedure in helping middle-aged people. But it might be well to point out that in order to make his reassurance convincing, the physician must really believe it himself. He needs to have genuinely positive attitudes about the aging process.

The Male Climacteric (Menopause)

The male climacteric is a sly, subtle change which makes no such dramatic announcement as the stopping of menstruation in women. There are no sudden physical changes which can be noted. No night sweats or hot flashes occur, neither does impotence or premature ejaculation or lack of sex interest (those dramatic evidences that "something is wrong" with the male machinery).

The male menopause is a term that should never have been coined, yet it is with us for some time to come. It has no physical basis. It does not mark the stopping of sperm formation or of male hormone production. Instead, it is an emotional-attitudinal change.

The man in his late 40's may suddenly realize that his physical powers are limited somewhat. He does not bounce quite so well the next morning. He may be confronted with the realization that he has gone about as far as he will go—or can go—in his job. Younger men suddenly seem to have loomed as challengers. Also, his children seem to doubt many of his ideas and values and to seek his advice less often. But then, so does his wife, who seems to be emotionally upset most of the time. His behavior toward her has not changed, he thinks, yet all he gets is into trouble.

In other words, his entire world seems to focus upon him as if he were at fault, or as if his values were not as good as he had always thought they were, or as if whatever he has accomplished is not very worthwhile. These things bring many uncertainties at a time when he suddenly realizes that there *is* only one real certainty—he is on the downhill slide.

He realizes that he is mortal, is aging and will someday die. True, he has left children as evidence of his immortality, and possibly a number of fine works. This is the time when the professional fund raisers hit him for stained glass windows for the church, for alumni gifts or for endowment of any of many monuments to show that he once was alive.

It can be a very unsettling moment of truth for the strong and for the weak, for the religious and the irreligious, for the happy man and the unhappy man. This is a spiritual menopause which often has been precipitated by certain physical realizations.

If this man can turn to his wife—as we hope she can turn to him for support and understanding—their marriage may go on for another very happy 30 years (remembering our current life expectancy).

On the other hand, if he has no support from his life partner, from his job situation, from his financial planning for the future, from a progressively devaluated dollar or from his physician-counselor—what may he do?

He may check his sexual prowess with another partner.

He may say "To hell with it !" and chuck the whole thing and go over the hill.

He may look his situation over and decide that it is better to stay where he is, unhappy though he may be, rather than to change his familiar road for unknown new responsibilities.

None of these alternatives offers any real solution to his problem.

This man at this juncture needs understanding, help, sympathy and reinspiration for what could be productive years ahead.

Treatment for Men

For the man, medical treatment is largely that of counseling and not of endocrine therapy. If we note the fact that the male has a higher incidence of cardiovascular problems than the female up until the age of 60, it would seem that the use of androgens for "supportive" reasons has little value. Any improvement in libido is thought to be largely a placebo effect. Estrogens are being used experimentally in males for definite indications, such as coronary heart disease. However, at the present dosage levels there are some side effects of note—increase in breast size, and loss of libido. At the moment, these side effects may outweigh routine use of estrogens in the male for cardiovascular prophylactic purposes.[3]

A sympathetic discussion and hearing on the part of the interested physician is a treatment must for the middle aged male. Simply helping a man of this age group to understand the physiology involved, both in himself and in his wife, can be reassuring. While he may be on the "downhill metabolic slide," it can be presented in such a fashion that it represents a happy challenge for the next 30 years. The man mentioned above who thought only of stepping out, going over the hill or resigning himself to unhappiness really has another possibility which, perhaps with a little counseling help from the physician, he can come to see. He can, if he will, pull himself up by his own bootstraps. He can take the initiative and say to his wife, "These are green years. Our children are launched. Our responsibilities now are only for you and me. Let's start these new fruitful years, not fruitful from our loins but from our minds."

THE FAMILY CLIMACTERIC

The "family climacteric" is not often discussed as such. But in its own way it may be most dramatic. It occurs when the family has a "change of life" and the children are suddenly gone.

One parent pair may have trained their children for maturity and for leaving the nest. They will be delighted by the children's adulthood and independence. After this graduation from the family, the children may take on the status of good friends to their parents because of mutual enjoyment and respect.

But another parent pair may despair at the departure of the children, the loneliness of life with only themselves, the overwhelming boredom of facing the future with only the other sterile partner. Put this way, these are melancholy prospects.

In middle age, we find only too many couples who no longer "are in love with each other." On the other hand, the old familiar resentments have become chronic and there is not enough motivation to cause either to want a divorce.

The physician is in an ideal position not only to counsel but to suggest avenues of a new enriched life—to go back to school—to return to a job, whether paid or volunteer, part-time or full-time—to exploit a latent talent. Whatever the doctor's prescription, it should emphasize the need for the couple to become interesting to themselves as individuals and then to each other as individuals and partners.

This is not just sentimental talk. As we live with our patients and watch the human patterns form again and again, certain patterns for helping emerge. The basic problems are the same. Just the individuals change. Often the physician-counselor is able to make a larger contribution to his patient's mental health than any other helper, because of the intimate association he has had with all the family members over the years. The counseling he can provide in the latter years of the family life cycle may be as important as the prescriptions and treatment he gave when the family was just beginning to grow.

REFERENCES

1. BAKKE, J. L.: A teaching device to assist active therapeutic intervention in the menopause. West. J. Surg., **71**: 241–245, 1963.
2. ALBRIGHT, F.: Studies on ovarian dysfunction. III. Menopause. Endocrinology, **20**: 24–39, 1936.
3. Editorial: Estrogens in the treatment of atherosclerosis. J. A. M. A., **183**: 682, 1963.

ADDITIONAL REFERENCES

MARMORSTON, J., MOORE, F. J., HOPKINS, C. E., KUZMA, O. T., AND WEINER, J.: Clinical studies of long-term estrogen therapy in men with myocardial infarction. Proc. Soc. Exper. Biol. & Med., **110**: 400–408, 1962.

OLIVER, M. F., AND BOYD, G. S.: Influence of reduction of serum lipids on prognosis of coronary heart disease—a five-year study using oestrogen. Lancet, **2**: 499–505, 1961.

PICK, R., STAMLER, J., RODBARD, S., AND KATZ, L. N.: Estrogen-induced regression of coronary atherosclerosis in cholesterol-fed chicks. Circulation, **6**: 858–861, 1952.

PICK, R., STAMLER, J., RODBARD, S., AND KATZ, L. N.: Inhibition of coronary atherosclerosis by estrogens in cholesterol-fed chicks. Circulation, **6**: 276–280, 1952.

RUTHERFORD, R. N.: Editorial: Eternal Estrogen? (With or Without Progestogen). West. J. Surg., **71**: 158, 1963.

WILSON, R. A., BREVETTI, R. E., AND WILSON, T. A.: Specific procedures for the elimination of the menopause. West. J. Surg., **71**: 110–121, 1963.

chapter twenty-three

Family Planning as a Marriage Problem

MARY S. CALDERONE, M.D., M.P.H., *Executive Director, Sex Information and Education Council of the U. S., New York, New York*

In the well-established, stabilized and harmonious marriage, the family planning counseling expected of the physician will consist of providing, in uncomplicated fashion, the method most suitable to the consciences, capacities and health needs of the family unit.

It is for the marriage in trouble that the physician needs to muster all of his skill and knowledge. Here it will be important for him to ascertain whether contraception *per se* is a difficulty in the marriage, or whether it is being exploited by one or the other of the partners as a symbol or mask for deeper difficulties. The woman who has been unable to achieve full sexual expression and who subconsciously wants to avoid intercourse, may use one or another of the contraceptive methods as an excuse to accomplish this end: the wife who consistently "forgets" to insert her diaphragm before she is in bed, the wife who leaves her ovulation thermometer at home when going off for a week-long trip with her husband, the wife who compulsively insists she must douche immediately after intercourse because of the "messiness" of a contraceptive cream or jelly— these are women who need help in the total psychosexual area rather than in contraception *per se*, for changing the method will not change the problem. The same is true with the husband who refuses to use a condom because "it dulls my sensation" yet objects to both the diaphragm because "I feel it" and an oral contraceptive because "it might hurt my wife's nature."

The physician should also be on his guard for the individual who may fail to use indicated contraception in the unexpressed hope that another child may save a failing marriage. This, of course, is a dangerous and useless gambit, resulting only in bringing into the world a child who must bear the burden of failure to achieve for the parents what they could not achieve for themselves.

Requests for counseling on family planning problems may often give the physician the first opportunity of sensing deeper troubles in a marriage, particularly in the psychosexual area. Medical training has up to the present not included orientation in the very common sexual problems that are inevitably met in ordinary practice: impotence, premature ejaculation, infertility, frigidity—any of these may occur at any stage of marriage, or may recur, and inevitably constitute sources of severe marital stress. The partners happily wedded for many years, one of whom loses sexual desire earlier than the other, may grow apart just when their children are moving into adolescence and are most in need of a united family. Another couple may have had no pregnancies, or only one child, or a series of abortions, and the failure to achieve further successful pregnancies may cause tension and neurotic interplay between husband and wife. A woman very happy in her marital relationship even though not achieving full orgasmic response, may be so oversensitized by magazine articles and wifely gossip, that her concern over what she thinks she is missing may well threaten the stability of the union. These and many other complex factors may have little or nothing to do with the kind of contraceptive method to be prescribed, yet because they play a decisive role in the strength and continuity of the marriage relationship, they should be considered to lie within the broad meaning of the term "family planning."

As with all processes that deal with conflicts and changing attitudes in the human psyche, and particularly in the delicate and emotionally-charged psychosexual area, the physician whose patient approaches him with problems in this area must long before have come to comfortable terms with his own sexuality. This is a prerequisite that is not as easy to achieve as it sounds because of two reasons: (1) our social attitudes about sex are so unresolved and confused that human beings grow up with all sorts of resultant distortions in their sex knowledge and attitudes to which physicians are not magically immune,[1] and (2) the usual medical school curriculum makes little or no provision either for helping the medical student to resolve his own sexual problems, or for orienting and preparing him to meet the psychosexual problems of his future patients.[2] Indeed, emphasis in medical training is almost exclusively on the reproductive, as contrasted to the sexual, functions of the genital systems.[3]

If the physician—or, for that matter, the social worker, the nurse or the clergyman—has not pretty well succeeded in integrating sex into his own life pattern as a positive force, he may unconsciously under- or over-react to the sexual problems of his patients, perhaps out of anxiety over his own, and may thereby fail to help the troubled person, or may even compound an already complicated situation.

This does not, by any means, imply that every physician needs psychotherapy or marriage counseling. It does mean, however, that he must be sufficiently honest and courageous to face his own attitudes about sex, and realistically assay his readiness and capacity to help his patients with theirs. If he has any doubts about himself, the safest procedure to follow is referral.

One other problem area is the failure of couples to use contraception even though they openly desire no more children. It used to be thought that this was because the methods available were unacceptable, and indeed the advent of the oral contraceptives has proved that, given acceptable methods, many more people can accept contraceptive techniques. Nevertheless, studies[4, 5] indicate that the slips twixt the cup of desire to limit one's family and the lip of motivation strong enough to accomplish this desire, are many indeed. The need for continuing depth studies on motivations for successful contraception is very great.

SUMMARY

It may be difficult to disentangle and identify problems relating to contraception *per se* from problems having to do with disturbed psychosexual patterns and attitudes in one or both partners, or with neurotic interreaction between husband and wife. Rarely is contraception itself the basic problem, although it may be the presenting one.

The attitudes and orientation of the physician himself about human sexuality are important factors in successful counseling. Ethel Nash has summed it up well:

"Those who deal with patients in connection with their contraceptive needs will have much greater success if they give as much attention to the emotional and interpersonal aspects of the problem as they give to the technical and physiologic aspects. It is important to remember that in terms of its *rational* components, contraception with any method is actually a fairly simple matter. It is because people often have *feelings* and irrational attitudes that interfere with and disrupt good intentions, and because husbands and wives do not truly communicate and cooperate with each other as fully as they need to, that many couples have difficulty in limiting their families to the desired number. The physician or other family planning worker will have success with the highly motivated and well-controlled patient although he attends only to the technical aspects of the problem, but these are people who would probably get along without advice if they had to. Those who really need his help need him as counselor and understanding advisor as well as in the role of medical expert." [1]

REFERENCES

1. NASH, E. M.: Attitudes of physicians affecting contraceptive practice. In *Manual of Contraceptive Practice*, edited by M. S. Calderone. The Williams & Wilkins Company, Baltimore, 1964.

2. LIEF, H. I.: Orientation of future physicians in psychosexual attitudes. In *Manual of Contraceptive Practice*, edited by M. S. Calderone. The Williams & Wilkins Company, Baltimore, 1964.

3. CALDERONE, M. S.: Sexual energy—constructive or destructive? West. J. Surg., **71:** 272–277, 1963.

4. FREEDMAN, R., WHELPTON, P. K., AND CAMPBELL, A.: *Family Planning, Sterility and Population Growth*. McGraw-Hill Book Company, Inc., New York, 1959.

5. RAINWATER, L.: Attitudes of patients affecting contraceptive practice. In *Manual of Contraceptive Practice*, edited by M. S. Calderone. The Williams & Wilkins Company, Baltimore, 1964.

chapter twenty-four

The Overdominant Partner Problem

JOHN R. CRIST, Ph.D., *Department of Sociology, Denison University, Granville, Ohio*

Marriage counselors—or physicians serving as marriage counselors—frequently see the overdominant partner problem, sometimes referred to as "the aggressive-submissive constellation." Overdomination is frequently a form of aggression and is often manifested in hostile or destructive acts, usually the outgrowth of frustration or opposition. While the frustration or opposition may be occurring because of the present relationship with the spouse, it can also be related to past marital experiences or to problems with parents, siblings or others.

It should be noted, however, that domination by one spouse does not always imply hostile aggression or even necessarily indicate a marriage in difficulty. In some marriages, a dominant-submissive relationship is quite adequate, as it may satisfy complementary needs to be dominant or to be submissive. To disturb such an adjustment may in itself create trouble. This sometimes happens in the course of individual psychotherapy when a troubled spouse who is making considerable progress in working through his own neurotic state will then come into open conflict with the spouse who had previously been adjusted to him the way he was.

Then too, there are other normal marriages involving a dominant and a submissive personality which are adequately stable and satisfying to the partners. An example would be one in which both husband and wife were conditioned to believe that it is right and proper for the man to be the boss, and the wife accepts this. In this type of marriage the role expectations of both marriage partners are satisfactorily met.

The major problems concerning the overdominant partner arise when the dominant-submissive pattern is in conflict with, instead of in accord with, the role expectations of the partners. If, for example, the husband considers it his prerogative to play the dominant role and thinks that the wife should be submissive, while the wife feels an equalitarian role should be played by both, some trouble is inevitable for, by the wife's definition, her husband would be overdominant.

Perhaps there is an even greater overdomination problem when the wife wishes to be dominant and her husband refuses to play a passive role. And there is also a difficult situation when the wife feels forced into a position of dominance she really doesn't wish to play by an oversubmissive husband who insists on making her the boss.

All of these problems are amplified by the fact that our social norms have been in a state of flux, and this has led to anxiety, uncertainty and confusion over what kind of relationship is proper in marriage today. In this situation, occasionally one partner or the other has stepped in to fill the vacuum caused by a lack of social definition, and almost immediately the other accuses him of overdomination. Since this overdomination is perceived as a form of aggression and hostility, the mate often gives aggression and hostility in return.

Often these reactions to an overdominant mate are learned in the childhood home. The patient may have experienced a great deal of frustration and anxiety in relation to an overdominant parent, and he attempts to use the earlier learned behavior pattern in his relationship with his spouse, in an effort to relieve his feelings of guilt, frustration and anxiety. Actually, the objective behavior of the spouse accused of overdomination may provide no rational justifiable basis for the aggressive reaction. The latter can be explained as a kind of transference response, generalized from the earlier childhood situation where it was learned.

We can see, therefore, that the overdominance problem can be related to several factors:

1. Disagreements and misunderstandings regarding role expectations of dominance—who is boss in the family or who should "wear the pants."

2. The confusion on the part of the persons concerning the roles that they should be playing. Women are particularly caught in this dilemma in an era of changing roles of women.

3. The meaning of this domination or submission to each of the persons involved. The "facts" of domination or submission have little meaning or significance in themselves.[1] The significant element is how we perceive these "facts" and thereby arrive at our concept of reality. The only reality for the individual is that based upon his own unique experience and background.

4. Deep-seated emotional psychologic disturbances involving one or all of the above and others. In these cases the physician will probably wish to refer the patient to a psychotherapist for intensive treatment.

In this chapter we shall concern ourselves with the relatively normal couple in relation to whom we may find one of the following situations:

1. The husband is overdominant or perceived to be so by his wife.

2. The wife is overdominant or thought to be so by the husband.

3. Either spouse is oversubmissive or considered so by the partner.

Counseling with the Overdominant Husband

If the physician does not already have an intimate firsthand knowledge of the patient's parental family experience, he should get as much of this as possible in a case history report. This can help the physician counselor to understand more clearly the reasons for the difficulty and can be used to help the couple convey to one another their own expectations and needs. Since collecting such information is time-consuming, there are certain aids which the physician can use which can be administered by the nurse or receptionist. Examples of these are "Form M—Marriage Role Expectation Inventory" by Marie S. Dunn, "Marriage Adjustment Form" by Ernest W. Burgess and "Background Schedule" and "Marriage Adjustment Schedules, 1-A and 1-B" from the Marriage Council of Philadelphia.* The usefulness of such aids (and this is all they should be considered, as nothing can take the place of the personal relationship with the patient) is, of course, enhanced when one has the results from both husband and wife to compare. With this background material, the physician counselor is in a better position to help his patient more readily face the difficulties and seek solutions.

As an example, the husband may have grown up in a family where the father was the undisputed head of the household. He made the major decisions in the family; his word was law. The mother in the parental family also came from a region where this was the normal pattern for marriage. Thus, our patient is very upset when he finds his wife, who grew up in a more equalitarian family, cannot accept his "demanding, hostile and aggressive behavior." The husband must be helped to see that his wife's "rebellion," her "cold attitude," her "refusal of sex," her "clamming up" and the like are not necessarily attacks upon him, but may be her efforts to deal with her own frustrations and anxieties upon finding herself in what she considers an intolerable situation. The husband can, therefore, be helped to understand why he and his wife reacted as they did, and how they are failing to fulfill the needs of the other. He must be helped to see:

1. How his expectations may not be entirely acceptable and appropriate to the contemporary emancipated woman.

2. That he must learn to listen and try to understand his wife's feelings and needs.

3. That he should try to lessen his need to defend himself by argumentation, but should rather try to understand his spouse.

4. That discussion of basic issues should take place at times other than those when points of tension have arisen.

* The Dunn and Burgess forms may be obtained from Family Life Publications, Inc., Box 6725, Duke Station, Durham, North Carolina. The "Background Schedule" and "Marriage Adjustment Schedules, 1-A and 1-B" may be obtained from the Marriage Council of Philadelphia, Inc., 3828 Locust Street, Philadelphia 4, Pennsylvania.

5. That many hostile words and actions are attempts to cover up one's own inadequacy and to relieve anxiety and guilt feelings, and, if so understood, they can be more readily accepted for what they are with less need to strike back with more hostility.

6. That to face the issue of whether he has any responsibility in the difficulty will help him see what he can do about it.

7. That his expectations may have been appropriate for his grandparents or even his own parents but that they are not necessarily appropriate with his own spouse.

8. That he can not change his spouse; that he must learn to accept her as she is; that only by doing this will she be free to bring about any change on her part, if it is possible or advisable for her to change; that without this acceptance, her time and energy are spent in fighting him and not in further growth and development on her own part.

9. That contemporary women in our changing society are often confused about what is expected of them as a wife, mother or career woman, and that a great deal of patience and understanding is needed in helping them find their place in the contemporary world.

10. That in those cases where he may be overdominant in an effort to relieve his own feelings of inadequacy, he may find more constructive ways to deal with his inadequacies and recognize and accept his strengths. (In such cases the physician should let the patient know that he has real strengths and assets which can give him the courage to tackle his problems.)

11. That mood swings are associated with the menstrual cycle for many women. Even "educated" men need this reminder.

12. That he should try to be less demanding, especially in the sexual area, and to understand that women generally find it more difficult to go from discord to sexual expression in the same evening, and to learn to express feelings of affection without necessarily expecting sexual relations.

Through all of these, the counselor should be helping the patient to see alternative courses of action and to choose for himself those which he feels he can most honestly accept and implement. It is generally not best to tell the patient what to do, but rather to help him in making a wise choice which he feels is his own and that he can implement and act upon.

Counseling with the Overdominant Wife

Most of the points made under the previous section for counseling overdominant men are equally relevant for counseling overdominant women, and there is no need to repeat them. There are a few things that should be pointed out, however, in counseling such women:

1. They should be helped to know that most men are more oriented toward the traditional male authoritarian pattern than are women.

2. They should realize that many men find it too much of a threat to the "masculine ego" to accept wholly even an equalitarian role, much less a submissive role, even though these same men may have *some* need for "mothering."

3. That some women suffer from "masculine protest" and have difficulty in accepting their own sex and sexuality. This lack of acceptance is the cause of the anxiety which, in turn, causes her need to overdominate her husband. Such women can be helped to see this and accept their position in life as women, wives and mothers.

4. In their desperation and need to dominate and control, some women use love and sex as weapons against their husbands by withholding, being too tired or passively submitting, which can be terribly devastating to the male ego.

After having helped the woman patient to recognize some of the above factors, if they are involved, the counselor is in a better position to help her take specific action to improve the relationship. For example, under number four above, the counselor might ask her whether she does have any love for her husband and, if she responds in the affirmative, she might be asked to suggest ways she feels that she could express this more directly to him.

Counseling with the Submissive Spouse

Just as in the case with the overly dominant partner, the overly submissive partner usually has a great deal of hostility and aggression. Instead of striking out against his opponent, he withdraws and turns his hostility and aggression inward. This does not mean, however, that he does not desire to hurt others, for his submission is often designed to do just that. It may be his way of fighting an overly aggressive spouse or it may be related to his own feelings of insecurity and inadequacy. In the case of the former, the counselor might gently get him to talk about why he is afraid to face unpleasant situations directly. His reasons may well be related to unpleasant memories of an earlier home environment. The counselor can help him to face this and to take more appropriate action.

If the submissiveness is related more directly to feelings of inadequacy rather than to spouse antagonism, the counselor, by a supportive relationship, can help the patient to build a more adequate ego concept and to recognize and accept his own value and worth. If, on the other hand, the submissive pattern is more related to inability to accept responsibility, the patient must be helped to see this and to take increasing responsibility a step at a time. The physician-counselor should remember that the patient's partner will often need help, too, in understanding and encouraging the patient.

Finally, it must be made very clear to each partner that a failure on the part of the spouse to carry through on agreements or plans of action which they may have devised does not necessarily mean dishonesty or "you did not mean what you said." What we understand and agree to intellectually, we may not be able to accept fully or act upon emotionally. It is therefore usually best for the counselor to discourage the making of large numbers of specific agreements or commitments. It is enough, usually, that the person will honestly do his best to improve his relationships and to understand and accept his spouse. This is in itself a large and difficult enough task.

A CASE ILLUSTRATION

To sharpen some of the concepts which have been discussed, a case illustration is appropriate. The following case excerpts are from an earlier paper on counseling an overdominance problem.[2]

Mr. and Mrs. Jenkins, 33 and 34 years of age, respectively, had been married for 14 years and had three children, ages 12, 8 and 6. She was employed as a clerk and he as a skilled workman. The Jenkins sought counseling on the advice of her attorney after she had filed suit for a divorce.

Mrs. Jenkins' complaints were that her husband was oversexed, moody, quarrelsome, took sides with his mother against her and controlled the money. She came for 11 counseling sessions.

Mr. Jenkins complained that his wife had been too interested in another man, that she made unfair statements about his mother and could not manage money. He came for a total of six interviews.

Mrs. Jenkins exhibited a considerable display of emotions and an ability to express her feelings in the counseling sessions. In contrast, Mr. Jenkins was withdrawn and found it more difficult to express both emotions of resentment and hostility and those of elation. He expressed his resentments about the domination and control of his wife and mother by his passivity and submission. Mrs. Jenkins, on the other hand, expressed her hostility and resentment toward her husband by attempted domination and the withholding of love, affection and sex. Both seemed to be motivated to attempt an improvement in their relationship.

Excerpts from Some Counseling Sessions

Mrs. Jenkins stated, "My husband feels inferior and jealous, and I think he has no reason to feel this." She finally came to face the fact that she contributed to these feelings. When the counselor inquired as to why her husband might feel inferior to her, she said, "I would like to know myself." After unsuccessfully trying to get the counselor to answer the question, she replied, "I wonder sometimes if I make him feel inferior, because usually, when we go places, I am the one who does all the talking, and I plan everything. I have always tried not to hurt his feelings, and to take care of him." After considerable exploration, Mrs. Jenkins concluded, "Well, maybe I have tried to run things too much." She posed the question of whether she should try to protect her husband, and push him into things which she thought he ought to be doing. The counselor reminded her that she had indicated in a previous interview that she felt she was trying to control things too much. "Might this have any bearing on your question?"

She then posed the question of whether all women wanted to change their husbands, and, after some deliberation, concluded that she did want to change him.

Mrs. Jenkins related many incidents expressing deep resentment and hostility toward her husband in their everyday relationships and the feelings of guilt about her actions. For example, she and the children did not wait for him for dinner one evening when he was late. She put the food away and let him find something to eat for himself when he returned. The story was told to the counselor in a very hostile and defensive way, with the complaint that if her husband cared for her, he could at least call her up. She at first rationalized her actions as justifiable, but after some exploration admitted that she really wanted to punish or hurt him. She would then show her guilt and anger over doing this by crying and pointing out that she knew that this was not the Christian way of living.

By a slow and arduous process she came to realize that she was deeply hurt by his earlier affair and that "I have really never forgiven him." The counselor was never condemning of her actions and constantly encouraged her to explore the meaning, motivations and results of actions. She gradually came to see that out of her desire to punish her husband and the fear of being hurt again she was rejecting him and withholding her love and that this in turn contributed to his moodiness, jealousy and "excessive" sexual demands. With this new insight she was able to be more affectionate, to express feelings of love toward her husband and even on occasion to initiate sexual relations.

In a defensive and hostile way, Mrs. Jenkins related their financial difficulties in terms of her husband's inability to understand how much it took to keep a family going, his control of the money and complaints about food and clothing bills. When the counselor inquired why she was so defensive about this, she began to cry and said that the psychiatrist had asked her why she was so defensive about everything. She said she really did not know, and this bothered her. Gradually, she came to the conclusion that some of her defensiveness was due to: (1) her inability to forgive her husband for his earlier affair, and (2) her desire to control him. In a later interview when the matter of finances arose, she reported that she was feeling much better about herself and her husband and that the matter of finances had not recently bothered her so much. This last is an excellent example of the idea that the facts of the relationship are not as important as how the couple feels about them.

In working through his sexual problems, Mr. Jenkins first asserted that he was not oversexed and that "sex once a day is not too much." As the counseling proceeded, he came to see that some of his demands grew out of his own insecurity with his wife, and that as he became more secure in his relationship with her, he had less need to make sexual demands. He also found that his wife's resistance to affection decreased as he was able to express affection without demanding coitus. Mr. Jenkins was able to gain new insights regarding his attachment to his mother and its effect upon his wife, and in so doing was able to establish more positive attitudes and actions toward her.

It should be noted here that the goals in the above counseling situation were limited. While ideally the couple, and particularly Mrs. Jenkins, might well have benefited from some more intensive psychotherapy aimed at their personal difficulties, their previous disappointment with other therapy and their present desires and circumstances limited how far it was possible to go at this time.

In this case the following objectives were realized: (1) good rapport was established with both husband and wife, (2) a marked reduction of hostility was achieved, (3) greater objectivity and insight were developed, (4) the couple was reoriented toward their roles in the relationship, (5) some new objectives were outlined, and (6) a new pattern of relationship in conflicting situations was developed.

While this much improvement may not be manifested in every case, these are reasonable aspirations for good marriage counseling with many partners.

REFERENCES

1. MOUSTAKAS, C. (Editor): *The Self*, Ch. 1. Harper & Brothers, New York, 1956.
2. CRIST, J. R.: Marriage counseling involving a passive husband and an aggressive wife. Marriage and Family Living, **20:** 121–126, 1958.

chapter twenty-five

Counseling in Infertility Problems

A. LAWRENCE BANKS, M.D., *Department of Obstetrics and Gynecology, University of Washington School of Medicine, Seattle, Washington*

The inability of married couples to have their own children usually produces a strain on a marital relationship. This may be attributed to the generally held premise in our society that a marriage is not really fulfilled until a couple has its own children.

Friends, relatives and neighborhood acquaintances are usually the first ones to wonder among themselves why the wife of the childless couple has not had a baby. A short time after this wondering begins, the bludgeon-like hints concerning the wonderful experience of having a new baby in the home descend upon the wife in an ever-increasing crescendo. She begins to worry, as did Rachel, why her womb is barren. She talks over these pressures with her husband and soon what has been a relaxed expectancy of eventual pregnancy becomes a source of tension and frustration. The arrival of each menstrual period builds more anxiety. The love, tenderness and affection in the marriage relationship threatens to give way to an obsessive drive for reproduction. It is understandable that this couple will soon seek the guidance of a physician who, by past performance, has shown an interest in and an understanding of the infertile couple.

THE INITIAL INTERVIEW

The physician's initial interview with the infertile couple is extremely important. He should be prepared to listen in a completely objective manner and to avoid imposing his values on the infertile couple. For, while many of those marriage partners who come to him will genuinely want him to use all his professional skill in helping them to have a child, there will be some couples in which only one partner has a real desire for pregnancy; there will be others in which neither partner really wants a child right now, but both have been pressured into feeling they ought to. All of these couples will initially need the physician's counseling help as much as —if not more than—his pills and prescriptions.

It is not uncommon to find during the initial interview that the wife is eager while the husband is, at best, lukewarm. Often the woman has assumed ever since she was a little girl that some time after marriage she would surely experience motherhood. If she does not easily have children her firmly entrenched expectation of emotional fulfillment is threatened. In many instances, this proves so disturbing that she forgets her role as a wife. She becomes thoroughly preoccupied with the desire for a child and may perceive her husband to be only a necessary cog in the role of procreation.

Ordinarily, the male in such a marriage is puzzled and hurt by his wife's seeming lack of attention to his needs. But usually he is willing to do anything to help her gain the fulfillment she seeks, even though, characteristically, he less often equates children with fulfillment in marriage, and even though he is half afraid that if there is a child he may lose even more of his wife's attention.

With such a couple as this, the physician's first task is to help the partners to evaluate their respective needs and goals and to arrive at some common understanding and purpose. Hopefully, with skillful handling by the physician and a few genuine insights on the part of the partners, in a relatively short time the wife may attain a more relaxed attitude toward her need for motherhood and the husband may no longer feel so threatened and neglected because of his wife's desire for a child.

There will however, be other cases in which previously well-adjusted couples have, by social pressures, been made anxious about their failure to have children even though neither one of them basically is ready for parenthood. Here, particularly, the physician-counselor will need to beware of allowing his own values to direct the course of the initial interview. There are, after all, a large number of couples who are completely happy and satisfied with the companionship and love afforded by their marriage, even though they are childless. It may be better for such couples to maintain their happy marriage without children than to risk an unhappy one with them. Perhaps the physician can best serve the marriage partners in this case by helping them to reinforce their conviction that it is better not to have children until they are really ready.

Explaining the Procedures

Once the physician is sure that there is mutual eagerness for solving an infertility problem, the next step is to help the partners to understand completely what is, or may be, involved. It should be impressed upon them that a complete sterility survey with professional supervision for at least a year following the survey is usually necessary. In addition, it is important for the couple to realize that the reasons for infertility can be equally shared between husband and wife and, therefore, it is imperative that both undergo a complete evaluation. The reproductive physiology should be explained in order to provide the couple with some insights into the physiologic and possible psychologic implications of their problem. The need for, and value of, a complete physical examination for each partner should be explained in such a fashion that they will realize the importance of overall physical well-being in the process of reproduction.

The need for a sperm study and the proper significance of motility, normal forms, number and survival time of the sperm can also be explained at the time of the initial visit. Such an approach can help to assure the husband's later cooperation.

The value of and need for such a careful evaluation of the infertile couple is implict in the eight factors for grading the partners proposed by Dr. Fred Simmons* at the Tenth Annual Conference of the American Society for the Study of Sterility in 1954. He proposed that couples be graded as to:

1. Peritoneal Factor	5. Ovarian Factor
2. Cervical Factor	6. Male Factor
3. Tubal Factor	7. Metabolic Factor
4. Uterine Factor	8. Psychologic Factor

His feeling was that if three or more factors were found against the couple, a successful conception was most unlikely. The ultimate validity of this proposal has yet to be established but meanwhile it serves as a convenient and thorough check-list.

While the need for culdoscopy may not arise in every case, there is no better time than the first interview to suggest its potential value if such a need should later occur.

The value of psychometric tests, whether carried out by the physician or by an associated psychologist, should be brought to the patient's attention. Such tests are often helpful in uncovering hidden tensions, motivations for desiring a child and personal and marital problems, including those involving sexual attitudes. In the experience of the writer, these tests have constituted a revealing and rewarding type of investigation and often help to explain the etiology of a particular case of functional infertility.

Most experienced physicians have seen the infertile marriage partners who have traveled from doctor to doctor. Usually they have received less than a complete evaluation but they have been told, without adequate

* "Analysis of Failure of Conception in One Hundred Completely Studied Infertile Couples," presented at the Tenth Annual Conference of the American Society for the Study of Sterility, June, 1954.

evaluation, either that there is no reason for infertility or that the situation is hopeless. This leads to tremendous marital confusion, increased tension and, unfortunately, a loss of confidence in the medical profession. It would be hard to overstress the importance of a *thorough* infertility examination and a considered, judicious and valid diagnosis.

Elsewhere, the writer has reported on the Accelerated Fertility-Study Plan,[1] which should take no longer than three months. Upon completion of the infertility survey, the couple should again be interviewed so that any factors—physiologic and/or psychologic—contributing to their problem can be explained to them. Therapy can then be undertaken.

MEDICAL TREATMENT

The physiologic problems usually lend themselves to a definitive approach. The correction of a Stein-Leventhal syndrome, closed tubes, abnormal uterus, hydrocele and so forth are well covered in the existing literature and need no comment here. I have found a few additional measures to be of considerable help in the correction of infertility, though they are infrequently written about:

1. The use of special formula multivitamin capsules (Hep-Forte for our patients), three daily, tends to increase the sperm count in the male and, even more important, may increase his general body vigor which in turn tends to increase his sexual desire and so the number of exposures to pregnancy.

2. The use of liothyronine in dosages varying from 50 to 150 mg. daily for the male sometimes produces a marked increase in sperm motility. This has been discussed both pro and con, but is recommended here without reservation.

3. The empirical use of thyroid for the infertile wife has, in my experience, appeared to be of real value in increasing fertility.

4. Newly developed pharmaceuticals not currently available, such as Clomophene, show some promise in stimulating ovulation in previously anovulatory women. Their experimental progress should be carefully watched in the medical journals.

PSYCHOGENIC FACTORS IN INFERTILITY

It is now widely believed that in many cases of infertility, psychogenic factors such as tensions and anxiety, are primarily causative. Many authorities feel that uterine irritability, tubal spasm and blockage, insufficient endometrium, and alteration of the specific chemical and physical properties of the secretions in contact with the sperm and the ovum, all take place as a result of disturbed emotional states in the woman. As evidence for the spasm and blockage they point to such similiar emotional effects resulting in bronchial, gastrointestinal and bladder spasm. As evidence for the chemical changes, they point to modifications of the salivary and gastric secretions as a result of anxiety.

Such psychogenic infertility presents many treatment problems. There is a growing psychiatric literature reporting success in psychotherapy with infertile women, but statistical validation by carefully controlled studies is notably lacking. Furthermore, while the tensions believed to be the cause of infertility in some women are in the class of deep-seated hostilities and phobias which respond well to depth psychotherapies, in other women these tensions are more often chronic worries, rigidities and overconscientiousness which appear to offer the psychopathologist inadequate challenge for his techniques.

Not infrequently, however, the physician serving as counselor can have a therapeutic role himself. In some cases, the infertility-causing tensions are generated in response to an unhappy marriage relationship situation, and marriage counseling techniques, so thoroughly discussed in other chapters of this book, are the treatment of choice. Here there is a double benefit potential—a more happy, loving, relaxed marital relationship—in addition to a baby. So even if pregnancy is not achieved, the couple is often helped.

In other cases where the marriage is not the problem, simple support and reassurance from the physician-counselor may provide enough tension reduction within the individual woman to allow conception to take place. Walser[2] quotes Pratt as believing that even such simple reassurance as telling some psychogenically infertile patients that "Nothing is wrong in any way, so now all you need to do is go on home and get pregnant," has helped to bring on pregnancy in individuals whose tension might have been worry over pregnancy. To this Kroger and Freed add a classic understatement: "Obviously, refractory cases require more intense therapy."[3]

In addition to individual counseling, there are two other sometimes-overlooked possibilities for treating the suspected psychogenically infertile couple. The first involves the use of one of the recent psychopharmaceuticals. A study was carried out in the fertility clinic with which the writer is associated using a group of 66 infertile couples presenting no definite or obviously correctable fertility defects. Initially, the wives were placed on 100 mg of Nialamide daily for three months. If no pregnancy resulted, then both the husband and the wife were medicated in the same manner. It was noted that the majority of the patients realized a decided improvement in mood, as well as an increase in libido. During Nialamide therapy, 30 patients conceived. Twenty-six healthy children were delivered, and four of the pregnancies terminated in miscarriage. There seemed to be a correlation between the use of the antidepressant drug Nialamide and the ability of these previously infertile couples to reproduce. The inclusion of the male partner in this therapy produced two dramatic effects: (1) there were more pregnancies, and (2) the marriages were reported to be more satisfactory to both partners.[4]

The second possibility for treating the psychogenically infertile couple involves group counseling. The value of group therapy for the infertile couple has been considered only by a minimal number of those physicians engaged in the care of these patients. This is to be regretted. The childless partners are continually being pressured by their more fertile associates. It is extremely reassuring for them to be given an opportunity to associate with others sharing their problem, especially in the presence of a positive figure, the physician-counselor, who is striving to solve their problem.

I have found that such group sessions can be effectively started by showing a color film produced by our clinic with the cooperation of our infertile patients. This film demonstrates all of the steps carried out in an infertility survey and terminates in the obstetric suite of the hospital, picturing a happy young couple with their newborn infant. This permits the wife to see the procedures her husband undergoes and helps the husband to understand the procedures in which his wife participates. The film is always followed by group discussion.

In these sessions the doctor often learns more than does the patient. The infertile couples are usually the most apprehensive and confused patients in any practice; therefore, anything that can be done to produce empathy and confidence will be productive—not only in pregnancies, but in better marriage and better individual emotional health as well.

But one other suggestion made to the psychogenically infertile couple should be discussed here. Such couples are sometimes advised that if they adopt a child they will probably soon thereafter become pregnant. Several studies, including two by the writer,[5, 6] have shown that the adoption of a baby has absolutely no effect on infertility. The number of pregnancies occurring after adoption is no greater than chance. Old beliefs die hard.

There are two courses open to those married women who after all possible measures have been taken still cannot reproduce with their husbands. It is possible for married couples to adopt children through an adoption agency and/or a private physician. In carefully selected circumstances where the husband has proven to be irrevocably infertile and the wife has proven to be fertile, the sperm of another male may be used for artificial insemination. The couple thus has a choice; in the first instance, the child will be foreign to both. In the second, the child will be foreign only to the husband.

Prior to accepting either of these alternatives, the childless couple should again be carefully evaluated not only as to their fitness to be adopting parents as is customary, but also as to their attitudes about adoption or insemination. Often a psychologist can be helpful in the evaluation. But ultimately it is the physician-counselor, who by now knows the couple well, who can best help the partners to make the decision which will bring each of them the most happiness.

Those of us who treat infertile couples know what a severe strain this condition often places upon marital harmony. Not all infertility patients can achieve pregnancy, but for those who do, a marriage threatened because of the infertility once again becomes solid and satisfying. For those patients who must finally be labeled sterile, the physician and psychologist should make every available effort through adoption,[7] semiadoption or counseling aimed at adjustment to a marriage that can be happy though childless.

REFERENCES

1. RUTHERFORD, R. N., BANKS, A. L., AND COBURN, W. A.: An accelerated fertility-study plan. Fertil. & Steril., **14:** 13–20, 1963.
2. WALSER, H. C.: Fear, an important etiological factor in obstetric problems. Am. J. Obst. & Gynec., **55:** 801, 1948.
3. KROGER, W. S., AND FREED, S. C.: *Psychosomatic Gynecology*. The Free Press of Glencoe, Illinois, 1956.
4. BANKS, A. L., RUTHERFORD, R. N., AND COBURN, W. A.: A new medication for the psychogenically infertile couple. West. J. Surg., **71:** 9–11, 1963.
5. BANKS, A. L.: Does adoption affect infertility? Internat. J. Fertil., **7:** 23–28, 1962.
6. BANKS, A. L., RUTHERFORD, R. N., AND COBURN, W. A.: Fertility following adoption: report of 31 cases. Fertil. & Steril., **12:** 438–442, 1961.
7. RUTHERFORD, R. N., AND BANKS, A. L.: Semiadoption technics and results. Fertil. & Steril., **5:** 271–281, 1954.

chapter twenty-six

Legal Help in Marital Problems

LUVERN V. RIEKE, LL.B., LL.M., LL.D., *University of Washington School of Law, Seattle, Washington*

The general function of law in marital disputes, as well as elsewhere, is to create and maintain an environment within which individuals may work out solutions to their conflicting interests. The specific contributions of law with respect to this general function may be considered under four separate headings:

1. There are occasions when the physical or economic interests of one spouse are threatened and legal protection must be sought.

2. Situations often arise in which the validity, indeed the very existence, of the legal status is questioned and clarification becomes mandatory.

3. Various stresses may cause spouses to seek some means of living apart from each other, enjoying some incidents of the consortium package and avoiding others, without complete termination of the marital status.

4. Finally, there is the possibility of terminating the status and, by what is essentially a liquidation proceeding, making the best adjustment possible because of the conflicting demands.

In any of these instances, as is illustrated below, there are two things to be remembered. The first is that while legal technique will be useful in clarifying or giving stability and direction to a situation, law cannot change the individual. That is the function of the physician, psychologist, clergyman or other professional in the helping sciences. The lawyer works with that portion of the social environment composed of the legally controlled relationship between one individual and another or between an individual and some group of individuals such as government. The lawyer treats a situation, not a patient.

The second important point to remember is this: since the residents of various jurisdictions, by legislation, adjust the applicable law as they deem best for their own needs, there is no uniform set of rules which govern the details of domestic relations for the entire nation. Indeed, the law of a single state is often flexible, leaving many items to the discretion of the

246

judge who hears the case. It is possible, however, to identify the types of situations in which persons experiencing marital problems need the assistance of a lawyer.

PHYSICAL AND ECONOMIC PROTECTION FOR THE THREATENED SPOUSE

One of the common problems facing the marriage counselor—or the physician serving in the role of marriage counselor—is what can be done to restrain the irrational or intoxicated spouse who is bent upon inflicting abuse. The first course of action is generally for the threatened person to call the police.

But family fights are common and, simply because of volume, the police cannot intervene in every exchange of hostile words or blows. Nor is the police officer eager to expose himself to the risk of subsequent actions for false arrest, assault or trespass brought by spouses who prefer to battle without interference from outsiders. Police policy in many areas provides for intervention only in cases where there is a threat of immediate and serious physical violence. The spouse who needs more than stopgap emergency protection must procure a court order as a basis for obtaining police cooperation in the event of threatened disobedience by the party enjoined.

An order of court—whether called an injunction, restraining order or any other name—is not self-executing. It will not alone restrain the abusive spouse. The value of the order lies in the fact that police protection is more readily obtainable after a restraining order has been issued.

But it should be observed that our legal traditions are essentially those of freedom. A court is reluctant to interfere in the routine intrafamily determinations of a married couple. As long as the marriage continues, the partners are accorded considerable leeway in most personal matters— including family fights.

Only in rare instances will any long-term legal coercion be available to control a personal (*i.e.*, noneconomic) aspect of the marriage relationship. A few courts have exercised equitable powers to enjoin a spouse and a third person from engaging in conduct which is obviously incompatible with the integrity of an existing marriage.

There are cases on record in which courts have issued restraining orders prohibiting an abusive spouse from entering the apartment where his wife has sought refuge, from beating his stepchild and from seeing another woman with whom he has been known to be unfaithful.

But such attempts at control by injunction are usually thought unenforceable, impractical and, from a legal view, not desirable. Aside from occasional exceptions of the nature indicated above, orders directed toward regulation of personal aspects of a marriage will normally be issued only in conjunction with other, more traditional, legal proceedings.

This simply means that a spouse who desires physical protection on a continuing basis must also be willing to seek a decree of nullity, annulment, separate maintenance, in some instances a proceeding in a family court or divorce. The petition for such relief will indicate to the court that the couple are no longer able to control their own relationship and must accept discipline from society through a formal, judicial action. The restraining order, typically available as soon as the basic action is initiated, is entered *pendente lite* or "pending the litigation" of the underlying causes of action. Such temporary orders will be terminated, continued or modified at the time the basic action is decided.

The situation is significantly different when economic interests of a spouse are threatened. In most of the western world, and almost without exception among the United States, a woman may own property in her own right and may take appropriate action to protect her interests. Constitutional amendments and extensive legislation during the past century have given married women equality with their husbands in most matters. There are marked differences in local procedures, however, especially between jurisdictions which have the so-called "common law" and those having "community property" provisions regulating marital property interests.

It is, perhaps, remarkable that the emancipation of the property of married women from the control of the husband has not been accompanied by the elimination of the correlative obligation of the husband to support the wife. That this has not occurred is obvious, however, and there is currently available to the wife a broad choice of legal maneuvers designed to enforce the support obligation both during continuance of the marriage and after some formal separation or termination has occurred.

Virtually any court determination related to marital status may be accompanied by orders for support or for the division of property. The nature of these decrees is discussed below. The significant point here is that *a wife may obtain legal assistance in compelling the husband to furnish support during the continuation of the marriage.* Wilful failure to support is criminal conduct in many jurisdictions.

Several quasi-criminal enforcement devices have been developed to help the wife to obtain the support due her. Creditors who furnish necessary goods or services to the wife usually have an action against the husband, either pursuant to "family expense" statutes or under a restitutionary theory independent of legislation. In this connection it is often important to distinguish between the relatively narrow class of "necessaries" and the broader classification of "family expenses." The former indicates food, shelter, clothing, medical care and so on, at a basic level, while the latter often denotes many more amenities of life, limited of course by the test of reasonableness in all instances.

In many jurisdictions the wife also has an action to recover from the defaulting husband some contribution toward *any* expenditures she has made in providing for the family. Some jurisdictions have statutory provision for this type of reimbursement. Recovery may range from the entire amount spent to some much smaller portion. The specific facts and the local law are, of course, determinative.

Most significant among recent legislative developments is the Uniform Reciprocal Enforcement of Support Act. This act, or legislation similar enough in form so that genuine reciprocity is feasible, has been adopted by all states and territories of the United States. This reciprocal legislation enables a wife to obtain the concurrent assistance of courts in both her jurisdiction and the jurisdiction in which her defaulting husband is then residing, for the enforcement of family obligations. This multistate proceeding may be used before, after or in conjunction with other traditional marital actions.

An additional factor of considerable importance should be noted here. Spouses may contract with each other. The contract may be used to facilitate temporary, or continued, living apart. So long as fairly negotiated and not in violation of public policy, the separation agreement, separate property agreement or separate maintenance contract (or indeed all of these taken together) may control, *inter se*, extensive portions of the marital relation. The preparation of such a contract is technical work, very beneficial when done well and equally damaging when mishandled.

These agreements are of far greater significance than normally is recognized. Even custody rights may be put in doubt by provision of contract in some states. A husband living apart from his wife often needs the practical protection of contract as a defense against the possible subsequent assertion of abandonment.

Although contracts are normally subject to modification in connection with subsequent marital litigation, this is not always the case. A death, following contractual separation but before court action, may make modification impossible. Contractual obligation may arise quite informally, sometimes with unforeseen and unfortunate results.

Spouses who contemplate living apart for any reason should be encouraged to obtain legal assistance promptly, before the actual separation when possible.

When a marriage problem is brought to the counselor, the need for protection must be appraised carefully. Does the threatened spouse need physical, economic or both forms of protection? How long will the need continue? Is the rift in the marital relation already so severe that legal coercive action will not produce further alienation? Is the case one in which forthright, authoritative evidence of continuing legal obligations will help promote reconciliation? Protection, physical and economic, is available. These are not panaceas. The contribution of the law is to stabilize the situation while a correction is sought for the causes of the difficulty.

Testing the Validity of the Marriage

As a legal institution, marriage is both contract and status. It differs significantly from routine contract because of the tremendous social significance of the family. Courts have frequently suggested that marriage is a three-sided contract, the third party being the state or other governing body. Contract requires mutual assent and, if the state is viewed as a party, it must assent as well as the spouses. Marriages of questionable validity are almost always cases posing an assent problem. The problem may take various forms, such as total absence of assent, attempts to marry without the assent of the state or assent which is defective because it was procured by force, fraud or coercion.

In common parlance the term annulment is used to indicate the court's disposition of both void and voidable marriages. This is unfortunate because the two situations have important distinctions. These distinctions, to put them in terms of practical consequences, pertain to the grounds upon which the relation may be questioned, when and who may raise the question, and the relief which will follow a determination of "void" rather than "voidable."

The grounds for a decree of nullity or, to put in another way, the facts which show that an alleged marriage is void, will normally be a total lack of capacity. A person lacks capacity to marry because of consanguinity (the prohibited degree of blood relationships being variously defined by the states), lack of sufficient age or the existence of a prior marriage which has not been terminated. Some jurisdictions describe additional grounds, insanity or marriage-in-jest are common examples, for a void marriage. The remedy for a void relationship is properly a simple declaration that a marriage never existed—a decree of nullity.

Grounds for an annulment, by comparison, relate to impaired capacity and defective assent rather than no capacity and no assent. Most frequently, the ground is fraud, a term deceptive in its seeming simplicity. Fraud must go "to the essence" of the relation. In some states this is construed so narrowly that only misrepresentation concerning ability and willingness to engage in sexual intercourse are included. Other jurisdictions range broadly over statements relating to age, wealth, social standing or other factors inducing consent. Other grounds relate to limited mentality or age, duress and health. A marriage contracted under such circumstances has legal existence until, and unless, a decree is entered to obliterate the status. The annulment of a voidable marriage acts as an eraser—the legal effect, historically, being to wipe out the marriage *ab initio*, as if it had never existed. To this extent the ultimate consequence of the decree of nullity and the annulment are much the same.

The process of obtaining one decree or the other poses important variations. In many jurisdictions only the spouse under the disability or who was defrauded, coerced or tricked, can sue for annulment. Other states permit such action to be brought by the parent or guardian of the "injured" spouse, but other strangers almost never have standing to sue. By way of contrast, petition for a declaration of nullity may be sought by anyone who has an interest impinged upon by the alleged marital status. Further, the suit for annulment must be brought while both spouses are alive. The theory is that the proceeding is to change the status, and the marital status of a surviving spouse cannot be changed. The decree of nullity, which simply states a fact and changes no status, may be entered even after a death has occurred. Even more significantly, a voidable relation may be "ratified" by the injured party and thereafter not voidable while most jurisdictions hold a void marriage to be incapable of ratification.

The procedural distinctions above, and others not necessary to mention here, constitute the major reasons why one must distinguish suits for annulment from those for a decree of nullity. Historically, either decree, after entry, had dramatic consequences. This was especially true with respect to children born to a voidable marriage. Entry of the decree relegated the children to the position of bastards. The results concerning economic interests were, of course, also far reaching.

Many jurisdictions now have legislation (sometimes judicial decisions without statutory provision) saving the legitimacy of children despite the dubious marital status of the parents. Such legislation is rather common in cases of voidable marriage and is gaining popularity in instances of void marriage. One also finds, in some states, provision for alimony, child support, division of property and additional ancillary relief in these types of actions. It is not safe to generalize in this connection as the law is in a fairly rapid growth period.

The marriage counselor can help the spouse understand the nature and objectives of actions designed to test the validity of a marriage. It is of particular importance that a good paper record of marriage be obtained at the time of the marriage and be carefully preserved. This should be evident when one recalls how many legal consequences depend upon the existence of, and the spouse's ability to prove, a valid marriage. The record should be clarified whenever ambiguity exists. Sometimes a simple marriage ceremony will suffice. In other instances formal proceedings for a decree of nullity or an annulment are essential. Selection of an appropri-

ate proceeding is obviously a professional problem and the patient should
be encouraged to obtain help.

Separation without Termination of Marital Status

Decrees of nullity, annulment and divorce deal with marital status.
There exists another type of court decree concerning marital problems
which does not pertain to status, but only to the incidents of the relation.
These remedies are variously, and imprecisely, known as divorce *a mensa
et thoro* (divorce from bed and board), limited divorce, judicial separation
or separate maintenance. None of these terminates marital status.

Separate maintenance is, technically, not the same as the several forms
of limited divorce. The major difference is that the decree of separate
maintenance is terminated automatically upon reconciliation and resumption of marital relations by the spouses, while similar conduct would not
abrogate the limited divorce. This fine distinction, however, is widely
ignored and shortly may not exist at all. The real test is whether the court
decree itself, no matter by what name it is identified, prohibits further
cohabitation by the spouses permanently (or at least until modified), for
some specific time, or not at all. Aside from this factor, the various forms
of the decree permitting separation without termination of the marital
status are essentially comparable.

Several objectives are sought by this type of decree. The major purpose,
normally, is to make compulsory provision for the support of the wife and
children. The husband (very infrequently, the wife) is compelled to furnish a specified, usually periodic, amount of support even though living
apart.

Judicial separation has a bizarre and complex legal history, understandable only in light of circumstances which existed when the marital status
was regarded as a sacrament beyond the reach of civil law. The purpose
was to make legal provision for the wife who, although unable to divorce
her husband, found it impossible, because of his wrongful conduct, to
live with him. In the early law of this nation, a wife could obtain, at her
option, a divorce or separate maintenance for certain marital wrongs.
She could also, moreover, obtain separate maintenance for many abuses
not constituting grounds for divorce. This is still true in some states.

On the other hand, many jurisdictions, especially during recent years,
have limited the situations in which separate maintenance may be procured very narrowly. Sometimes this relief is granted only when the parties
are already living apart and the husband is in fact wrongfully refusing to
support.

Reflection will suggest reasons for this judicial animosity toward the
decree of separate maintenance. It creates, or at least perpetuates, a very

abnormal condition. The spouses are neither bound nor free, and the husband is visited with all the burdens of marriage while denied all benefits. Unless used with caution, the decree can be a damaging weapon in the hands of a vindictive spouse.

Upon occasion, however, the husband may desire legal authorization to live apart from the wife without being subjected to the accusation of desertion or criminal nonsupport. The decree may be helpful to him and is, in some jurisdictions, available for this purpose.

There are also situations in which, because of jurisdictional reasons, the spouses will not be eligible for any other form of judicial relief. The traditional actions dealing with marital status require that at least one spouse, typically the plaintiff, be domiciled in the state or territory where the action is brought. The decree of separate maintenance, not dealing with status, does not require a domicilliary connection between the plaintiff and the jurisdiction.

In other words, the separate maintenance action is normally regarded as transitory (*i.e.*, not restricted to the state of domicile), and may be instituted in any state where the plaintiff can obtain personal service of the defendant. The practical importance of this factor is demonstrated by the numerous cases in which the wife has been deserted by a husband who now resides in another state. This "migratory" problem has, it should be remembered, also been greatly ameliorated by the Uniform Reciprocal Enforcement of Support Act discussed above.

Separate maintenance decrees may be accompanied by restraining orders in many jurisdictions. Custody problems and child support may also be determined in this type of proceeding. Most states make provision for modification of separate maintenance orders in a fashion similar to that used in divorce.

There is one decided limitation to the relief available in separate maintenance—in addition, of course, to the fact that the marital status is not terminated and remarriage is not legally possible. The consequence of continued legal marital status is that property interests of the spouses are confused. There is not enough uniformity among the various jurisdictions to permit a general statement but, stated most broadly, the problems are that postseparation conduct of one spouse may impose legal obligation upon the other, that they may continue to share in each other's acquisitions and that they may have difficult problems to resolve in relation to succession of interests at death and tax complexities during life. Some of these uncertainties can be minimized by specific order of court. Unfortunately, some cannot. For example, some courts have held that a court cannot, in a decree of separate maintenance, make a division of marital property. In most states this problem will yield to a well-drawn separation agreement or a property conveyance. The spouses are unlikely, unless alerted by some advisor, to be aware of this needed supplement to a separate maintenance decree.

The one advantage of the decree stressed most frequently is that preservation of the legal status enhances the chance of reconciliation, an advantage lost when the parties resort to divorce. Perhaps there is some truth in this assertion. How much value it has must be judged by the marriage counselor. Perhaps the actual utility is much less than is popularly believed.

If a reconciliation is accomplished following the entry of a decree of separate maintenance, it is sometimes good practice to have a formal termination of the decree by court order. This is not required in most cases, and the abrogation is probably automatic upon a bona fide reconciliation. However, there is always the question of proof. Resumption of cohabitation for a short time, followed by a new period of living apart, can pose distressing factual and legal questions. A complete, unambiguous, paper record is always desirable.

COURTS OF CONCILIATION

Judicial attempts to promote conciliation are, of course, not new. The concept of a specialized conciliation court is fairly novel, however. By no means common as yet, and not uniformly successful where they do exist, the so-called "family court" is a resource available to at least some of our population.

The objective is to provide a specialized court equipped to handle domestic relation problems with the skills of the social scientist as well as those of the lawyer. Implementation assumes different forms from one court to the next, but the following basic elements appear in most of these tribunals.

The agency remains a court. It is controlled by a judge and supplied with broad powers to coerce obedience. The new ingredient added to the judicial form is the availability of staff with social work training. Most actual counseling is done by the staff, with the judge normally participating only when traditional judicial functions are required. Access to the court is simple as pleadings are held to a minimum and formal procedure is often eliminated totally. Parties may appear in family court before other litigation is started, in fact many judges give preference to "early" conciliatory efforts on the theory that it is then more effective than it would be at some later stage of the problem. The court is also used during divorce litigation, however, and even after divorce, in connection with enforcement and modification of divorce orders.

Lawyers play a minor role in the appearance of parties during this conciliation attempt. Counsel is valuable in the preparation of fact schedules, proposed plans, agreements, orders and other formal documents which may be required.

The usual proceeding in a conciliation court is patterned after the informal, casework type of interview. The goal is to help the parties reach voluntary agreement, and some conciliation judges refuse to enter an order without the assent of both spouses. More recently, the value of "gentle judicial coercion" is being rediscovered. It seems true that spouses often hope, secretly, that someone will stop the drift toward divorce commenced in anger and haste. The difficulty is that admission of the error, and withdrawal of the action, may cause a serious loss of face. The litigant in such a position will welcome an order of the court which compels him to do what he wishes to do, but cannot bring himself to do without "coercion."

The judge of a conciliatory court usually has power to make provision for support, custody and virtually all the restraining orders found in divorce litigation, plus some authority unique to this new type of proceeding. The question requiring diagnostic skill is to determine when spouses will profit from formal discipline. This decision must ultimately be made by the judge. His decision will be better or worse, depending upon the advice given to him and to the spouses. The physician or marriage counselor can, if he will inform himself of the resources available in his locality, make efficient use of the strengths which are unique to the law.

It may be that both the most encouraging and significant development in conciliation court practice is the bridge it offers between legal authority and the private services available in the community. The court can order a recalcitrant party to do things which a counselor could not otherwise accomplish. Third persons may be enjoined from interference. In short, an effective partnership can be developed between the court and the nonlawyer professional in family work. These contacts are highly valued and regularly used by most family court judges.

DIVORCE

The suggestion that divorce may be the best solution to a domestic crisis might appear misplaced in a discussion of marriage counseling. It is not. There are problems which, when evaluated honestly, simply will not yield to solutions which are consistent with preservation of the marital status. No pretense will be made here of furnishing guides for determining which cases are beyond repair. They do exist, and continued living together in those instances will produce only violence or hardship.

Divorce is never forced upon spouses when both protest. But when one spouse wishes a divorce, and the requisite grounds exist, it will almost certainly be obtainable. The duty of the lawyer in this event is to make the dissolution as beneficial, clean and painless as possible.

When a divorce is sought, the technical problems are the lawyer's and should be left to him. This does not mean that the patient no longer needs the assistance of the counselor. It is in fact tragic that the need for continued guidance at precisely this point is not more frequently recognized. Even the skillfully handled divorce produces trauma. No amount of legal ability can avoid this consequence.

Emotional damage and bitterness can be minimized, however, if the counselor uses his skill in preparing the patient for what must be faced. Considerable strength is needed to cope with loss of a companion—even an unwanted one—coupled with possible loss of children, economic stability, social position and similar consequences of divorce.

The adjustment to postdivorce living is frequently more difficult than when death of one spouse has terminated the marital relationship. Loss of a mate by death is not the occasion for public censure, personal qualms about adequacy or other unpleasant and continuing, often inescapable, concomitant effects of divorce. At this point the most fortunate patient will be the one who has the help of a lawyer and counselor who are able to work together. The marriage may not be saved—although many are by a subsequent remarriage after the emotional, physical or legal problems have been resolved—but the present emotional needs of the patient will certainly be better served.

part four

PREMARITAL
COUNSELING

chapter twenty-seven

Premarital Counseling

HERBERT A. OTTO, Ph.D., *Graduate School of Social Work, University of Utah, Salt Lake City, Utah*

If about-to-be-married men and women can be helped to express, explore and clarify their attitudes, feelings, desires and expectations, many misunderstandings and conflicts can be avoided later on. This kind of nonphysiologic counseling shares equal importance with the premarital physical consultation to be discussed by Dr. Rutherford in the following chapter.

Although the total preceding life experiences of both prospective partners are, in a sense, preparatory for their marriage, premarital counseling presents one of the last formalized occasions for helping the premarital partners prepare for marriage and life as a family. Often, standing at this critical crossroad in their lives, both partners are more open to the establishment of healthy patterns of marital interaction through counseling than they are likely to be at any subsequent time in their married life.

What Help Are the Partners Seeking?

As in all other forms of counseling, it is necessary for the premarital counselor—or the physician serving as premarital counselor—to have some idea of the nature and the scope of the patients' problem early in the counseling process. Couples who come for premarital counseling are often able to state their reasons for seeking help and may indicate specific areas where they feel assistance is needed. There are, however, exceptions to this and at times the stated reason may not be the actual reason why counseling help is sought.

For didactic purposes, persons who come for premarital counseling can be divided into three groups.

First, there is the group whose primary purpose is to seek information and to obtain reassurance. Included in this group are counselees who see themselves as having no particular problem and who are not attempting to secure any specific information, but who have concluded that premarital counseling is "the thing to do." In spite of the fact that this group does not appear to be in need of counseling, problems are often uncovered in the course of the interview. Experience has shown that such counselees usually value highly the time spent with them and the understanding the counselor has shown in helping them prepare for marriage.

The second group consists of those having moderate doubts about the marriage and themselves. These counselees, on the one hand, seem to entertain some serious doubts about the marriage (or whether they as a person are fit subjects for marriage); on the other hand, they are of the opinion that they should proceed with the marriage.

The third and final group has severe doubts as to whether they should get married and they seriously question whether they would be adequate as marital partners.

While individuals in each of these groups will have special needs which should be recognized at the outset and treated accordingly, all of them can benefit from a full exploration of their values, goals, attitudes and expectations concerning marriage. In general, any realistic set of objectives for the premarital counselor should be designed with the following purposes in mind:

1. To help the couple to relieve fears, worries and anxieties about marriage and to communicate these to each other.

2. To help them to express their feelings and attitudes in regard to marriage and to share these with a counselor.

3. To provide general and specific information, education and guidance about the problems and responsibilities of marriage.

4. To encourage the couple to explore and communicate their separate, individual needs, goals and values.

5. To provide an opportunity to practice the "problem-solving approach" by stimulating the couple to work together toward solution of their problems.

TREATMENT CONSIDERATIONS IN PREMARITAL COUNSELING.

Since the general principles of counseling, which premarital counseling shares with all other forms of counseling, are discussed in other chapters, only the unique aspects of premarital counseling will be discussed here.

The question as to whether to counsel a couple jointly or separately is often raised. Many counselors prefer to see the couple together for a short initial interview, which may last 10 to 15 minutes, and then to meet with them individually. The time together is used to briefly orient the couple to premarital counseling, but the primary purpose is to gain clinical impressions of the couple's interaction and to obtain a basic idea of their situation or problem. Each member is then seen separately for a 10- to

15-minute period. The objective at this time is to explore with him any doubts, areas of conflict or possible problems he may see in relation to the marriage. There is a tendency on the part of some counselees to deal with possible conflicts or problems by avoidance, although there may be a recognition that these need to be dealt with some time prior to marriage. The counseling setting, facilitated by the absence of the prospective spouse offers an opportunity to view these problems.

On the basis of the initial joint and two short single interviews, the counselor is able to exercise his judgment and gain a fairly clear impression as to what extent and in relation to what areas further counseling is needed. The last 15 to 20 minutes of the hour interview can then be used to acquaint the couple with the counselor's impressions and findings and to begin work on possible problems.

If no areas of difficulty or concern are discernible, the counselor can begin to briefly survey with the couple the key areas in premarital counseling which will be discussed in detail subsequently. Where no apparent difficulty or problems can be identified, many counselors either conduct one long interview or schedule two hour-long sessions. The latter scheduling method is preferable as the time lapse between interviews allows for futher interaction between the couple, which may result in the identification of areas of concern or possible difficulty. Many couples normally have some apprehensions, fears or misgivings about their marriage. The counselor should encourage the ventilation of these feelings, help the couple to examine them realistically and give support and reassurance as needed.

Two time-honored maxims are still of value. They are: (1) "When in doubt, hold off diagnosis and schedule more counseling sessions. When still uncertain, refer," and (2) "When in doubt, ask for postponement of the wedding so that the problems can be worked out." It is well to be frank with couples and, when indicated, to make clear to them that a series of counseling sessions should be scheduled so that a specific problem can be adequately dealt with and worked out before the wedding. The preventive nature of premarital counseling can be stressed at this point.

A Diagnostic Screen for Premarital Counseling

To enable the counselor to gain a clear perspective of the couple's situation and needs, a diagnostic screen is available. This screen consists of six areas which can be explored to gain a thorough understanding of the patient's situation:

1. Courtship history. An overview of the courtship history should be obtained beginning with the question, "How and under what circumstances did the couple meet?" In addition, the length of dating prior to "going steady" or engagement should be clarified. Date of engagement should be secured and related to the date of the planned marriage. Do both partners feel the engagement period was long enough? It can be pointed out that for many couples the engagement represents a preparatory period for marriage, and that this time is often used to explore the expectations from marriage of each partner as well as for realistic planning. The counselor here needs to get a clear idea as to whether the romantic elements or "blind infatuation" have played a dominant part in the courtship history and whether these factors have kept the couple from "really getting to know each other," *i.e.*, from communicating about values, goals and expectancies in relation to marriage. Finally, the reasons why the couple decided to get married should be explored. What were the circumstances surrounding this decision and why did they choose to get married at this particular time are two key questions.

2. Comparative background of the couple. In general, research studies have shown that men and women with a similar background of experience, social level, values, goals and interests tend to date and marry each other, and that *such marriages are generally more successful.* However, there are a sufficient number of exceptions to this finding to indicate that the counselor should refrain from discouraging those couples who have grossly dissimilar backgrounds and interests. In these instances, it is the counselor's function to help the couple to become fully aware of the range and extent of their differences and to help them explore what effect these differences may have in relation to their marriage.

What is the *educational background* and training of the couple and what is their work history? Sometimes excessive differences in the educational background of couples may be a source of problems. The employment history can give valuable clues as to the counselee's capacity for assuming responsibility, for getting along with co-workers and with superiors. In the event of uneven or "spotty" employment, the reasons or causes of this history should be considered in detail. Conversely, an outstanding record of vocational performance can be considered as a strength or resource.

Differences in *family culture and social class* need to be noted and, if necessary, fully explored. It should be kept in mind in this connection that there is a general tendency for women to "marry up" in the socioeconomic scale and for men to "marry down." The principle of "like marries like equals better chances of success in marriage" also applies in this area. If there are obvious and marked differences in the family culture and socioeconomic background, it is again the counselor's function to help the couple to explore the implications of these differences for their marriage.

Similarly, differences in *ethnic background* usually indicate that the counselor may need to give special help with adjustment problems. This seems especially to be the case in second generation marriages, those in which the parents were not born in this country. *Religious differences* may pose a major counseling problem, especially in cases where the theologic divergencies are obvious and marked. Most religious denominations are opposed to interfaith marriages. Both the Catholic and Jewish faiths, for example, discourage such marriages. Research studies have shown that divorce rates are higher for couples having different faiths than those having the same faith.

Due to the intricate nature of personal value systems, each case of interfaith marriage is unique and usually is complex. Two volumes[1,2] are available to the counselor who wishes more detailed preparation for working with this type of case.

Other matters which need to be taken into consideration in obtaining an overview of the comparative backgrounds of a couple include such factors as *genetic and health status* (treated at a later point in this chapter) and the matter of *comparative age*. Special attention must be paid to early marriages where the prospective partners are excessively youthful and give the impression that they lack maturity. Although the trend is toward earlier marriages, research has shown that such unions have fewer chances of success than marriages contracted at a later age. If the couple's age differential exceeds a decade, a thorough exploration of this factor needs to be undertaken, both in terms of the causes and the implications of this age differential for the marriage.

3. Attitudes of both families. It is necessary to obtain a clear understanding of the attitudes of both sets of prospective in-laws toward the marriage. The emotional (and sometimes economic) support of the families is often as important as is their opposition or disapproval. Is there a likelihood that one or the other partner may be excessively dominated by in-laws? Does one or both prospective partners show a marked dependence on a particular parent? Has an effort been made to help both sets of parents become acquainted? These are some of the questions which need to be covered in detail.

4. Realistic planning for the marriage. An index of the couple's ability to assume responsibility is presented by the quality of their preparations and planning for the marriage. This includes not only active participation in the plans surrounding the wedding itself, but also formulations of plans and concrete preparations which have been made both for the honeymoon and for life together as a married couple. For example, what housing arrangements have been made, have matters of income and budget been discussed?

5. Psychologic and personality factors. Of major importance in the assessment of a couple's situation are psychologic and personality factors. To a considerable extent the counselor must here be guided by his clinical impressions of each of the prospective marriage partners. However, a number of criteria can be helpful in this assessment. Important among these is *sex role differentiation*, i.e., whether both mates are dissimilar in respect to masculinity and femininity. Is the man essentially masculine and the woman essentially feminine? If not, are their masculine-feminine components essentially complementary? What is each partner's idea of his role in the marriage? Closely related is the criterion of *body-image* and *self-image*. From the manner in which a person uses his body, the way he holds his body, his posture and physical characteristics, as well as dress and grooming, clues are conveyed as to how he feels about himself as a person and about his sense of self-worth and self-esteem. Is help needed in relation to the self-image? Does there seem to be an imbalance in the partners' masculinity-femininity components?

6. *Procreative attitudes.* A particularly important and sensitive area is concerned with each counselee's attitude toward sexual relations and their individual attitudes about having children. How to help counselees to acquire sound attitudes about the sexual aspects of their marital relationship will be discussed in detail subsequently under the heading "Key Areas in Premarital Counseling." The counselor also needs to explore with the couple their viewpoints about beginning their family. Have they discussed whether they wish to have children, and, if so, when they are planning to have their first child? Has the subject of raising the children been talked over in detail?

Aids in Premarital Counseling

A limited number of premarital counseling aids are available. The first of these is a "self-diagnostic form" used by some counselors. This is simply a mimeographed or printed form with the heading, "We wish to discuss these subjects with the counselor:" The rest of the sheet is blank. Counselees are handed the form with the instructions to first talk over together what they would like to discuss with the counselor in preparation for their marriage, then to list these subjects on the form.

An alternative to this procedure is to give each counselee a form and ask him to fill it out alone, without comparing results until after each has filled his in. It has been found that often individuals are able to pinpoint problem areas and areas of concern with considerable accuracy.

Several printed premarriage check lists are available, including Burgess' "A Marriage Prediction Schedule,"[3] McHugh's "A Courtship Analysis"[4] and Dunn's "Marriage Role Expectation Inventory."[5] Each of these is intended, in its separate way, to help the partners understand some aspects of each other's behaviors and attitudes. McHugh's "Sex Knowledge

Inventory"[6] is specifically directed toward ascertaining some of the respondent's sex knowledge and values.

As a result of extended research and the clinical findings of over a decade of counseling practice, the writer has, himself, developed a set of premarital counseling schedules designed to help couples to explore their values, attitudes and expectations prior to marriage. These schedules have now been published as "The Otto Pre-Marital Schedules"[7] and are available with an accompanying direction book, the *Manual for Pre-Marital Counseling*,[8] from the Consulting Psychologist Press in Palo Alto, California.

"The Otto Pre-Marital Counseling Schedules" consist of three separate parts, two of which explore in greater depth areas touched upon in the first schedule, which is entitled the "Pre-marital survey section." The survey section is routinely used with all counselees, and includes questions about housing, money matters, the couple's relationship, education, employment, health, religion, in-laws, children, leisure time, wedding preparations and future plans. Questions are open-ended and are designed to require expression of opinion and feeling by each of the partners before they decide jointly how to mark the question. Space is also provided for the couple to make brief notes. An additional feature of the survey section is a self-diagnostic form which offers the couple an opportunity to reveal areas in which further counseling or education is needed. The self-evaluation by the counselees can furnish many clues to the counselor and can also serve as a guide for further counseling or other assistance which may be needed.

A two-page "Sexual adjustment section" and a one-page "Family finance section" are also available. These may be employed routinely with all couples or selectively with those expressing an interest in them or demonstrating in the survey section that they need further help with sexual or financial problems. All sections are designed to be filled out by the couple together, and the "Sexual adjustment section" has been constructed for the purpose of helping the couple to acquire information as well as to explore and share their attitudes and feelings about sexual relations in marriage. Similarly, the "Family finance section" is designed to assist a couple to clarify their thinking about monetary matters in marriage and to make concrete plans in relation to such subjects as budgeting, housekeeping allowance, joint or separate checking account, life or health insurance and so forth.

Other premarital counseling aids include assigned readings and "assigned discussion." For example, a counselor may wish to recommend that a couple do a certain amount of reading in relation to a specific area such as family finance. It is also possible to ask counselees to read specific chapters or passages and to discuss these fully with the understanding that they will talk over with the counselor the substance of their discussions and conclusions.

KEY AREAS IN PREMARITAL COUNSELING

A number of key areas can be distinguished which should be routinely covered or explored during premarital counseling.

Their prospective *sexual adjustment* in marriage is a major area of concern for many couples. It is in the discussion of this area that the counselor's frankness, openness and healthy attitude can do much to allay fears and anxieties and to build a sound foundation for the marital relationship.

The counselor may wish to cover the following items which have been selected from the sexual adjustment section of the writer's previously mentioned counseling schedules:

1. If a couple has some fear or uncertainty about the wedding night, it may be helpful to talk about it and share their feelings together.

2. After marriage, many couples find that husband and wife should feel free to tell each other of any irritations or satisfactions that they may experience in their sexual relations.

3. If a couple is concerned about reaching a climax or orgasm together, it may be helpful to realize that it often takes time to make this adjustment.

4. It can be helpful for couples to have an understanding of the importance of tenderness and affection before, during and after sexual intercourse.

5. Many authorities agree that couples should work out their own standards about what is "right" and "wrong" in loveplay and sexual expression in marriage—what really matters is giving love and happiness to each other.

6. Since many women take longer in being sexually aroused than men, the husband needs to devote more time to foreplay (such as stimulating the wife's clitoris and breasts) in order to give satisfaction to both.

In addition to the preceding, a series of key areas should be routinely reviewed with the couple. For the counselor's convenience, a number of questions have been placed under each area which can be used with the counselees. It should be understood that these questions are not exclusive and that other questions can be added, based on the counselor's judgment.

1. Housing
    a. Have you talked about where you will live?
    b. Are you satisfied that you have adequate living space and sufficient privacy?
2. Money matters
    a. Have you decided how to handle your family finances?
    b. Have you discussed budgeting?

3. Have you talked over what you consider the basic necessities and luxuries?
4. Relationship factors
    a. To what extent are you able to express to each other your real feelings?
    b. How do you handle your arguments and quarrels?
5. Education
    a. What are your educational or vocational interests?
    b. What are your plans for further educational or vocational training?
    c. Are there any skills or hobbies which you may wish to develop together?
6. Employment
    a. Have you talked about whether the future husband is in the right job?
    b. How do you feel about the subject of the future wife's working after marriage?
7. Health
    a. Have you both had a premarital medical examination and are you planning to have a yearly medical examination after marriage?
    b. Is there a possibility of hereditary or genetic factors in both of your family backgrounds which may affect your having children?
8. Religious matters
    a. Have you decided about a church which you may wish to attend?
    b. Have you discussed the question of the denomination or church you may wish to have your children reared in?
9. In-laws
    a. Do you consider that you each know the other's parents well enough?
    b. Have you talked about how you may deal with possible interference from in-laws after marriage?
10. Children
    a. Have you discussed when and if you wish to have children?
    b. Have you shared some of your ideas about the care and training of children?
11. Sexual adjustment
    a. Have you expressed your real feelings to each other about sexual relations in marriage?
    b. Do you need more information about the male or female bodies, contraception or pregnancy?
    c. Have you discussed what effect your parent's attitudes about sex may have on your marital relationship?
12. Leisure time
    a. Have you talked over your selection of friends?

    b. Have you agreed on your favorite kinds of recreation and how to spend much of your leisure time?

13. Wedding preparations

    a. Have you discussed the financing of your wedding and decided on what type of wedding you want?

    b. Have you talked over and made plans for your honeymoon?

REFERRAL IN PREMARITAL COUNSELING

As in other forms of counseling, *referral in premarital counseling is a process.* The same principles and practices which have been described in Chapter 9, "Evaluating the Patient's Problem for Counseling or Referral," govern referral in premarital counseling. Only one additional factor needs to be kept in mind, due to the educational elements of premarital counseling— in cases where intricate or difficult problems exist, or where the couple appears to need a great deal of information or instruction, referral can be made to a number of specialists who are equipped to furnish specific information and help. Included in this group are specialists in home economics, family finance and budgeting, and the clergyman. Last, but not least, is the geneticist who should be consulted in relation to problems which exceed the competence of the practitioner.

The major crises in the lives of individuals present special opportunities for personality growth and maturation. Marriage, as at no other point in life, represents such a life crisis. Communication in depth of basic feelings, values and attitudes becomes an important medium of growth and is so utilized to a varying degree by most couples. It is the purpose of counseling, then, to help the couple to explore areas of concern through communication and to help them obtain an overview of key areas of interaction in relation to marriage. *The counselor's professional skill, his understanding and help can make a major contribution in assisting the premarital couple to build the sound foundations needed for a happy and productive marriage.*

There is a reading list of books for those ready to be married in Section V of the Appendix.

REFERENCES

1. BOSSARD, J. S. H., AND BOLL, E. S.: *One Marriage, Two Faiths.* The Ronald Press Company, New York, 1957.
2. PIKE, J. A.: *If You Marry Outside Your Faith.* Harper & Row, Inc., New York, 1962.
3. BURGESS, E. W.: A marriage prediction schedule. Family Life Publications, Inc., Durham.
4. McHUGH, G.: A courtship analysis. Family Life Publications, Inc., Durham, 1961.

5. DUNN, M. S.: Marriage role expectation inventory. Family Life Publications, Inc., Durham, 1961.
6. McHUGH, G.: Sex knowledge inventory, forms X and Y. Family Life Publications, Inc., Durham, 1955.
7. OTTO, H. A.: The Otto pre-marital schedules: educational instruments for use in pre-marital counseling. Consulting Psychologist Press, Palo Alto, 1961.
8. OTTO, H. A.: Manual for Pre-marital Counseling. Consulting Psychologist Press, Palo Alto, 1961.

chapter twenty-eight

The Premarital Physical Examination

ROBERT N. RUTHERFORD, M.D., *Department of Obstetrics and Gynecology, University of Washington School of Medicine, Seattle, Washington*

The premarital physical examination usually is one of the most emotionally charged experiences either the bride or groom has ever had. True, each may have had other encounters with a physician before, but none when there was such a sense of ultimate intimacy. Of all the physician's many responsibilities, this can be the most satisfying and rewarding.

Why such a statement? Because here is the opportunity for the physician to play many roles—as a sympathetic expert advising in emotional and body relationships, as one who is doing proper preventive medicine in the finest sense, as one who is helping a new family unit to form when it is ready for a child and, finally, as an available friend and advisor for their marriage problems and adjustments as the years unfold.

The beginning of this satisfying helping process is the premarital examination. Here many aspects of human experience are discussed as a part of a very necessary marriage education process. One subject of primary importance is, naturally, the sexual relationship. In our practice, we often start our premarital examination with such a discussion.

Discussion of the Sexual Relationship

It comes as a surprise to many of the young couples we see to learn that the physical enjoyment of sex is a learned technique. Without ever having been told so, each of the partners may have assumed that when the proper time comes, all will be revealed to them. They are, they say, IN LOVE. Isn't that enough?

While there is a great need to provide these prospective marriage partners with some thorough, accurate and unabridged information, there is no reason, in the premarital physical consultation, for an exhaustive discussion of the horrendous problems which can beset the sexual relationship. Ordinarily, there is no occasion for an emotionally charged excursion into sexual psychopathology or the controversies of Freudian psychology.

Instead, it would seem from practical experience that a great deal of positive reassurance is indicated. The couple should be told that immediate spontaneous exaltation and satisfaction are not always possible from the marriage night onward. Instead, usually there develops an increasing ability for each to enjoy the other's body. It may take weeks or months or even years before total satisfaction is possible.

It is also important for the physician to mention planning for children. Too often the couple will create life without a thought for the long-term chain of events triggered by an unplanned pregnancy. Here again the physician may live his preventive and educational role—not advising *against* children, but instead planning *for* them when the couple has proved its maturity and ability to accept increased responsibility.

The Male Examination

There is a general professional disregard for this type of examination. If a man shaves daily, has a resonant voice and pays his bills, the implication seems to be that he will be an entirely satisfactory physical specimen as a husband. Indeed, any male reproductive deficit is more evident than in the female; that is, the size and development of his external sexual organs are more readily observed. However, other things are difficult to anticipate—premature ejaculation, inability to achieve an erection, a paucity of sperm—just to mention a few of the more common male problems which may make their appearance only *after* the marriage has been consummated. As reassurance, the physician may mention casually that "if there are any problems in sexual adjustment after marriage, come back for discussion. Today, on your examination, you seem to be in excellent health and a virile man." Obviously, if some problem is found, it should be handled appropriately at that time. But the large majority of men in this age group will be found ready for sexual activity.

At one time in our private practice consultations with the couple to be married, we entertained the thought of a premarital semen examination. We discarded this rather promptly, since we agreed that semen analyses were often difficult of interpretation at best, and were anything but esthetic and romantic for the young prospective bridegroom. Moreover, since the couple were already in love, they could not be dissuaded anyway by our finding of a doubtful sperm count. Further examination and reexamination of this concept seems to bear out the wisdom of omitting this earthy bit of male reproductive information, especially since our definition of an "adequate" sperm count is still most inaccurate.

If the young man is found healthy, this assurance is of utmost value. He then can be asked to return with his fiancee for a mutual consideration of marriage physiology and child spacing.

THE FEMALE EXAMINATION

It was with considerable professional shock that the writer found some years ago that the usual "physical examination" for unmarried young women was superficial to say the least. In those days of 25 years ago, whether the examination was for insurance purposes, to enter the nursing profession or to enter college, rarely was more done than the thrusting of a stethoscope gingerly through the patient's dress in order to listen to the aortic or the pulmonic valve heart sounds.

This kind of premarital physical examination had inevitable consequences. The writer has encountered many wives coming as infertility patients after some years of barren marriage who had never had a pelvic examination. When the examination was made, the woman often would be found to have an underdeveloped uterus—a probable cause of her infertility. Most physicians know the difficulty of growing the uterus if hypodevelopment is found after the age of 20.

In the virginal woman a rectal examination is often more revealing than a vaginal examination. However, in the virginal woman who is to become a bride, it is paramount to know that the hymen is soft and distensible for proper marital acceptance. If not, corrective procedures may be employed long before a possible traumatic first wedding night experience.

But internal examination is the last item in our premarital examination protocol. It is our practice to begin in a relaxed consultation room visit where the patient has been allowed to sit by herself for a few moments before the physician enters. Near her is a carved ivory Chinese figure some six inches in length, reclining, nude, within a glass case. There is within the case an explanatory note that this is the kind of doll used by Chinese doctors. It was considered improper for the Chinese doctor actually to examine his patient. Instead, the patient would point out on the doll wherein her problem lay, and the doctor would then prescribe suitably. This is an excellent mood creator for simple conversation with even the most modest young woman.

Then the physical history is taken simply and without an immediate writing of it on a record in front of the patient. Next, a line drawing of the femal genitalia is discussed with the patient so that the physician can be sure she understands the proper naming of the organs, the function of menstruation and the physiology of reproduction. This will be gone over again with both premarital partners in a later interview, since each partner often has a considerable amount of misinformation and questions.

The patient then is introduced to the nurse with the statement that the nurse will prepare her for the doctor's examination to see if she has properly matured.

It is our custom to have the nurse at this time instruct the patient in the techniques of douching, which is to be performed immediately after each menstrual period, and to answer any questions regarding the examination to come. The nurse explains that douching usually is not necessary in the unmarried girl, but that the married woman usually has more shedding of the surface lining of the vagina and more secretion of mucus from the cervix. Douching is described simply. This can be done sitting on the toilet, using a fountain spray nozzle and a bag, and inserting the nozzle an inch within the vagina for irrigation of the canal. This may be done several times weekly, but especially the first day or so after the period has ended, to cleanse the vagina. Normal vaginal acidity is maintained by the conventional douche of four tablespoons of vinegar per quart of warm water. Some may prefer the various prepared douche powders. Emphasis is made that it is not necessary to douche—it is entirely a matter of personal choice. Douching should be encouraged by the doctor only for specific medical problems if the patient is reluctant to douche.

The physician enters the room and begins the usual careful routine examination, which includes use of the ophthalmoscope, the otoscope for both ears and nostrils; then he procedes with the conventional physical examination. The doctor explains to the patient, now draped for pelvic examination, that there is a very strong protective muscle at the outlet of the birth canal. If the patient expects to be hurt and tightens this muscle, proper examination is impossible. Hence, the patient is to lie with her hands folded on her chest, breathing normally, allowing her knees to fall three feet apart and allowing her hips to remain resting on the examining table.

The physician may then separate the labia and visualize the external genitalia and hymen. If the hymen is soft and easily distensible, vaginal examination may be completed. If the hymen is not, rectal examination may be used for outlining the pelvic viscera.

We have not had to do hymenotomies for years because we have a better technique—*not* because we are reluctant to impair presumed virginity. If the hymen is soft, and one and one-half fingers' breadth diameter or greater, the statement is made that "You are virginal but the hymen can be stretched easily by your husband if you both are well lubricated." Explanation is made that proper sex excitement will usually self-lubricate the young woman. However, often at first it is wise for both to use a surgical lubricant. On the other hand, if the hymen is less than the above dimensions, we advise the patient of this fact. She is taught to dilate herself after a hot bath (which relaxes her pelvic structures), by inserting her thumb into the vagina. With gentle pressure against the perineum she can dilate herself with little discomfort.

If she is unwilling to undertake this procedure (very few demur if the rationale is discussed and diagrams used), then the hymen dilatation is done at a later date under Pentothal or similar anesthesia in the office. Then, the patient is instructed to continue her self-dilatation.

Great care is used in explaining to the woman that the vagina is capable of stretching to pass a 10-pound baby. The woman who is "too small for her husband" really is saying that the defense reflex valve muscle at the outlet has been mobilized for her protection against her husband, sex or some other phobia. The patient who fails to respond to this education usually will need more profound investigation of her past training and present attitudes regarding her feminine role, sex, acceptance of her husband, fear of pregnancy and the like.

The patient may be advised at this time regarding the use of internal tampons for protection during menstruation instead of the usual external pad. Many physicians have been very reluctant to make positive and definitive statements in this area, yet a number of studies have shown that this is entirely safe, does not introduce infection into the birth canal, does not destroy the virginal hymen and allows the young woman a great latitude of activity which the external soaked menstrual pad does not. For example, this internal protection will allow the young lady to swim in a swimming pool without offense or danger to herself or others. Moreover, since it has been demonstrated that menstrual blood does not become odorous until after it has left the birth canal, even normal daily activities can usually be carried on with less fear of embarrassment.

Despite these well-known advantages, the patient on her first contact with the doctor rarely feels brave enough to ask his advice regarding the use of tampons for internal protection. In our opinion, it is entirely proper for the physician to introduce the subject and to make a positive recommendation, even though unsolicited by the patient.

Laboratory Studies

The routine laboratory studies which we use in premarital examinations can be duplicated in any doctor's office where there is a technician available. These are the same for both partners except for the Papanicolaou smear for the woman. This latter is less to exclude cancer than to measure ovarian function. The tests used for the couple are:

1. Complete blood count and smear
2. Complete urine study
3. Sedimentation rate
4. Guaiac test on the stool
5. Blood serology

In the event of any medical problem, the physician may proceed appropriately—again in the corrective and preventive role which is truly his.

Sexual Techniques

To reiterate, most couples in our experience actually have very little factual knowledge regarding the sexual act. The depth of our working ignorance has been demonstrated by the studies of the Kinsey group, by the pioneering work of Dickinson and more recently by Masters and Johnson[1,2] in their basic studies of the physiology of reproduction.

We have found it valuable to reemphasize, at the close of the premarital examination, several important points about the sexual relationship.

First, enjoyment of the sex act is not always natural, instinctive or guaranteed. Only in the human being is the sex act separated from the primary function of reproduction. In the human being, sex for producing children is less used than sex for pleasure. The confusion and interplay of these two motives within the sexual world of human beings would seem to be basic causes for many of our problems.

Secondly, the female is a much slower responding person than the male. During certain phases of the menstrual cycle, some females seem to be more receptive than at other times. In general, however, the female requires a period of preliminary sexual foreplay in order to ready her.

Thirdly, the clitoris is the main "trigger point" for the woman. Its manipulation plus vulvar, thigh, breast and lip stimulation all are important in the foreplay period. The eager husband sometimes does not understand this. However, tactile sensation is not enough. Mood creation for loving is most important. Failure to do this can nullify techniques of stimulation. It is hard for a wife to quarrel with her husband and then to respond to him sexually.

Fourthly, the vagina is essentially a canal with very little sensation. This is an excellent device for delivering a baby, but when it is used in the sexual function, often there is very little if any sensation other than deep pressure. More sensation may develop as the marriage goes on. Orgasm takes place as a result of sensation originating in the clitoris. (This is discussed in several other chapters.)

When the physician explains these various physiologic mechanisms to the couple, then the techniques outlined in careful objective detail in our modern marriage handbooks can be better understood. We regularly supply our premarital examination patients with a copy of a marital guide.[3]

Summary

One of the most fruitful areas for the physician to explore is the forming family unit, wherein the bright-eyed couple join with him in exploring life's most exciting and potentially most rewarding relationship. Here can begin preventive medicine at its finest with a lifetime association and friendship. It is not for the casual physician. Better that he not appear on the scene at all than in haphazard or disinterested fashion.

REFERENCES

1. MASTERS, W. H., AND JOHNSON, V. E.: The physiology of the vaginal reproductive function. West. J. Surg., **69**: 105–120, 1961.
2. MASTERS, W. H., AND JOHNSON, V. E.: The sexual response of the human male. I. Gross anatomic considerations. West. J. Surg., **71**: 85–95, 1963.
3. GREENBLATT, B. R.: *A Doctor's Marital Guide for Patients*. The Budlong Press, Chicago, 1962. (Available in Regular Edition or Rhythm Edition.)

chapter twenty-nine

Counseling for Family Planning

MARY S. CALDERONE, M.D., M.P.H., *Executive Director, Sex Information and Education Council of the U. S., New York, New York*

This book is in and of itself an indication of the deepening attitude and understanding by the medical profession—indeed by all of the helping professions—of their role in helping people to build good marriages. Similarly, awareness that family planning constitutes one of the elements essential for a good marriage has also broadened and deepened.

The term family *planning* is too often narrowly interpreted to mean family *limitation*. Less narrowly, it can also mean spacing between children. More broadly, it can mean conscious timing of the advent of desired children over the life span of a marriage. From the total point of view, however, and in its broadest sense, family planning must mean planning *for* one's family, and might be said to begin when life and environment first start building attitudes about sex into the young child.

There is presently little question that family planning as a basic principle has nearly universal acceptance. No one of the major religions or philosophies expects a woman to bear as many children as she theoretically could, nor countenances thoughtless and irresponsible procreation as moral. Quite the contrary, religious groups echo and reecho the concept that the creation of a new human being is an event of supreme importance, one that should be undertaken only within a setting of family stability, in full awareness of the solemn responsibilities involved for the future of this new person. It follows then that it is not merely a medical obligation, but the highest privilege, for a physician to aid couples in such responsible family planning.

PREMARITAL COUNSELING ON FAMILY PLANNING

It is during adolescence that much positive planning for the future family can be encouraged by the physician who seizes opportunities whenever they offer themselves. Providing a young person with protective information about venereal disease and the dangers of illegal abortion is essential, and should be done even if the consultation was only for acne. Furthermore, the physician may well exercise affirmative influence as the young person moves towards choosing a mate. Whenever the physician can help a young person to understand his own sexual nature and to act in such a responsible way that final choice of a mate is made on as mature a basis as possible, rather than on mere physical attraction, he is teaching the best kind of family planning.

Discussion of the inadequacy of sexual attraction alone as a basis for marriage provides an opportunity to open up the topic of sex and the part it can play in the relationship between mates. Sex as a channel of deepening communication between husband and wife should be stressed, with emphasis away from its exploitative and purely pleasure aspects—of which most young people today are all too well aware. The ability of the prospective mates to bring to conscious level, and to verbalize to each other, their feelings and attitudes about sex should be encouraged. It cannot too often be stressed that the experience of thus talking to a mature adult who has obviously and successfully come to grips with his own sexuality, will for most young people, be a releasing one, the effects of which will be felt in the future marriage as continuingly therapeutic.

The physician who has the opportunity of counseling with a young couple before their marriage should make the most of it. All of the skill, acumen and intuition that he has developed over the years should be brought into play as he attempts to assay what kinds of people they are and what their potential is for development as mates and as parents. If they are very young or immature, he will make them aware of the high divorce statistics weighing against such a marriage, and will counsel them to wait, if not for marriage, at least for two or three years before their first child, to allow their individual maturation to proceed, and the husband-wife relationship to stabilize. He must, however, clearly indicate that waiting too long before trying for pregnancy also has a danger, as it may mask an existing but undeclared fertility problem, at a time when the age factor is on the side of the angels. Such counseling constitutes the best kind of preventive medical practice, and also lays the groundwork for the time when the young couple will undertake the sex education of their own children.

In summary then, whether premarital family planning counseling[1, 2] must be given in single dose form at the premarital examination visit, or whether it has ideally been part of a long-continuing process during the entire conscious life span of each young individual, the couple and the physician should have as much understanding as possible of the following considerations:

1. Sound bases for choice of mate—including ages (measured in terms

of emotional maturity as well as chronologically) of the prospective marriage partners.

2. Their health—physical, mental and emotional.

3. Any evidence of fertility impairment that would make family planning *for* fertility essential.

4. Their genetic backgrounds.

5. Their psychosexual attitudes.

6. Their socioeconomic situation—that is, if they can be self-supporting or must still depend on parents, whether they are wage earners or still preparing for careers, whether the education of one or both is terminated or ongoing, whether or not the wife must work while the husband finishes his education or embarks on career or enterprise, whether this marriage at this time will open—or close—doors into an expanding future.

7. The characters of the young people—of limited potential for carrying the psychologic burdens of a family, or with capacity for continued growth and development under the stresses inevitable to family life.

8. The social milieu in which the family will have its being—whether the couple will live in an expanding society, or in an area that is severely overpopulated, or where there is unemployment or other socioeconomic stress.

9. The various methods of contraception to fit the varying and changing individual needs of couples.

METHODS

Consideration of the methods presently available to implement family planning decisions is left to the end of the premarital counseling interview. Fortunately, the era of only one or two means of fertility regulation is past, and in the light of the rapid development of new useful and effective methods, it behooves the physician to keep currently informed on these developments, so that he may best serve the special needs of each couple.

In deciding which methods to offer for choice, a preliminary consideration must of course be the religious conscience of the couple. In being scrupulous to present the available data on the relative effectiveness of all methods, the non-Catholic physician must be equally scrupulous not to appear to be trying to subvert Roman Catholics by seeming to undersell or decry the rhythm method. Theirs must be the decision, and his the obligation to serve that decision by knowledge and effort to help them learn and practice, *as well as possible*, the only method permissible to them, in the face of the inescapable fact of its lower effectiveness in comparison with other methods.

The available information on this method is not as well understood nor as widely spread as it should be, even by Roman Catholic scientific individuals and institutions, but happily, work and research on it are increasing.[*, 3, 4] Generally speaking, the calculations carried out according to Ogino are considered by authorities to provide the highest safety factor. Most important, of course, is that the woman should have an accurate record of, at a minimum, her 10 most recent cycle lengths. Until she has this, she must be supervised in carrying out her calculations as if her cycle lengths had the widest variations. Descriptions of the method and directions for patients are available,[5, 6] and all physicians should be sure that they understand its intricacies before trying to teach it.

It is the medical methods of contraception that have received most scientific attention and are now many.[7, 8] More are under intensive study.[7, 9] Roman Catholic physicians should be aware of the Protestant denominations that now regard the practice of family planning, using medical contraceptive methods, as a religious obligation. Even if their own consciences do not allow them personally to serve the needs of patients of faiths other than their own, they nevertheless have a professional obligation to refer such couples to non-Catholic colleagues or to other resources competent to do so.

Fitting the method to the particular needs of each family unit is of prime importance, for the consensus is that acceptability plays a decisive role in the effectiveness with which a couple will practice contraception. The wide variety of methods now available makes it possible for a couple to try several, if necessary, to discover the one that suits them best. Because new methods are being developed with such rapidity, the full roster is not detailed here. The writer has recently edited a comprehensive textbook[7] which attempts to synthesize recent developments in methods and practice. Particularly important for a physician to understand are the principles of *use* as contrasted with *theoretic* effectiveness.

The following listing of *accepted* contraceptive methods taken from the writer's *Manual of Contraceptive Practice*[7] (p. 232) is arranged in descending order of relative theoretical effectiveness. Ratings are based upon clinical experience and statistical studies.

Theoretical Effectiveness Ratings of Nonsurgical Contraceptive Methods

Group 1. *Most effective:* suppression of ovulation by oral contraceptives.

Group 2. *Highly effective:* diaphragm or cervical cap with cream or jelly; "combined" method; condom.

* Georgetown University in Washington, D. C. has established a Center for Population Research, one program of which is research to perfect the rhythm method.

Group 3. *Very effective:* aerosol vaginal foam.*

Group 4. *Less effective:* creams and jellies used alone; foam tablets; suppositories; coitus interruptus; rhythm (safe period); sponge with foam.

Group 5. *Least effective:* breast feeding.

Group 6. *Probably ineffective:* vaginal douche, plain or with chemicals added.

It should be noted that preliminary results on the intrauterine devices (still undergoing wide and intensive research trials) indicate that it will rank between Groups 1 and 2, very close to the orals.

To help physicians arrive at a judgment of best method, and best product within that method for each individual patient, the full discussions of methods in the manual include their advantages and disadvantages. All the products in Group 4 are also listed in the descending order of their *in vitro* spermicidal effectiveness.

Teaching resources, for both professionals and the public, include a voluntary health agency, The Planned Parenthood Federation of America, Inc., with its over 100 affiliates in various cities,† and the obstetric departments of an increasing number of medical schools and hospitals. The American Public Health Association, 1790 Broadway, New York, New York, has established two committees—a Maternal and Child Health Section Subcommittee on Family Planning and a Program Area Committee in Population and Public Health, both of which may be expected to serve as resources for the family planning programs rapidly proliferating in the tax supported health services of an increasing number of states, counties and cities. It is noteworthy that family planning is more and more being looked upon as an integral part of total community health services. Some schools of public health now offer year-long seminars in population and family planning, or short, intensive postgraduate teaching institutes in the subject. The American Medical Association has established a Committee on Human Reproduction, and recently recommended that prescription of birth control should be made available to all patients who require it, whether through private doctors or community sponsored health services. "An intelligent recognition of the problems that

* Preliminary results on the pregnancy rates of approximately 588 women who used an aerosol vaginal foam for a period of one year or more indicate that its effectiveness falls approximately mid-way between that of the diaphragm and that of a group of the jellies and creams manufactured for use alone. The rate of change from the aerosol foam to other methods also falls approximately midway between the rates of change from the other two methods. It is postulated that the persistency with which a woman uses a method reflects the acceptability to her of that method.

† The "List of Planned Parenthood Affiliates" may be obtained from The Planned Parenthood Federation of America, Inc., 515 Madison Avenue, New York, New York.

relate to human reproduction, including the need for population control, is more than a matter of responsible parenthood; it is a matter of responsible medical practice." [10]

Family planning should not be looked upon as an end in itself, nor as a means merely of family limitation. Instead it should be regarded as one broad approach to total planning for the family, and as a preventive health measure to be applied in all services established for the support of marriage, of the family and of society as a whole. The physician must become aware that he can and should play a key role in family planning as a field of health.

REFERENCES

1. FLOWERS, C. E. JR.: Premarital examination and counseling. Obst. & Gynec., **20**: 143–147, 1962.
2. KAVINOKY N.: Premarital medical examination. J. A. M. A., **156**: 692–695, 1954.
3. HARTMAN, C. G.: *Science and the Safe Period*. The Williams & Wilkins Company, Baltimore, 1963.
4. ROCK, J.: The rhythm or periodic continence method of birth control. In *Manual of Contraceptive Practice*, edited by M. S. Calderone. The Williams & Wilkins Company, Baltimore, 1964.
5. The safe period. The Planned Parenthood Federation of America, Inc., New York, 1963.
6. GUTTMACHER, A. F.: *The Complete Book of Birth Control*. Ballantine Books, Inc., New York, 1963.
7. CALDERONE, M. S. (Editor): *Manual of Contraceptive Practice*. The Williams & Wilkins Company, Baltimore, 1964.
8. Methods of contraception in the United States. The Planned Parenthood Federation of America, Inc., New York, 1963.
9. Spirals, loops and rings tested as contraceptives. Medical World News, November 8, 1963.
10. Trustees urge A.M.A. to back birth control and sex education. The New York Times, December 2, 1964, p. 30

part five

MARRIAGE COUNSELING INSTRUCTION IN THE MEDICAL CURRICULUM

chapter thirty

Marriage Counseling Instruction in the Medical Curriculum

ETHEL M. NASH, M.A., *Department of Preventive Medicine and Genetics, Bowman Gray School of Medicine of Wake Forest College, Winston-Salem, North Carolina*

Until a short while ago only one medical school in the United States made instruction in marriage counseling techniques a part of the required curriculum. Today, interest in marriage and sexual behavior education as a part of the medical school curriculum has grown to the point where it is difficult to keep up with the developments. Several schools have recently introduced course work, others have it scheduled for introduction and still others are in the early exploratory phases.

This new interest has resulted both from the increase in marriage and sexual problems brought to the physician in recent years, and from an increased awareness that little has been done in the past to help the physician deal with these problems. Recently, the American College of Obstetricians and Gynecologists sent to its members this questionnaire which reflected the new concern.

"Since one approach to our national problems of criminal abortion, illegitimacy, venereal disease, perinatal mortality and high divorce rate, particularly among our young people, is through the education of young people, particularly in problems of marriage adjustment, marriage disharmony, sex education in general and sexual maladjustments, you are asked to answer the following questions:

'Do you believe that you are sufficiently trained to counsel patients in the problems of sex and marriage? Did you receive adequate, organized instruction in the problems of sexual maladjustments and marital disharmony in your medical school, internship and residency training or elsewhere? Do you believe that more training is needed in these subjects for doctors in your field doing private practice? Do you counsel patients with the above problems? If not, do you send such patients to marriage counselors, clergymen, psychiatrists or others?' "

The results* indicated that one doctor in three considers himself not qualified to counsel patients about sexual and marital problems. Ninety per cent think that more training is needed by practicing physicians since neither the medical school nor the internship-residency program prepared them properly.

The results of a previous study,[1] in which one-fifth of all practicing North Carolina physicians were interviewed in relation to their premarital and marriage counseling practices are also revealing. The large majority (93 per cent) of physicians reported that when patients consulted them about marital problems or if the nature of the illness indicated the likelihood that marital stress was a factor, then they tried to counsel. However, a large majority also stated that their medical training had not prepared them adequately for this aspect of patient care. Most reported that they had received no instruction in normal marital interaction, in normal adult sexual behavior or in marriage counseling techniques during their entire medical training. Only a few of the better residencies in obstetrics and gynecology and in psychiatry were partially exempt from this blanket indictment. Ninety per cent of those interviewed expressed the conviction that instruction in the accumulated scientific data about family interaction, normal sexual behavior and marriage counseling techniques should be included in the required medical curriculum.

PRECURSOR IN REQUIRED COURSE WORK

The precursor in required medical course work in marriage and sexual problems was the Bowman Gray School of Medicine of Wake Forest College. There, since 1955, a three-pronged approach has been in use under the direction of the writer. This program presently includes: classroom instruction, clinical experience in the diagnosis of marital stress symptomatology† and the availability of premarital consultations and marriage counseling to medical students, their wives and fiancees. The aim is to equip graduates of the medical school to deal with this aspect of patient care at individual and community levels and in terms of prevention as well as salvage.

Classroom instruction begins in the first semester of the first year when 16 hours are allocated to the possibilities and problems of marital interaction, premarital preparation for sexual adjustment in marriage, the

* From "The Challenge of Change," an inaugural address presented by Frank R. Lock at the Twelfth Annual Meeting of the American College of Obstetricians and Gynecologists on May 20, 1964 at Bal Harbour, Florida.

† The writer is uncomfortably aware that as yet the students have no opportunity to develop skills in marital counseling beyond diagnosis. However, it is planned that they soon will have opportunities for clinical experience in marital therapy and follow-up of patients.

development of sexual satisfaction, varied coital techniques, and the general importance of a noncritical attitude towards others along with an understanding of the paradox that the marriage relationship is one of acceptance and yet of pushing and pulling each other into new attitudes and ways of behavior. The emphasis throughout is on the normal processes of adjustment, not on the pathologic states. Subjects such as illegitimacy, infidelity and the effects of alcoholism on the marital relationship are reviewed in the light of the potential for a rewarding solution. Throughout, the emphasis is on the prevention of marital maladjustment or on early salvage when the soma first begins to indicate effects of marital stress.

Since marital problems occur in the patients of all specialties, pediatricians, surgeons, internists and general practitioners are asked to help with this course by sharing clinical experiences which indicate that the "missing patient" is the marital relationship.

In the second year, in the course in preventive medicine, one hour is allocated. This is used to illustrate the process of crisis. Either the sequelae of long term hospitalization as it affects the stable but low income family, or the steps in the alienation process that precede divorce are subjects usually discussed.

An introduction to the theory and practice of marriage counseling is included in the third year curriculum in preventive medicine. Five hours are allocated. The foci are on the differences between the counseling approach and the directive approach used by a physician when prescribing, and between individual and marital counseling. Using his previously acquired knowledge of the marriage patterns evolving in America at the present time, of sexual adjustment and maladjustment, of marital and family interaction, of individual emotional maturation and of the "collusion" operative in the reactions of spouses to each other, the student now learns something of the science of marriage counseling. He is taught that his goal as a physician-counselor is to get a patient to sift his motivations and to decide for himself the consequences of a given course of action. Emphasis therefore is on the development of the ability to listen investigatingly and to create a relationship through which the patient can find a new way of viewing and solving his problems.

The differences between minor and major counseling and psychotherapy are stressed. The distinctions used are that through minor counseling a patient comes to understand better himself, his partner and their conflicts, and is able to utilize formerly unused abilities to bring about a solution. Through this type of counseling the patient remains what he is, but is better organized. Major counseling is depicted as the type in which many of the patient's suppressed desires and feelings are brought to the surface and integrated into his conscious personality. Thereby he reaches a new stage of development. His infantile approach to life is replaced by a more adult one and a marked reduction of egocentricity takes place. The students are taught that as nonpsychiatric physicians they should limit themselves to one or the other of these two approaches. They should not attempt depth psychotherapy, since in this the negative images of the unconscious, which cause addictions, obsessions and anxieties, are brought to light. To change these into something positive requires more training and more time than the nonpsychiatric physician is likely to have or want to give.

The Department of Obstetrics and Gynecology has instituted an experimental course which includes conceptive physiology, contraceptive physiology and methodology, abortion, adoption and the problems of the "special family" such as the one-parent family, the family with stepchildren, the infertile couple, and the family with a retarded child. Varied religious attitudes towards contraception, abortion, sterilization and interfaith marriages are presented. Frigidity, dyspareunia, impotence, premature and retarded ejaculation, homosexuality and transvestism are discussed in relation to treatment and referral. So too are the possibilities of family life education through the premarital medical examination, and through group premarital counseling with couples about to marry. This is reinforced by the clinical experience of third and fourth year students who are presently required when on the obstetrics-gynecology service to obtain from two patients a marital and sexual history and to present these to the group for discussion. It should be noted that throughout the entire course work every effort is made to insure student participation in discussion and presentation.

At the house-officer level, residents and their wives attend a two-hour week seminar for five or six weeks. Course content is concerned with the communication processes and the taking of marital and coital histories of patients in a manner productive of insights and clues about family and sexual problems. The attendance of residents' wives is based on the premise that physicians who understand their own marital situation and who have developed healthy attitudes and practices toward their own human sexuality are in a better position to understand and help patients with such problems.

The third prong of the Bowman Gray approach is the availability of premarriage and marriage counseling to medical students and house officers, their wives and fiancees. The presupposition is that a counselor should know something of the dynamics of his own inner life. Also, he needs to understand the mechanisms of transference and projection because these are the ways that both he and his patients try to escape their own responsibilities. We believe that one means whereby a physician can become aware of the unconscious diplomacy operating in himself and his patients is by his experience as a counselee. This, we think, will be a good way for him to avoid being perplexed by his own responses. Knowing himself, he will not be befuddled by his patients' admiration or disillusioned by their apparent ingratitude.

PIONEERING WORK AT THE UNIVERSITY OF PENNSYLVANIA

The pioneer in giving elective courses has been the University of Pennsylvania Medical School through its Division of Family Study in the Department of Psychiatry. In 1952 the first course on family attitudes, sexual behavior and marriage counseling was made available to senior medical students under the direction of Emily Mudd, Ph.D. The course material includes discussion of teen-age marriage, unwanted pregnancies, religious viewpoints on sex, marriage and divorce, divorce and its repercussions, premarital, marital and family problems in general practice, sexual adjustment during marriage, heterosexuality and homosexuality, the meanings of love, and fidelity and infidelity in marriage. It is taught by a team which includes not only medical personnel but also a Roman Catholic priest, a rabbi and a Protestant clergyman. Approximately 50 per cent of senior students have elected to take this course in the 12 years since its inception. In addition, the Department of Psychiatry has offered research and study facilities in the Division of Family Study and the related Marriage Council of Philadelphia to medical students who have been awarded fellowships. This course work has been more fully described in *Marriage Counseling in Medical Practice*.[2]

COURSE WORK RECENTLY INTRODUCED AT OTHER MEDICAL SCHOOLS

The Department of Obstetrics and Gynecology of the Washington University School of Medicine at St. Louis uses four-ninths of its allocated lecture time for eight lectures covering the general area of reproductive biology. The subjects taught include male and female sexology, conceptive and contraceptive physiology, impotence and frigidity. One lecture hour is given to a discussion of any subject requested in advance by the students. Usually these are transvestism or homosexuality.

The Department of Psychiatry at the University of Virginia has recently introduced a lecture series which discusses the meaning of sexual behavior in terms of psychodynamic considerations, sexuality from the viewpoint of growth and development, marriage and divorce, illegitimacy, homosexuality and the sexual neuroses.[3]

The Department of Obstetrics and Gynecology of the Albert Einstein School of Medicine has also become one of the growing number of medical schools who have introduced or plan to introduce course work in some aspects of marriage counseling. They have small seminar discussions on the premarital consultation, on marital problems in medical practice and on the sex education of the adolescent. These are their first steps towards a more comprehensive approach to sex education.[4] Previously, units of this type have sometimes been included in the instruction in several medical schools, but until now have been dependent on the concern and interest of a particular professor rather than a definite departmental or school policy. However, letters of inquiry indicate that plans are being made by other medical schools, including Harvard, to start similar course work.

At the University of Washington School of Medicine in Seattle, regular lectures on marriage counseling in medical practice for senior students by Richard H. Klemer, Ph.D., under time allotted to the Department of Psychiatry, are the hopeful precedents of a more extensive program in this area. These lectures provided the impetus and some of the basic material for earlier chapters in this book.

A Holistic Approach to Teaching Essential

Finding teaching methods which can be effective within the limited hours available in a medical curriculum is not going to prove simple. Despite the fact that marriage problems are of themselves seldom open to simple solutions, if it were only a question of subject matter, this would call merely for ingenuity of approach. Like actual performance of surgery, this would not prove too difficult. The complication stems from the necessity of attempting to teach the "whole" medical student. It can be done successfully only if attention is given to three special factors: the personality type of most medical students, their emotional developmental stage and the closed nature of their environment during their years of medical training.

Psychologic studies of medical students by Dr. Harold Lief[5] of Tulane University Medical School have shown that approximately 50 per cent are obsessive-compulsive in personality type. This means that they work hard, even if they dislike the subject; they are exacting of themselves and others; they tend to be shy, hard to draw out, and do not express their feelings easily. They are emotionally somewhat inhibited and have little capacity to relax. These are not characteristics typical of the person naturally oriented towards counseling, which requires being free enough in one's own self to enable another person to explore parts of his personality of which he has been previously either unaware or afraid. The obsessive-compulsive type of personality finds it easier to give clear, concise direction than to enable someone else to sift, weigh and slowly choose a course of action. However, even though physicians would not, in general, choose a counseling role, the public, plus the now recognized interaction of the psyche and the soma have combined to assign it to them. Even if unwillingly, the physician in America today functions in a social climate in which a majority assume that he is the best source of help for problems related to sex.

Lief also developed the concept of a continuum of adjustment with contrasting categories of "mature" and "conflicted" at the extremes, and with intermediate groupings of "emergent" and "normaloid." Upon this scale each medical student can be placed approximately into one of these groups. The "normaloid" type, which will probably comprise about one-third of any class, will tend to be uneasy with his own and with patients' feelings, preferring to approach himself and others on a socially conformist, superficially adjusted basis. He, along with the "conflicted," will have difficulty in assimilating material related to sexual behavior and to marital interaction. The "emergent" is essentially in flux emotionally. His general approach to life will be somewhat typical of late adolescence, but he is on the road towards maturity and will, along with the "mature" student, who combines the social adjustment of the "normaloid" with much greater creativity, introspective ability and ease with his own feelings, find it a relatively easy task to feel secure in the exploration of sexual and marital interaction in patients.

Allowance has to be made also for the effect of the extraordinary concentration of medical training which confines the student to classroom and laboratory, to clinic and ward. Success requires almost a monastic devotion to study. Much of ordinary living experience inevitably passes medical students by during the years of 22 to 28. Yet they have to learn to counsel men and women whose own experience of living has been more varied.

Methods of teaching, therefore, have to be devised which will modify the effect of the medical environment and enable the student to utilize his own personality type by developing its latent strengths. For example, the "normaloid" will need to find ways to become more introspective and the "conflicted" will possibly need to find ways to become more socially adjusted. All have to learn that the counselor must not impose his own concepts on the patient.

Special stresses are encountered in the marital adjustments of medical students and their wives. The student often is torn between his need to study and his own and his wife's desire for companionship. Financial insecurity is also the lot of many married students, along with role reversal if they are dependent upon their wives' working to put them through school. The total circumstances of medical education weight the scales against students being able to counsel patients regarding sex and marriage on the basis of their own deep marital intimacy and satisfying shared sex life. Therefore, as teaching is developed, it is imperative that built-in evaluation techniques be devised.

Many More Programs in Prospect

Prominent medical educators such as Dr. Harold Lief are urging that the time is now "ripe for conferences among medical educators and for more research in order to determine means for counteracting these deficiencies in medical education so that graduate physicians will be confident of their ability in responding to the enormous demand for services by the patients asking for help in the most delicate and potentially the most satisfying of all human relationships—marriage." [5]

Especially significant for the future is the formation of a liaison committee representative of the American College of Obstetricians and Gynecologists and three family-centered, multidisciplinary and nonsectarian national organizations—the American Association of Marriage Counselors, the National Council on Family Relations and the Groves Conference. The next step forward, as suggested by the President of the American College of Obstetrics and Gynecology, Dr. Frank Lock, who initiated the conference which led to the formation of this committee, is to work together on a national program of family life education, which will begin with the education of the medical profession in family life aspects of patient care.

The development of this as an effective program at a national level really extends beyond instruction to medical students to the training of house officers and physicians already in practice. The period of house officer training is one in which lifetime patterns of patient care are formed. Most house officers today have not been exposed to any instruction in marriage counseling techniques and are as likely as medical students to try to mask inadequate knowledge and embarrassment about sex behind a facade of pseudosophistication. Seminars in marriage counseling techniques together with a requirement that they get a marital and sexual history as part of the evaluation of most patients could help to bridge this gap in their medical education.

A few postgraduate courses for physicians in marriage counseling have already been offered under various medical auspices and more are planned. The response has been so good that it has surprised the initiators. Marriage counselors and social workers requested permission to attend one of these courses. The interaction that resulted made it clear that cooperation between medical and nonmedical personnel is most rewarding.

Certainly, for the development of an effective program at a national level, the supply of highly trained paramedical personnel to work with physicians in marriage counseling must be increased. At present both trained personnel and facilities for their training are inadequate. A resolution passed in May 1963 by the Medical Society of North Carolina urged the development in the state of a Marriage Counseling Training Center under medical direction and using the resources of the state's three medical schools. If this is both implemented and copied, such centers would provide training for nonmedical marriage counselors, clinical training for medical students, house officers and interested physicians, service facilities for patients and opportunities for research.

SUMMARY

In the U. S. A. today one child in every nine is a stepchild. Marriages with bride and groom under 20 are on the increase despite the fact that 50 per cent end up in divorce within five years. One in every six marriages begins with the wife pregnant at the time of marriage. Approximately 780,000 persons within any year of the 1960's have taken or will take the significant step of divorce. Concern about the family as an institution can hardly be considered alarmist.

Physicians are aware that marital stress often produces illness and that ill health can adversely affect a marriage. Patients do consult their doctors about marital problems and especially about sexual difficulties. A new freedom about sex is endemic throughout the country, a fact reflected in the popular press. Yet a recent survey showed that in the five medical schools located in Philadelphia, one faculty member in five believes the now discredited idea that mental illness is frequently caused by masturbation.[6] So, before introducing too much about marriage counseling and sex education into the medical curriculum, some interdepartmental faculty education would seem essential.

Instruction to students will need to be multidisciplinary since marital problems crop up in almost all specialties. Medicine, obstetrics and gynecology, surgery, pediatrics, preventive medicine, genetics, urology, physiology, endocrinology and psychiatry all have their contributions to make through teaching and research.

The availability for students and house officers of consultations about premarital and postmarital problems can make it possible to capitalize on two existing factors. Many students are married and therefore are better prepared to understand the interaction of family life. The climate in which medical students have grown up has been more free in its discussion of sex than any previous one. These environmental conditions may make possible the success of this educational program.

REFERENCES

1. HERNDON, C. N., AND NASH, E. M.: Premarriage and marriage counseling. A study of the practices of North Carolina physicians. J. A. M. A., 180: 395–401, 1962.

2. MUDD, E. H.: Marriage counseling instruction in the School of Medicine curriculum, University of Pennsylvania. In *Marriage Counseling in Medical Practice*, edited by E. M. Nash, L. Jessner, and D. W. Abse. University of North Carolina Press, Chapel Hill, 1964.
3. SHEPPE, W. M., JR.: Personal communication. March, 1964.
4. DAVIDOFF, I. S.: Personal communication. February, 1964.
5. LIEF, H. I.: Sexual attitudes and behavior of medical students. Implications for medical practice. In *Marriage Counseling in Medical Practice*, edited by E. M. Nash, L. Jessner, and D. W. Abse. University of North Carolina Press, Chapel Hill, 1964.
6. GREENBANK, R. K.: Are medical students learning psychiatry? Pennsylvania M. J., **64**: 989–992, 1961.

Reading List

i. For Physician-Counselors

A. Psychosocial background to marriage problems

Bell, N. W., and Vogel, E. F. (Editors): *A Modern Introduction to the Family*. The Free Press of Glencoe, New York, 1960.

Bell, R. R.: *Marriage and Family Interaction*. The Dorsey Press, Inc., Homewood, Illinois, 1963.

Berne, E.: *Games People Play, the Psychology of Human Relationships*. Grove Press, Inc., New York, 1964.

Blood, R. O., Jr.: *Marriage*. The Free Press of Glencoe, New York, 1962.

Bossard, J. H. S., and Boll, E. S.: *Why Marriages Go Wrong*. The Ronald Press Company, New York, 1958.

Christensen, H. T. (Editor): *Handbook of Marriage and the Family*. Rand McNally & Company, New York, 1964.

Gruenberg, S. M., and Krech, H.: *The Many Lives of Modern Woman*. Harper & Brothers, New York, 1952.

Haussamen, F., and Guitar, M. A.: *The Divorce Handbook*. G. P. Putnam's Sons, New York, 1960.

Kenkel, W. F.: *The Family in Perspective*. Appleton-Century-Crofts, Inc., New York, 1960.

Kephart, W. M.: *The Family, Society and the Individual*. Houghton Mifflin Company, Boston, 1961.

Landis, J. T., and Landis, M. G.: *Readings in Marriage and the Family*. Prentice-Hall, Inc., Englewood Cliffs, New Jersey, 1952.

Landis, P. H.: *Making the Most of Marriage*. Appleton-Century-Crofts, Inc., New York, 1960.

LeMasters, E. E.: *Modern Courtship and Marriage*. The Macmillan Company, New York, 1957.

Mace, D., and Mace, V.: *Marriage East and West*. Doubleday & Company, Inc., Garden City, New York, 1960.

Martinson, F. M.: *Marriage and the American Ideal*. Dodd, Mead & Company, New York, 1960.

Nimkoff, M. F., *Comparative Family Systems*. Houghton Mifflin Company, Boston, 1965.

Nye, F. I., and Hoffman, L. W.: *The Employed Mother in America*. Rand, McNally & Company, New York, 1963.

Polatin, P., and Philtine, E. C.: *Marriage in the Modern World*. J. B. Lippincott Company, Philadelphia, 1956.

Rogers, C. R.: *On Becoming a Person*. Houghton Mifflin Company, Boston, 1961.

Schur, E. M. (Editor): *The Family and the Sexual Revolution*. Indiana University Press, Bloomington, Indiana, 1964.

Smith, I. E.: *Readings in Adoption*. Philosophical Library, Inc., New York, 1963.

Steiner, L. R.: *Romantic Marriage, The Twentieth-Century Illusion*. Chilton Books, Philadelphia, 1963.

Sussman, M. B.: *Sourcebook in Marriage and the Family*, Ed. 2. Houghton Mifflin Company, Boston, 1963.

Vincent, C. E.: *Unmarried Mothers*. The Free Press of Glencoe, New York, 1961.

Winch, R. F., McGinnis, R., and Barringer, H.: *Selected Studies in Marriage and the Family*, Rev. ed. Holt, Rinehart and Winston, Inc., New York, 1962.

B. Marriage counseling

Cuber, J. F.: *Marriage Counseling Practice*. Appleton-Century-Crofts, Inc., New York, 1948.

Johnson, D.: *Marriage Counseling, Theory and Practice*. Prentice-Hall, Inc., Englewood Cliffs, New Jersey, 1961.

Mudd, E. H.: *The Practice Of Marriage Counseling*. Association Press, New York, 1961.

Mudd, E. H., and Krich, A. (Editors): *Man and Wife*. W. W. Norton & Company, Inc., New York, 1956.

Mudd, E. H., Stone, A., Karpf, M. J., and Nelson, J. F.: *Marriage Counseling: A Casebook*. Association Press, New York, 1958.

Nash, E., Jessner, L., and Abse, D.: *Marriage Counseling in Medical Practice*. University of North Carolina Press, Chapel Hill, 1964.

Stone, A., and Levine, L.: *The Premarital Consultation*. Grune & Stratton, Inc., New York, 1956.

Vincent, C. E.: *Readings in Marriage Counseling*. Thomas Y. Crowell Company, New York, 1957.

C. Psychopathology

Arieti, S. (Editor): *American Handbook of Psychiatry*, Vols. I and II. Basic Books Publishing Company, Inc., New York, 1959.

Cameron, N.: *Personality Development and Psychopathology*. Houghton Mifflin Company, Boston, 1963.

Gregory, I.: *Psychiatry, Biological and Social*. W. B. Saunders Company, Philadelphia, 1961.

Knight, A.: *Psychiatry for the Family Physician*. McGraw-Hill Book Company, Inc., New York, 1955.

Noyes, A., and Kolb, L.: *Modern Clinical Psychiatry*, Ed. 6. W. B. Saunders Company, Philadelphia, 1963.

Stevenson, I.: The psychiatric interview. In *American Handbook of Psychiatry*, p. 197. Basic Books Publishing Company, Inc., New York, 1959.

Stevenson, I., and Sheppe, W. J.: The psychiatric examination. In *American*

Handbook of Psychiatry, p. 215. Basic Books Publishing Company, Inc., New York, 1959.

D. Sex problems

Beigel, H. G. (Editor): *Advances in Sex Research*. Harper & Row, Publishers, Inc. (Hoeber Medical Division), New York, 1963.

Calderone, M. S. (Editor): *Manual of Contraceptive Practice*. The Williams & Wilkins Company, Baltimore, 1964.

DeMartino, M. F. (Editor): *Sexual Behavior and Personality Characteristics*. The Citadel Press, New York, 1963.

Dickinson, R. L.: *Atlas of Human Sex Anatomy*. The Williams & Wilkins Company, Baltimore, 1949.

Duvall, E. M., and Duvall, S. M. (Editors): *Sex Ways in Fact and Faith*. Association Press, New York, 1961.

Ellis, A., and Abarbanel, A.: *The Encyclopedia of Sexual Behavior*, Vols. I and II. Hawthorn Books, Inc., New York, 1961.

Hastings, D. W.: *Impotence and Frigidity*. Little, Brown and Company, Boston, 1963.

Henry, G. W.: *Sex Variants*. Harper and Row, Publishers, Inc., New York, 1941.

Himelhoch, J., and Fava, S. (Editors): *Sexual Behavior in American Society*. W. W. Norton & Company, Inc., New York, 1955.

Kirkendall, L. A.: *Premarital Intercourse and Interpersonal Relationships*. Julian Press, Inc., New York, 1961.

Lloyd, C. W. (Editor): *Human Reproduction and Sexual Behavior*. Lea & Febiger, Philadelphia, 1964.

Oliven, J. S.: *Sexual Hygiene and Pathology*. J. B. Lippincott Company, Philadelphia, 1955.

Reiss, I. L.: *Premarital Sexual Standards in America*. The Free Press of Glencoe, Illinois, 1960.

Stokes, W.: *Married Love in Today's World*. The Citadel Press, New York, 1962.

Vincent, C. E.: *Unmarried Mothers*. The Free Press of Glencoe, New York, 1961.

E. Parent-child relations

Apley, J., and Mackeith, R.: *The Child and His Symptoms: A Psychosomatic Approach*. F. A. Davis Company, Philadelphia, 1962.

Bossard, J. H. S.: *Parent and Child*. University of Pennsylvania Press, Philadelphia, 1953.

Bossard, J. H. S., and Boll, E. S.: *The Sociology of Child Development*, Ed. 3. Harper & Brothers, New York, 1960.

Cole, L.: *Psychology of Adolescence*. Rinehart & Company, New York, 1959.

Finch, S. M.: *Fundamentals of Child Psychiatry*. W. W. Norton & Company, Inc., New York, 1960.

Garrison, K. C.: *Psychology of Adolescence*, Ed. 5. Prentice-Hall, Inc., Englewood Cliffs, New Jersey, 1956.

Ginsberg, E. (Editor): *The Nation's Children: The Family and Social Change*, Vol. I; *Development and Education*, Vol. II; and *Problems and Prospects*, Vol. III. Columbia University Press, New York, 1960.

Grinder, R. E.: *Studies in Adolescence.* The Macmillan Company, New York, 1963.

Kuhlen, R. G., and Thompson, G. G.: *Psychological Studies of Human Development.* Appleton-Century-Crofts, Inc., New York, 1952.

Muuss, R. E.: *Theories of Adolescence.* Random House, Inc., New York, 1962.

Peck, R. F., and Havighurst, R. F.: *The Psychology of Character Development.* John Wiley & Sons, Inc., New York, 1960.

Seidman, J. M.: *The Adolescent, a Book of Readings.* Holt, Rinehart and Winston, Inc., New York, 1960.

Stone, L. J., and Church, J.: *Childhood and Adolescence: A Psychology of the Growing Person.* Random House, Inc., New York, 1957.

Watson, R. I.: *Psychology of the Child.* John Wiley & Sons, Inc., New York, 1959.

F. Alcoholism

Blakeslee, A., Jr.: *Alcoholism—A Sickness that Can Be Beaten,* Pamphlet No. 118. Public Affairs Committee, 30 Rockefeller Plaza, New York 20, New York.

Block, M. A.: *Alcoholism Is a Disease.* National Council on Alcoholism, Inc., 2 East 203rd Street, New York 29, New York.

Ford, Rev. J. C., S.J.: *The General Practitioner's Role in Alcoholism.* National Council on Alcoholism, Inc., 2 East 103rd Street, New York 29, New York.

Ginsberg, D. M.: *Treatment of Alcoholism by the Family Doctor.* National Council on Alcoholism, Inc., 2 East 103rd Street, New York 29, New York.

Himwich, H. D. (Editor): *Alcoholism: Basic Aspects and Treatment.* American Association for the Advancement of Science, Washington, D. C., 1957.

Mann, M.: *How to Know an Alcoholic.* National Council on Alcoholism, Inc., 2 East 103rd Street, New York 29, New York.

Mann, M.: *New Primer on Alcoholism,* rev. ed. Rinehart & Company, Inc., New York, 1958.

McCarthy, R. G.: *Facts about Alcohol.* Science Research Associates, Inc., 57 West Grand Avenue, Chicago 10, Illinois.

Presnall, L. F.: *The Wife of the Alcoholic.* Utah Alcoholism Foundation, Salt Lake City, Utah.

The Al-Anon Family Groups. A Guide for the Families of Problem Drinkers. Al-Anon Family Group Headquarters, Inc., New York, 1955.

The Alcoholic Husband. Alcoholics Anonymous World Services, Inc., P. O. Box 459, Grand Central Annex, New York 17, New York.

Weeks, M. T., Jr.: *Thirteen Steps to Alcoholism.* National Council on Alcoholism, Inc., 2 East 103rd Street, New York 29, New York.

Other information may be obtained by writing to:

Alcoholics Anonymous, Box 459, Grand Central Annex, New York 17, New York.

National Institute of Mental Health, Reports & Publications Branch, Public Health Service, Bethesda 14, Maryland.

The National Council on Alcoholism, 2 East 103rd Street, New York 29, New York.

Your state Alcoholism Authority or local Alcoholics Anonymous or Council on Alcoholism.

G. Conjoint counseling with partners and family members

Ackerman, N. W.: *Exploring the Base for Family Therapy.* Family Service Association of America, New York, 1961.

Ackerman, N. W.: *The Psychodynamics of Family Life.* Basic Books, Inc., New York, 1958.

Bell, J. E.: *Family Group Therapy.* U. S. Department of Health, Education and Welfare, Public Health Monograph No. 64, Washington, D. C., 1961.

Freeman, V. J. *et al:* Allegheny General Hospital Family Study Project, Final Report, 1964.

Midelfort, C. F.: *The Family in Psychotherapy.* The Blakiston Division, McGraw-Hill Book Company, Inc., New York, 1957.

Richardson, H. B.: *Patients have Families.* The Commonwealth Fund, New York, 1948.

Satir, V.: *Conjoint Family Therapy.* Science & Behavior Books, Inc., Palo Alto, California, 1964.

H. Aging

Anderson, J. E. (Editor): *Psychological Aspects of Aging.* American Psychological Association, Washington, D. C., 1956.

Barron, M. L.: *The Aging American.* Thomas Y. Crowell Company, New York, 1961.

Birren, J. E. (Editor): *Handbook of Aging and the Individual.* University of Chicago Press, Chicago, 1959.

Tibbitts, C., and Donahue, W.: *Aging in Today's Society.* Prentice-Hall, Inc., Englewood Cliffs, New Jersey, 1960.

Williams, R. H., Tibbitts, C., and Donahue, W.: *Processes of Aging*, Vols. 1 and 2. Atherton Press, New York, 1963.

ii. For the Married Partners

Birch, W. G.: *A Doctor Discusses Pregnancy.* The Budlong Press Company, Chicago, 1963.

Daniels, A. K.: *It's Never Too Late to Love.* Prentice-Hall, Inc., Englewood Cliffs, New Jersey, 1953.

Fromm, E.: *The Art of Loving.* Harper & Brothers, New York, 1956.

Genne, W. H.: *Husbands and Pregnancy: Handbook for Expectant Fathers.* Association Press, New York, 1956.

Guttmacher, A. F., Best, W., and Jaffe, F. S.: *Planning Your Family.* The Macmillan Company, New York, 1961.

Havemann, E.: *Men, Women, and Marriage.* Doubleday & Company, Inc., New York, 1962.

Hilliard, M.: *A Woman Doctor Looks at Love and Life.* Doubleday & Company, Inc., Garden City, New York, 1957.

Himes, N. E., and Taylor, D. L.: *Your Marriage.* Rinehart & Company, Inc., New York, 1955.

Hunt, M. M.: *Her Infinite Variety.* Harper & Row, Publishers, Inc., New York, 1962.

Kelly, G. L.: *A Doctor Discusses Menopause*. The Budlong Press Company, Chicago, 1959.

Levy, J., and Monroe, R.: *The Happy Family*. Alfred A. Knopf, Inc., New York, 1938.

Pilpel, H., and Zavin, T.: *Your Marriage and the Law*. Holt, Rinehart and Winston, Inc., New York, 1952.

Schifferes, J. J.: *The Older People in Your Life*. Washington Square Press, Inc., New York, 1962.

iii. For Patients with Sexual Problems

Baruch, D. W., and Miller, H.: *Sex in Marriage: New Understanding*. Harper & Row, Publishers, Inc. (Hoeber Medical Division), New York, 1962.

Calderone, M. S.: *Release from Sexual Tension*. Random House, Inc., New York, 1960.

Davis, M.: *Sexual Responsibility in Marriage*. The Dial Press, Inc., New York, 1963.

Robinson, M.: *The Power of Sexual Surrender*. Doubleday & Company, Inc., Garden City, New York, 1959.

Stone, H. M., and Stone, A.: *A Marriage Manual*. Simon and Schuster, Inc., New York, 1952.

Van de Velde, T. H.: *Ideal Marriage: Its Physiology and Technique*. Random House, Inc., New York, 1930.

iv. For Unmarried Women

Glover, H.: *Sense & Sensibility for Single Women*. Doubleday & Company, Inc., Garden City, New York, 1963.

Klemer, R. H.: *A Man for Every Woman*. The Macmillan Company, New York, 1959.

v. For Those Ready to be Married

Blood, R. O.: *Marriage*. The Free Press of Glencoe, New York, 1962.

Boll, E. S.: *The Man That You Marry*. Macrae Smith Company, Philadelphia, 1963.

Bossard, J. H. S., and Boll, E. S.: *One Marriage, Two Faiths*. The Ronald Press Company, New York, 1957.

Bowman, H. A.: *Marriage for Moderns*, Ed. 4. McGraw-Hill Book Company, Inc., New York, 1960.

Butterfield, O. M.: *Sex Life in Marriage*. Emerson Books, Inc., New York, 1952.

Cavan, R. S.: *American Marriage—A Way of Life*. Thomas Y. Crowell Company, New York, 1959.

Duvall, E. M., and Hill, R.: *Being Married*. Association Press, New York, 1960.

Duvall, E. M., and Hill, R.: *When You Marry*. D. C. Heath & Company, Boston, 1960.

Duvall, S. M.: *Before You Marry*. Association Press, New York, 1959.

Greenblatt, B. R.: *A Doctor's Marital Guide for Patients*. The Budlong Press Company, Chicago, 1959.

Krich, A. (Editor): *Facts of Love and Marriage for Young People*. Dell Publishing Company, Inc. (Laurel Book), New York, 1962.

Landis, J. T., and Landis, M. G.: *Building a Successful Marriage*, Ed. 4. Prentice-Hall, Inc., Englewood Cliffs, New Jersey, 1963.

Landis, P.: *Making the Most of Marriage*, Ed. 2. Appleton-Century-Crofts, Inc., New York, 1960.

Mace, D. R.: *Marriage, The Art of Lasting Love*. Doubleday & Company, Inc., Garden City, New York, 1952.

Mace, D. R.: *Success in Marriage*. Abingdon Press, Nashville, 1958.

Peterson, J. A.: *Education for Marriage*. Charles Scribner's Sons, New York, 1964.

Peterson, J. A.: *Toward a Successful Marriage*. Charles Scribner's Sons, New York, 1960.

Popenoe, P.: *Marriage Is What You Make It*. The Macmillan Company, New York, 1955.

Stone, H., and Stone, A.: *A Marriage Manual*. Simon & Schuster, Inc., New York, 1952.

vi. For Parents

Child Study Association of America: *A Reader for Parents: A Selection of Creative Literature about Childhood*. W. W. Norton & Company, Inc., New York, 1962.

Despert, L.: *Children of Divorce*. Doubleday & Company, Inc., Garden City, New York, 1953.

Duvall, E. M., and Duvall, S. M.: *Sex Ways in Fact and Faith*. Association Press, New York, 1961.

Farnham, M. F.: *The Adolescent*. Harper & Brothers, New York, 1951.

Frank, M., and Lawrence, K.: *Your Adolescent at Home and in School*. The Viking Press, New York, 1956.

Fromme, A.: *The Parents Handbook*. Simon and Schuster, Inc., New York, 1956.

Gallagher, J. R., and Harris, H. I.: *Emotional Problems of Adolescents*. Oxford University Press, New York, 1956.

Gottlieb, B. S.: *Understanding Your Adolescent*. Rinehart & Company, Inc., New York, 1957.

Gruenberg, S. M.: *Encyclopedia of Child Care and Guidance*. Doubleday & Company, Inc., Garden City, New York, 1963.

Hymes, J. L.: *The Child Under Six*. Prentice-Hall, Inc., Englewood Cliffs, New Jersey, 1963.

Sakol, J.: *What About Teen-Age Marriage?* Avon Book Division, The Hearst Corporation, New York, 1963.

Schwartz, A.: *A Parent's Guide to Children's Play and Recreation*. Collier Books, New York, 1963.

Spock, B.: *Problems of Parents*. Houghton Mifflin Company, Boston, 1962.

Wittenberg, R. M.: *Adolescence and Discipline: A Mental Hygiene Primer*. Association Press, New York, 1959.

vii. For Teen-Agers

Duvall, E. M.: *Family Living*. The Macmillan Company, New York, 1961.

Duvall, E. M.: *Love and the Facts of Life*. Association Press, New York, 1963.

Duvall, E. M., and Hill, R.: *When You Marry*. D. C. Heath and Company, New York, 1962.

Landis, J. T., and Landis, M. G.: *Building Your Life*, Ed. 2. Prentice-Hall, Inc., Englewood Cliffs, New Jersey, 1959.

Landis, P. H.: *Your Marriage and Family Living*, Ed. 2. McGraw-Hill Book Company, Inc., New York, 1954.

Levinsohn, F., and Kelly, G.: *What Teenagers Want to Know*. The Budlong Press Company, Chicago, 1962.

Menninger, W. C., and others: *Blueprint for Teen-Age Living*. Sterling Publishing Company, Inc., New York, 1958.

Menninger, W. C., and others: *How to Be a Successful Teenager*. Sterling Publishing Company, Inc., New York, 1954.

Osborne, E. G.: *Understanding Your Parents*. Association Press, New York, 1956.

Richardson, F. H.: *For Teenagers Only*. Tupper & Love, Inc., Atlanta, 1957.

viii. For Sex Education

Davis, M.: *Sex and the Adolescent*. The Dial Press, Inc., New York, 1958.

Duvall, E. M.: *Love and the Facts of Life*. Association Press, New York, 1963.

Duvall, E. M.: *Why Wait Till Marriage?* Association Press, New York, 1965.

Duvall, E. M., and Duvall, S. M.: *Sense and Nonsense about Sex*. Association Press, New York, 1961.

Gruenberg, B. C., and Gruenberg, S. M.: *The Wonderful Story of You*. Garden City Books, Garden City, New York, 1960.

Gruenberg, S. M.: *The Wonderful Story of How You Were Born*. Doubleday & Company, Inc., New York, 1952.

Lerrigo, M. O., and Cassidy, M. A.: *A Doctor Talks to 9-to-12-Year-Olds*. The Budlong Press Company, Chicago, 1964.

Museum of Science and Industry: *The Miracle of Growth*. University of Illinois Press, Urbana, 1950.

Schauffler, G.: *Guiding Your Daughter to Confident Womanhood*. Prentice-Hall, Inc., Englewood Cliffs, New Jersey, 1964.

Scheinfeld, A.: *Why You are You*. Abelard-Schuman Limited, New York, 1958.

Index

Sexual motivation in women
  causes of lack of, 107
  low, as related to physical abnormality, 108
Sexual problems, *see* Problems, sexual
Sexual techniques, 274
Sleep consciousness, importance of touch and body contact during, 182
Social relationships, rebuilding of, 214
Sociopathic personality, 49
Sperm, medical treatment to increase count and motility of, 242
Sponge, foam and, *see* Foam
Suicide
  checklist for evaluating suicidal risk, 35
  preoccupation with, discussing with patient, 31
Suppositories, effectiveness as contraceptives, 280

Tablets, foam, *see* Foam
Tampons, internal, recommendation for use of, 273
Television, *see* Mass communication
Therapy
  in marriage problems, establishing communication between the partners, 13
  in sexual and marriage problems of older patients, 172
Thyroid, as medical treatment for infertile wife, 242
Touch as communication, 181
Transsexualism, 144
Transvestism
  causal factors in, 144
  characteristics of, 143
Turner's syndrome, 71

Unfaithfulness, *see* Infidelity, marital
Uniform Reciprocal Enforcement of Support Act, 249, 253
United States
  divorce in, as compared to rates in Canada, 5
  effect of recent social changes on marriage problems, 11
  homosexuality in, 142
University of Pennsylvania Medical School, as pioneer in offering elective courses in marriage counseling, 288

University of Virginia, course work in marriage counseling, 288
University of Washington School of Medicine, course work in marriage counseling, 289
Unmarried never married women, counseling with, 210, 212, 215
Unwed fathers, 154
Unwed mothers
  married and divorced "unwed" mothers, 156
  public image of, 149
  see also Pregnancy, premarital
Uterus, abnormal bleeding of, as inhibitor of sexual satisfaction, 72

Vaginal canal
  atrophy of, as cause of dyspareunia, 170
  lack of lubrication of, as cause of dyspareunia, 170
Vaginal creams, *see* Creams
Vaginal jellies, *see* Jellies
Vaginal lubrication, sources of, 76
Vaginismus
  as cause of dyspareunia, 170
  as cause of marriage problems, 74
  associated with lack of sexual desire, 75
  depth psychotherapy in treatment of, 75
Vaginitis
  as cause of dyspareunia, 71, 170
  treatment for, 173
Values, marriage, 14
Venereal diseases, as pathologic causes of marriage problems, 71
Ventilation, as a step in functional marriage counseling, 22
Verbal communication, importance of, 179
Vincent, C. E., 149
Voyeurism, 55, 138
Vulvitis, as cause of dyspareunia, 170

Washington University School of Medicine, course work in reproductive biology, 288
Widows
  counseling with, 210
  helping the widow to help her children, 213
Wimberger, H. C., 186